itbooks

AN IMPRINT OF HARPERCOLLINS PUBLISHERS

MY JOURNEY INTO THE UNKNOWN

PARANORMAL STATE™

RYAN BUELL

AND STEFAN PETRUCHA

PARANORMAL STATE. Copyright © 2010 by A&E Television Networks, LLC. All rights reserved. Printed in the United States of America. No part of this book may be used or reproduced in any manner whatsoever without written permission except in the case of brief quotations embodied in critical articles and reviews. For information, address HarperCollins Publishers, 10 East 53rd Street, New York, NY 10022.

HarperCollins books may be purchased for educational, business, or sales promotional use. For information, please write: Special Markets Department, HarperCollins Publishers, 10 East 53rd Street, New York, NY 10022.

FIRST EDITION

Designed by Ashley Halsey

Library of Congress Cataloging-in-Publication Data
Buell, Ryan.
    Paranormal state: my journey into the unknown/Ryan Buell and Stefan Petrucha.—1st ed.
        p.   cm.
    ISBN 978-0-06-176794-4
    1. Parapsychology. 2. Paranormal Research Society. 3. Paranormal state (Television program) 4. Buell, Ryan. I. Petrucha, Stefan. II. Title.
BF1040.B75 2010
130—dc22
2010005748

10 11 12 13 14   OV/RRD   10 9 8 7 6 5 4 3 2 1

This book is dedicated to all members of my family and friends that supported me and my unusual obsession in to the unknown all these years:

To Mom (Shelly), Herb, and Dad (Tim): Thank you for your love and support.

To Grammer, to whom I promised at a young age that I would dedicate my first book.

To Gramma and Grampa Buell: All those years of watching *Scooby-Doo!* undoubtedly had an effect.

To Christina, for being my first paranormal partner in crime.

To Lorraine Warren, for being an inspirational mentor.

To Penn State: Thank you for tolerating my weirdness.

To Josh, Heather, Katrina, and all members of PRS, past and present, for supporting me and helping me along this quest. To Eilfie and Serg: Thank you for being by my side, both through the good times and bad.

To Helen Isenberg, for helping me realize my strengths.

And lastly, to all those who have had experiences with the supernatural and felt alone, this book is for you.

Contents

Foreword

Some journeys change you as you walk them. After taking the first several steps, you can never return to the person you once were. Ryan Buell's journey started when he was a child. He was the victim of a persistent and malevolent haunting, but when he reached out for help, no one believed him. He felt abandoned, alone, and ignored. Some people would use such an experience as an excuse to become bitter and angry as they grow into adulthood. Others would use it as a reason to resent their parents as well as the society that taught those parents that things such as ghosts could not exist.

But Ryan Buell is not like most people.

He endured his experience, and as he grew older, he transformed his fear into inspiration. He sought answers and he sought allies. More than that, he worked to establish a way to reach out to people in similar situations, to offer them help and support. That work ultimately led him to found the Paranormal Research Society at Penn State University in State College,

Pennsylvania. You probably know PRS best as the team of young investigators featured on A&E's hit, *Paranormal State.*

I first met members of the Paranormal Research Society in 2006 at their annual event, UNIV-CON. UNIV-CON is one of the largest paranormal conventions in the country, and it attracts high-profile people from every aspect of the community. It was one of Ryan's ongoing projects, bringing people from the paranormal community together to dialogue, share ideas, and learn from one another.

Back then, I wasn't what you'd call high profile, at least not as far as paranormal circles were concerned. In the nineties, I'd done work as a paranormal investigator off and on, but my real focus was psychic development and energy work. I had several books out, and was best known for my work on psychic vampires. As it turned out, PRS's resident occult expert, Eilfie Music, and tech specialist, Josh Light, were both fans of my writing. I'm not sure which of them was responsible for convincing Ryan that I should give a presentation at UNIV-CON. I'm just glad that they did. It allowed me to meet Ryan and his amazing team.

During that first year of our association, my interactions with Ryan were minimal. To be honest, I was a little ambivalent about meeting him. I'd heard that he was a devout Catholic, and I really wasn't sure how he'd react to someone like me. Aside from my involvement with psychic vampirism, I'm also a practicing pagan. Neither were widely accepted topics within the paranormal community, so I decided it would be safer to lie low than run afoul of someone else's sincerely held beliefs. I shouldn't have worried. Ryan's approach to religion and the paranormal is one of open-minded tolerance. Of course, the fact that Ryan had two openly pagan members on his team, Eilfie and Josh, should have been a tip-off.

In fact, promoting tolerance was one of the points of UNIV-CON. Ryan had a vision about the future of paranormal research. In order to gain acceptance and understanding for the paranormal, he felt it was necessary for those interested in studying it to accept and understand one another first.

The year 2006 was especially huge for the Paranormal Research Society, not simply because of UNIV-CON's massive success but also because it was the year that A&E came to the convention to lay the groundwork for *Paranormal State*. I had no idea about that when I showed up, and I'm not even sure it sunk into my head by the end of the convention. Because we had been working in parallel communities that rarely converged, I hadn't even heard of the Paranormal Research Society. Heck, I was just tickled that this huge paranormal convention was being held—and accepted—at a major college.

That was the first thing that stood out. I could hardly believe that the organization contacting me to speak was a university-recognized student group. Maybe that's not so hard to accept now, but when I was in college, we had trouble trying to get the university to sanction a gaming group, let alone something devoted to the investigation of ghosts, demons, and the occult. Yet somehow Ryan Buell had managed to do it, at a major university in the mountains of central Pennsylvania. It was a fight at first, and not everyone welcomed the idea of the Paranormal Research Society with open arms. To this day, it has its detractors, but Ryan never let this stop him. He wanted to make changes in the field of paranormal research, and he knew that those changes would happen only through dedication and perseverance.

When I learned that Ryan Buell was the founding force behind the Paranormal Research Society, I wasn't sure what to think. From what I saw of him during my first UNIV-CON, he seemed quiet, earnest, and even a little shy. I could not imagine what had inspired this clean-cut Catholic boy to develop such a passion for the paranormal. I was curious to learn more, but at first our very different faiths kept us from connecting well. I spent a lot more time getting to know Josh, Eilfie, and even tech specialist and photographer Serg Poberezhny. Ryan was the quiet guy who politely acknowledged my existence just as he went dashing off to handle some administrative business.

I was still very much on the fringe of things when the first season of *Paranormal State* began. I interacted with Ryan only rarely. Most of my communication with PRS involved answering questions behind the scenes for a couple of their early episodes (mostly when Eilfie felt that I might have more resources in my occult library on a certain topic than she had on hand). Obviously, as the years went by, my involvement grew, until now when I'm pretty much an honorary team member. But that initial outsider perspective allowed me to watch the people of the Paranormal Research Society change and grow as *Paranormal State* really took off. Ryan's journey through this process was perhaps the most fascinating of all.

Judging by the content of some reality television shows, there are those who'd literally sell their own mothers for a shot at those proverbial fifteen minutes of fame. A lot of people who see Ryan Buell on *Paranormal State* assume he started out *wanting* to be a star, pursuing the show for nothing more than attention, money, and celebrity. But this projected image stands in stark contrast to the reality of the person I've come to know.

It's probably difficult to imagine from the other side of the television screen, but Ryan is an intensely private individual. Although he can handle himself eloquently in front of a crowd, deep down he's actually rather shy and introspective. He takes his work with *Paranormal State* very seriously, but would genuinely prefer to stay at home, far from the limelight, quietly writing and taking time now and then to enjoy the company of his close friends and his beloved dog. The important thing to remember about television is that every show—even reality-based documentary shows like *Paranormal State*—sets out to tell a story. That story, however, is just one thread in the extremely rich tapestry of a person's life. There's always more to be told.

This book reveals much more of Ryan's story, and it's a story that needs to be told. There are sides to him that never really come to the forefront of the show, mainly because only so much can be condensed into twenty-two minutes. For anyone who wants to understand the reasons behind his involvement with *Paranormal State*, as well as more about the investigations themselves, this book is crucial.

I believe that one reason for the show's success is that Ryan did not pursue *Paranormal State* for the attention or even the monetary incentives it offered. In fact, Ryan is the type of person who would gladly sacrifice his position on the show in the interest of integrity. He's fought long and hard to keep the show as real and honest as possible so that it can continuously push boundaries that educate, inform, and open people's minds to new and sometimes radical possibilities. For Ryan, it's all about the message and the good it can do. It's a message that ties back to Ryan's early years, back when he was a scared little boy, lying awake at night wondering what sort of terror haunted him in the dark. Now, as an adult, *Paranormal State* has offered him the very best vehicle for getting that message out to the world: It's not your imagination.

Michelle Belanger
Author of *The Ghost Hunter's Survival Guide*

Introduction

I don't know about you, but my parents never hoped I'd grow up to be a paranormal investigator. When I was young I was told that there's no such thing as ghosts. For my own reasons, I didn't buy it. Nor should you, whether it's from your parents or a scientist who thinks he has all the answers. Truth is, like with everything else, no one can give you all the answers. You have to find them for yourself.

When I meet with people or speak at a college, most hope I have the one piece of evidence or testimony that definitively proves the existence of life after death. But I don't. All I have are my stories and experiences, sometimes with really compelling evidence to go along. Do I want to find the smoking gun that proves God exists, that we're not alone in the universe, or that we survive after death? Always. But that's only part of my search.

If you've watched the TV show *Paranormal State*, which documents our cases, you know that I had paranormal experiences as a child. Not just one, but several. My mother was open-minded about it, to a point. I think it genuinely frightened her. I remember her calling members of my family and asking for advice. They didn't exactly know how to handle a child who claimed to see things, so they did what they thought best. They told me to ignore it and did the same themselves.

After the experiences had gone on for a while, I had a meeting with my Catholic priest. Although he was a very kind man, he wasn't helpful. I don't think he knew what to say. He seemed glib, like he didn't believe me, and just told me to pray more. I remember being baffled by that, because he was, after all, a man of God. If he didn't have the answers, then who did?

In time, as my encounters escalated, my mother decided it was easiest to ignore them. I even recall the moment it felt like she stopped believing me. She never came out and said it at the time, but it was there, on her face, in her body language. Everyone I reached out to couldn't, or wouldn't, help me. I was on my own. Even though the terror continued, I gave up.

To my surprise, as quickly as the phenomena started, they stopped. Completely. I don't know what upset me more: the torment or the fact that it had ended without explanation.

My life did not go back to normal. I tried as hard as I could to forget, and for a while I did. But I was angry—angry at my family for acting like nothing happened or that it was all a joke, angry at myself for being victimized, angry that no one believed me. It strained my relationship with my family and friends. I didn't trust anyone.

In the end, I was able to find a way to bottle it all up. The anger was still there, of course, but over time I forgot why. My family and I continued to fight. And my behavior became somewhat destructive. For the most part, though, as I got older I tried to blend in and be normal. Then, when I was around fifteen, something great happened.

I picked up a book by legendary investigators Ed and Lorraine Warren. Reading about their lives felt like a trip around the world. From haunted dolls to demonic possession, it was all there, complete with documentation and testimony. Hungry for more, I soon discovered the works of Dr. Hans Holzer, John Keel, and even Carl Sagan. Almost everyone had a differing viewpoint, but they had one thing in common: They were dedicated to pursuing answers about the unknown.

The Internet was just becoming a household phenomenon. When we finally got our computer online, as I was turning sixteen, I discovered an even bigger world. To my amazement, there were ghost hunters and investigators all over the country. I can easily remember listening to my first EVP (electronic voice phenomenon), seeing my first ghost photograph, and more important, realizing for the first time that I was not alone.

A single, overpowering thought invaded my mind. I'd become an investigator. I'd find my own answers about what I'd experienced, solve mysteries around the world, and, along the way, help people out.

A childhood friend, Christina (Chris for short), was my first partner. She also happened to be a staunch skeptic. She kept my feet on the ground—or tried to, anyway—as I searched the wondrous state of South Carolina for ghosts, ghouls, and lizard people (South Carolina had lizard man sightings in the late 1980s). For three years I investigated churches, cemeteries, and old, abandoned (and of course, creepy) buildings.

In those first days I found cases mainly by asking around— talking to friends and neighbors about local hauntings. There were a few times though that I did have more inventive moments, and actually posed as a reporter. Well, technically I *was* the managing editor of the high school paper, *The Cock's Quill*, and had the school ID.

There was one particular place I was interested in—a plantation that was rumored to be haunted—but I was told the owner was vehemently against discussing it. Christina was the school photography editor, so she and I knocked on the door and said we were doing a feature on fantastic places in Sumter. The owner let us in. As Chris took pictures, I asked about the history and so on, but eventually I got to my questions about the ghosts, and it worked out fine. That was a little trick I used a few times, even in college. Personal quest aside, I was just having fun investigating and unafraid of the consequences.

Like a lot of life dreams, though, things didn't work out exactly as I pictured. I didn't come up with many answers. In fact, I wanted to believe that there was *something* there so badly, at times I overlooked more obvious natural explanations. If something even *seemed* paranormal—creaking floorboards, winds—I was easily convinced it was. I've since learned that finding those more common explanations always comes first. Having faith in the existence of the paranormal, like faith in anything, means believing that it can stand up to honest skepticism.

Nowadays, I'm far from being a ghost hunter, going out only to document evidence or look for thrills. Most of my clients, the families I meet, aren't just looking for that scientific validation. They want to grasp what's happening to them, and, if possible, find a resolution. They need to be understood and helped. And that's what I try to do.

The skeptics' best reason for condemning paranormal experiences is always sadly lacking: If they didn't see it, it can't be true. Some can't even believe things they *do* see. I know. I spent the first sixteen years of my life trying to deny what I knew in my heart to be true—that there *is* something out there. That's why I don't immediately laugh when a child tells me he saw a monster claw its way out from underneath his bed, or write a woman off as crazy when she says she's hearing voices or having visions.

It may be the nature of the unknown to remain unknown, even unknowable. That doesn't mean the veil between the worlds doesn't slide back now and again, letting a select few see behind it, creating experiences that change them forever.

That doesn't mean I always take everyone at his or her word. Even though I want to believe—in ghosts, demons, beasts, and little green men—I'm not just going to buy anything. I've got standards, you know! But when the other side comes knocking, I can't ignore it, especially when it breaks down my door and invites itself in.

It's important to point out, though, that the way things look to me and what someone watching *Paranormal State* sees aren't always the same thing. Like any television series, in the interests of time and good entertainment, the show presents reality through a particular lens. Out of more than forty-eight hours or more of tape, the talented producers and editors have to boil the story down to twenty-two minutes. I wish I could say that I'm always that sensitive, caring, and selfless person seen on the show every week, but I'd be lying through my teeth.

My original reason for investigating was completely selfish.

I wanted answers for myself. I wanted to find the darkest side of the paranormal and confront it. It's like that scene in *Twister*, when Helen Hunt's character (who'd seen her father and home destroyed by a tornado when she was a child) disregards her own safety just to get closer to the center of the tornado. She *had* to see it, no matter the cost.

The paranormal experiences I had as a child were like that tornado. If you find that laughable, don't worry. I won't get offended. Most of my high school peers thought it was a joke, too.

So despite what some might believe, I didn't become a paranormal investigator to do a TV show. Exploring the unknown is something I'll be doing until I find the resolution I'm looking for, until I have my answers.

At the same time, clients often come to us because they're genuinely suffering, so I've learned to put my personal obsessions aside—sometimes grudgingly. Even when I do, though, deep down I'm still thinking that maybe I'll figure something else out as well.

In this book I try to capture that: my motives, my journey, what I've learned, and what I've had to unlearn. It's only a piece of a lifelong story involving over two hundred cases and twelve years, but it covers the crucial beginnings and most of the first season of *Paranormal State*.

I'm very proud of a lot of the work we've done throughout the four seasons we've completed at the time of this writing. Importantly, I believe we've stayed true to my original goals. I feel very fortunate to be where I am, with plenty of energy and plans for the future. Our successes inspire me to keep pushing the envelope, and I'm always learning new ways to do that, this book being one. Here you'll read many things about the cases that never made it to the screen, a lot of the hows and whys behind not only the show, but my personal journey as well, and how my attitudes and beliefs have changed along the way.

At the end of the day, though, the final thing on my mind, the thing I'm still chasing, is the truth. The show's intro gets it right. Each time I help someone I feel like I'm one step closer.

1

A Dark Crossroads

I hope you understand that what you're doing is not just hauntings. You're helping people in a lot of different ways that maybe you don't even realize.

As it says at the beginning of every episode of *Paranormal State*, my name is Ryan Buell and I became interested in the paranormal because I'd experienced some very frightening phenomena as a child. As I got older, I wasn't afraid anymore, but I was curious and fascinated. I studied the paranormal as much as I could. In high school I wrote about the paranormal for the school paper so often that people called me Mulder, after the character from *The X Files*. My interest continued as I became an undergraduate at Pennsylvania State University. On September 16, 2001, I founded the Paranormal Research Society (PRS) out of a clubroom in State College.

I discuss some of our very early cases later on, but PRS's first *major* investigation took place at the Pattee Library, the location of one of the only murders that ever occurred on campus. To give you the backstory, on November 28, 1969, a twenty-two-year-old graduate student in English named Betsy Aardsma was in the library stacks when someone stabbed her once in the heart. According to reports at the time, the librarian heard two men saying, "Somebody better help that girl." Upon inspection, she found Betsy with books toppled over her. There was no blood visible, so the librarian didn't even realize she'd been stabbed. By the time they got Betsy to the hospital her lungs had filled with blood and she was dead. The murder was never solved.

I learned the story soon after starting school. When I first came to Penn State in August 2001, I had two jobs: one at the cafeteria in the Student Union, the other as a telemarketer. During the telemarketing training we were asked to say something true and something false about ourselves. The true thing I said was that I was a young paranormal investigator. Don't know why I said that. Everyone looked at me like I was a fruit loop.

But after the training session, a supervisor came up and told me she found what I said really interesting. We got to talking and she mentioned how some people thought they'd seen Betsy Aardsma's spirit in the library. I did the telemarketing thing for a day, realized it wasn't for me, and quit, but the story stayed with me.

I was new at the school and didn't know anyone, so one Friday night, I went to the library microfilm section and started researching Betsy. It took hours, but I finally found the date of the murder, and with that it was easier to get more articles.

Within a month, I was forming PRS. I posted flyers in the community center of the school, the Hub, campus dorms, bulletin boards, and so on. Four people showed up at the first meeting, and the club was on its way.

One of our first members worked at the library and knew a lot of people who'd had experiences there. Some claimed to have seen Betsy in the stacks, in the red dress she wore when she was killed. Others reported more unpleasant experiences, seeing black shadows, being touched. Some even said they were assaulted by a figure that would disappear into thin air when they screamed.

With all this activity, it was clear this should be our first case. I headed down with some of our members during library hours to get a feel for the place. The stacks where the murder occurred were pretty empty. There were no desks, just old books in foreign languages that very few people looked for.

At this point we had no training program. PRS pretty much accepted anyone. Unfortunately, three of our members, self-proclaimed witches, attempted to contact Betsy. Using permanent marker, they drew what they considered a magic circle on the library floor. I think to this day you can still see a faint outline. Then they freaked out, thinking we'd angered the spirit of the murderer. It was totally out of control. It did make me realize, however, that not everyone who wanted to join PRS had the same aspirations I did.

But the club progressed. In 2002, we established UNIV-CON (some people think it's an acronym, but it's simply short for University Convention for Paranormal Research). An ambitious project, it was an attempt to offer paranormal enthusiasts an educational summit on paranormal research in an academic setting. Every year, we saw attendance grow, up to the thousands. At UNIV-CON I've met not only more fellow paranormal enthusiasts, but also many experts and professionals in fields like psychology, chemistry, and forensic science, which has helped make PRS a lot more than just a group of students who share an interest.

Events have a way of weaving patterns you can't see at the

time. The beginnings of the television series worked that way, starting with a tragedy. On Halloween 2001, a Penn State student, Cindy Song, disappeared. Following a night of campus parties, she was last seen outside her apartment building at 4:00 A.M.

The police worked the case hard—and the campus community followed closely—but there were no leads. Seven months later, in April 2002, she was still missing. It was then I took the step of contacting the police and suggesting they use a psychic. Since the Cindy Song case hadn't gone anywhere using other means, I thought it was worth a try.

The reaction from the police surprised me. Not only were they open to the idea; they were also willing to publicize their involvement with PRS. They explained that part of their reasoning was that the local news had stopped covering the case. Whether psychics were real or not, they hoped it might draw more media attention and with it, new information.

With their approval, I contacted Carla Baron, a psychic who later became involved in the nationally covered Elizabeth Smart kidnapping investigation.

Things worked out as the police had hoped. When word got out that a psychic was involved, the press picked up on the case with renewed interest. We spent a lot of time that summer trying to find Cindy Song, but, sadly, never did. Years later, Brian Sprinkle, the lead investigator, concluded she was likely dead. By 2005, there were no new leads. These days Cindy is used as a cautionary example by the State College mayor to remind students to stay safe at night, and not to drink too much.

That failure was very emotional for me. In my heart, I believed we'd find her—that it was meant to be. That only shows how naïve I was at the time. I still hope that the Aardsma and

Song cases will be solved one day. But Betsy died forty years ago. How much more information are you going to get? Cindy Song disappeared eight years ago. In that time the university town has changed populations twice, so I doubt her case will be solved either.

As a result, though, for the first time PRS was in the center of a surreal media spotlight. During our search, I was contacted by a documentary crew that wanted to follow psychic Carla Baron and the investigation. Those efforts later became the basis for *Psychic Detectives*, the first big paranormal series on TV. My name was also passed around in media circles and soon I was fielding more and more offers for interviews and show appearances. Wanting to do my part to expand awareness of paranormal phenomena, I was eager to accept, but, once again, the truth was not as I'd pictured it.

I quickly learned that the media thought of the paranormal as a novelty. During Halloween season everyone would air all these terrible paranormal specials that followed "real" ghost hunters on "real" ghost hunts. It just wasn't interesting or important to me. I wanted to do something better, with integrity, something that showed what a paranormal investigation was actually like.

At the same time, PRS was evolving. When it began, we were mostly interested in gathering evidence, proof. As I came in contact with more clients who were under duress, the focus shifted more toward trying to help. Failing to find a murderer aside, I learned there were other real ways to help, one of which was just believing what people had to say.

There's a huge taboo against openly discussing otherworldly experiences. People are afraid to talk about their experiences for fear of being judged, losing their jobs and families, or being discounted as crazy and getting locked up in some institution. As a result, they carry around this huge secret about experiences that deeply affect them on an emotional and mental level. Some of those who came to us were relieved just to have someone listen. Given my own experiences as a child, I was very sympathetic.

Having a television series is a fantasy lots of people probably have at some point and I was no different. As a result of the media attention, and *Psychic Detectives*, I'd been speaking to two producers from LA about a show. It was just talking, no contract, but as a result I started thinking about what *kind* of show I'd want to be involved in.

I decided I'd want it to try to accomplish two things: The first would be to show the realities of the investigation process, the trials and tribulations of the investigators, the quest for information, and the difficulty in getting proof. Second, I would want to fight that taboo, let people know that they're not alone, not crazy, that there *is* something going on in their lives that can be dealt with.

Don't get me wrong. I respect some of the other paranormal reality shows, but they focus on that first part, the evidence. The client becomes a side story at best, whereas to me, they're equally, if not sometimes more important. Having gone through it myself, I wanted to hear their stories, learn how it's affected their lives, *then* try to find the connection to the paranormal—if one exists. That way, we learn about the people involved and can do our best to help them, even if the final truth can't be known.

As I was mulling all this, PRS was increasingly active, doing as much as an investigation per month, which seemed like a lot at the time. I'd also experienced my first demonic cases and had begun doing some work with the church. It was then my own life took a dark turn.

During my senior year, I became involved in two very extreme cases that turned out to be related. One began in October 2004, the other in January 2005, but the cases overlapped, required frequent visits, and together lasted until May 2005. The church was involved, and in the process I witnessed the most intense activity I've ever seen.

The complete details are worthy of their own book. Suffice it to say that while the rest of my peers were worrying about paying bills, passing classes, or what nightclub to go to on the weekend, I was helping a family survive a demonic attack in a house that, according to a psychic priest, sat on a portal to hell.

At one point, I begged a professor for an extension on my final term paper because I had to participate in a formal rite of exorcism. When he stopped laughing, he managed to say it was the most creative excuse he'd ever heard (he later passed me, but only because I threatened to fight my grade with the dean for as long as I lived).

Toward the end of those cases, an Emmy-nominated producer and president of Four Seasons Productions Intl. named Betsy Schechter got in touch. She asked if we had any footage we could show her. The Friday before spring break 2005, long-time PRS member and close friend Sergey Poberezhny, another member, and I stayed up all night assembling interview clips and evidence. Finally finishing by 7:00 A.M., we burned it to a DVD and FedExed it out.

Exhausted, I crashed, and then headed home the next day. When I arrived, an e-mail was waiting for me from Betsy. I e-mailed back, expecting she'd answer in a few days' time, but she wrote back immediately, asking to speak to me on the phone. We wound up talking for two hours. I told ghost stories and Betsy avidly listened.

In May a two-man camera crew came to Penn State for a test shoot: producer Dave Miller, who later became coexecutive producer for the series, and his assistant. They planned to film us socializing at the school then follow us on an investigation for two days.

That first night, after trying to get into a crowded local bar, we went to a party. Dave filmed us playing pong, drinking beer, and flirting with girls. It was exciting, but weird. The partygoers were playing things up for the camera. I tried to act natural, but if you're thinking about it, it's not natural, right? Over time you wind up forgetting the cameras are there, but that time had yet to come.

The next day we went to Pittsburgh, the location of one of those two extreme demonic cases. As we stayed the night, things became intense. Our client began speaking incoherently, saying things that sounded like language, but weren't. The fancy term is *glossolalia*, a condition where someone constantly, fluidly vocalizes in speechlike patterns that aren't easily recognizable. It's part of some religious practices, but also considered a symptom of demonic possession.

Adam, an early PRS member, tried hypnosis on her. He was older than the rest of the team, and working on his PhD in clinical psych. During the session, different personalities came through the client and we became convinced an exorcism was needed. Driven by the client's husband, we ran out in the middle of the night to find a priest.

As we searched, it began to snow, which was very unusual,

since it was May. Arriving at a large church, we tried to locate the rectory, the residence for clergy. A narrow alley held some metal steps to a door with a mail slot, so we figured that had to be it. I rang and knocked, with no response. I was about to give up when a light came on from a floor above us. Shortly, an older priest, wearing pajamas adorned with images of Kermit the Frog, opened the door and eyed us suspiciously.

There we were: a college kid, a balding psychologist, and a cameraman, asking for an exorcist. He looked as if he would've been happier to find three muggers standing at his door. I started to throw out a lot of information, so he asked me to slow down. I did, and having worked with the church before, I also dropped some names from the diocese as references.

He explained I didn't need to convince him. He believed in the demonic, but he did not perform exorcisms. It wasn't something he could do. Instead, he gave us some holy water* and a rosary.

I remember him saying, "I hope you know what you're doing. You walk where angels fear to tread. I'll pray for you." Then he shut the door.

With the family under duress, Adam and I felt we had to do something to help them until we could get a priest. We planned to go back and try a house blessing.

Meanwhile, Dave, our visiting producer, was flipping out. "You actually believe this stuff?" he asked. "I'm in a desolate area of Pittsburgh in an alleyway begging a priest for an exorcism? What the fuck am I doing? This stuff is real?"

---

* For those who may not know, in the Catholic and other Christian traditions, holy water is sanctified by a priest and used in baptisms and other blessings. You usually find it in the font near the church entrance. Many believers bring some home as part of their worship.

I hadn't noticed Dave's reaction, but he was shaken. As we drove back to the house, he called Betsy and said, "I feel like I took the red pill from *The Matrix*." After a frantic conversation, Betsy told him if he wanted to, he could go.

I was surprised at Dave's reaction. Our worlds were colliding. It struck me then how completely and utterly absurd my life must have looked. Adam and I started laughing. Once we reached the house, we shared the story with some of the PRS team. Eilfie Music, who'd been in PRS practically since I founded the club, and Serg, who was there as part of the team, were as surprised as I was.

And we went back to the case.

Dave and his assistant met us again the next day and shot a little more footage before they headed back to New York City. Dave, who's a superfunny, laid-back person, later told me that when he got home, for the first time in a long while, he prayed. He also started sprinkling holy water around his room. Although we had an uneasy introduction to each other's worlds, Dave came back. He was a coexecutive producer for the first thirteen episodes in season one and for all of season two.

At the time, when I didn't hear anything, I figured the project was dead. But two days later, Betsy called, still very interested. Looking back, having a cameraman so freaked out he had to leave probably made her think she'd hit the jackpot with us.

For me, though, those two cases were profoundly different from wandering around an empty auditorium with a tape recorder and a camcorder hoping a chair would move by itself. I'd helped the families, yes, but I was also given a disturbing warning: The malevolent entities now knew me, and would one day return to attack me.

I was no longer an outside investigator looking in. I was not only knotted to the phenomena, I was left feeling as if these investigations nearly killed me. They certainly turned my life upside down. As a result of the fallout from these cases, which I discuss later in the book, I wound up dropping out of school in my senior year, and left at a very depressing crossroads.

I had to ask myself: If this was what it might mean, show or not, could I keep investigating? Was this *really* the direction I wanted to go in?

IMPORTANT DATES IN PRS HISTORY

Paranormal Research Society founded	09.16.01
First case (Betsy Aardsma/Pattee Library)	09.30.01
First full investigation (Schwab Auditorium)	03.02
First big case (Cindy Song disappearance)	04.02

First UNIV-CON	10.24–27.02
Test video	04.29–05.01.05
Pilot ("Sixth Sense")	03.31.06
Paranormal State begins shooting season one	11.08.06
Paranormal State season one premieres	12.10.07

SEASON ONE SHOOTING ORDER AND AIRDATES

Shooting Order	Original Air Date
"Sixth Sense"	12.10.07
"The Name"	12.10.07
"The Devil in Syracuse"	12.17.07
"Dark Man"	12.17.07
"Vegas"	12.31.07
"The Cemetery"	01.07.08
"Pet Cemetery"	01.07.08
"Man of the House"	01.14.08
"Beer, Wine & Spirits"	01.14.08
"Paranormal Intervention"	01.21.08
"Shape Shifter"	01.21.08
"School House Haunting"	01.28.08
"The Haunted Piano"	02.04.08
"The Woman in the Window"	02.11.08
"Requiem"	02.18.08
"The Asylum"	02.25.08
"Mothman"	03.03.08
"Freshman Fear"	03.10.08
"The Knickerbocker"	03.17.08
"The Sensitive"	03.24.08

2

Paranormal Pilot

Those black ones are the problem. Somehow I know they're danger.

Once the decision was made to shoot a pilot, the next step was to find a case. Naturally, I wanted it to be exciting and interesting, but there's no way to know for certain what will happen on an investigation until you get there.

It also wasn't as easy to find a case back then. These days we get lots of leads. Whenever I'm in State College, I get recognized. Sometimes I'll be sitting at a bar, someone says, "Oh my God, it's that guy from *Paranormal State*!" and twenty thousand people notice me. PRS wasn't unknown, but we weren't flooded with clients.

In conjunction with our producers, we issued a press release asking any haunted families open to being filmed to contact us. The search made the local news, and I wound up doing a couple of televised interviews with some of the team. That gave us a pool of responses to take a look at.

Eventually, we received a call from Shelly Seighman* in Mount Pleasant, not too far from Penn State. Shelly was an administrative assistant, her husband Bryan a retail manager. Both were very concerned about their eight-year-old son, Matthew, who was regularly seeing mists and spirits. If that weren't frightening enough, at times these mists told him to do horrible things like jump off the roof or stab his mother with scissors. One spirit seemed less malevolent, though, and Matthew knew him by name, Timmy.

The Seighmans had been to doctors and counselors and no one could figure out what was wrong. Of course they were extremely concerned.

When I spoke to them, they came across as unbelievably *believable*. To me, they felt like a normal family in despair, facing something they didn't understand, about to fall apart because of it. There were also indications of a possible explanation for the haunting. Shelly thought Timmy might be the spirit of a former resident. It sounded like a perfect opportunity to offer help, and a perfect case for our pilot. It even had a hook: With Matthew regularly seeing "dead people," it sounded like the film, *The Sixth Sense*.

While the case seemed perfect to me, for the first time, though, I had to consult people outside PRS. Our deal with Betsy and her company, Four Seasons Productions International and the production company, Go Go Luckey, was basically that while I had full control over what I knew best, the investigation,

---

* You'll notice that at times in this book and on the show I use full names for our clients and sometimes I don't. Last names are used only when permission's been given. In fact, since season three, we stopped using last names altogether, a decision I made collectively with production.

they had control over what they knew best, crafting the edited episodes. When we began, our investigatory process was new to them, while their concerns were new to us.

This would also be our pilot. We wouldn't get a second shot at impressing the network, so we all wanted the best possible case. Here there were concerns about Matthew's believability. He was a child, so how would we know what was an overactive imagination or not?

At the same time we've never gone into an investigation *knowing* there was true paranormal activity. Often we leave *still* not knowing. The only way to find out what's true is to do the investigation.

While I suspected something paranormal was going on, I knew deep down that this family needed the kind of help we could provide. Whether that meant uncovering an actual entity, finding ways to empower them emotionally so they could better deal with the situation, or empowering them just by providing explanations, would be something we'd have to find out along the way. At some point we had to roll the dice.

The family dynamic also seemed complicated for a twenty-two minute show. As Shelly indicates in the episode, the Seighmans' marriage was troubled. They also had an older child, Rachel, who was wheelchair-bound. She was suffering from a debilitating terminal illness that left her in an infant state. We agreed that since she didn't seem central to the haunting, there was no need for Rachel to appear on-camera.

In the end, we went ahead with the case.

New as I was to the whole process of discussing a case in terms of what made a good show, I soon learned that what might be considered risky one day, like shooting with children, could become standard the next. Once we had the experience of working with Matthew, it was easier to consider working with children, resulting in some of our best cases.

The only word to describe March 31, 2006—the first day of shooting—is *surreal*. One day life was relatively normal. The next, several vans full of technicians, camera people, directors, assistants, and equipment showed up at club headquarters.

Since this was the pilot, all the producers involved also showed up. In addition to my team, there were twelve or thirteen production people. Usually on a case, there'd be five or so of us, and whatever equipment we carried. Now we were quite a crowd. It was energizing, exciting, but also completely strange.

As everyone unpacked, I walked down the road with Eilfie. We were all excited about the show, but most of us had no longstanding desire to be on TV.

"Can you believe this is actually happening?" I asked.

"I just hope we don't get caught up in it," she said. "I hope they do a good job of documenting it."

Exploitation was certainly a fear I had. Television meant money and fame to a lot of people. Were we going to exploit the clients? Were they going to try to exploit us?

The producers, I assume, had their own worries. They were spending a lot of time and money on an expensive pilot. I could easily see them wondering, what if these college kids ruined it? What if the clients were lying? What if we didn't get any footage we could use?

The fact that our producers and the crew were extremely professional, hands-on, and communicative helped tremendously. Before anything was shot, we had a circle powwow with everyone to talk about the day.

I'd created an outline of how I felt things should go, starting with the briefing we always had before going out on an investigation. In a way, our briefing scenes are a real-life homage to *The X Files,* one of my favorite shows. They often have a scene with Mulder doing a slide show for Scully to explain their case. I think *every* paranormal investigator relates to Fox Mulder, but, to be a little cocky, I believe I have a stronger connection than most. As a child, Mulder experienced a sudden shift that changed his life. That was similar to what I went through.

When it came time to shoot, with all those cameras aimed at me, I was nervous. What was I supposed to talk about? How could I keep it interesting enough for a TV audience? In the end, I just went into the details about the case, like I had for years, and things worked out. "We were contacted back in February . . ."

That first briefing is particularly interesting to go back and watch. Aside from being our first shoot, there are people who have since left PRS and don't appear again. Except for the faithful few, the membership changed over time. People graduated, grew in different directions, and many months passed between shooting the pilot and shooting the series.

Adam was a special case. Though he wasn't technically our instructor, he'd been staff adviser for PRS. He came back for the pilot, but had already left the group. He'd told me that partly as a result of what we'd witnessed during those extreme demonic cases, he now had a more rigid view of doctrinal Catholic Church belief: Since every human spirit is sent to heaven, hell, or purgatory at death there can be no earthbound human spirits, no ghosts. Therefore any paranormal activity *must* be demonic.

It's funny, but because of the demonic cases we've done

on the show some viewers conclude that *I* think everything's demonic, but, based on my experience, I just don't believe that.

After the briefing, all twenty-three of us were on our way to Mount Pleasant. I called Shelly from the road, and, unfortunately, things were getting worse. Matthew's experiences were even more frequent now. The night before he'd felt something tighten around his neck.

As per the procedure we'd established over the years, when we arrived, Serg and the others set up our equipment while I sat down to talk with Shelly. Usually, though, I'd be alone with the client. Now I was surrounded by a film crew.

Beyond the short outline I'd written there was no sense of a formula, no plan. As it turned out, this worked very well. The producers and crew hung back and let us do our thing, a process that we've found leads to our best work and most exciting episodes.

It was easy to see that Shelly was upset. She told me how Matthew's experiences made him miserable and disruptive in school. He was even seeing the spirits manifest in class. They appeared more strongly at night, though, and Matthew was having a lot of trouble sleeping, despite medication.

One crucial thing I've learned is that there's nearly always an *emotional* aspect to hauntings. On the one hand, stress can make people see or hear things that aren't there. On the other, many believe that spirits don't have their own energy and have to borrow it. Stress can generate an excess emotional energy that attracts activity. Then again, encountering the paranormal creates stress, so it's hard to know how to unravel things.

I'd also learned, partly from Adam and his psychology training, to always proceed cautiously, with sympathy and concern. I try not to play pop psychologist. I leave the big issues to the professionals, which is why a counselor, like Adam, is an important part of the team. If the situation is clear to me, though, I do try to empower my clients to help themselves.

Here I felt a lot of sadness the moment I walked through the door. Caring for a daughter with a terminal illness had already put the marriage under pressure. Their new worries for Matthew, coupled with his refusal to sleep in his own bed, put an even greater strain on things. There was clearly a lot going on emotionally.

While I spoke with Shelly, Adam spent time with Matthew, trying to establish a relaxed, friendly atmosphere in which it would be easier for him to open up. You can see right away in the episode that Matthew wasn't a typical kid. He was often quiet and withdrawn.

As I mentioned, it's important to look at nonparanormal explanations first. Here, while it doesn't appear in the episode, a number of psychological checks were performed on Matthew. Though he had some speech problems, his doctors did not feel he was autistic or developmentally challenged. We were also comfortable there wasn't any question of physical or verbal abuse.

At the same time he seemed very shut down. I don't believe his parents directly told him his sister was dying or about their marital problems, but kids can sense what's going on in a household, and those factors may have contributed to his seeming withdrawal. It's sad to see that in any kid, but particularly with Matthew. My own childhood experiences also made me feel close to him. He had a very active mind, but it was occupied by dark concerns.

When he talked about the spirits, he said, "Those black ones are the problem. Somehow I know they're danger."

He described them as smoky shapes without full human form. "Mists" was the best he could come up with. He didn't know why they were around, but definitely thought they were after him, telling him, as I mentioned, to "stab Mommy" or "jump off the roof."

That kind of malevolence is sometimes demonic, but not all of his experiences were threatening. One spirit he saw, Timmy, not only had a human shape, but Matthew wasn't particularly afraid of him. Their conversations were, I guess, what you'd call a little more "normal."

One of the things that drew me to the case was the possibility of explaining the haunting historically. Shelly suggested to us that Timmy might be the spirit of Timothy Shirey, a former resident of the house. Research, both about the location of the activity and its past occupants, is always important. Here we were able to piece together Timothy's story in a way that strikingly fit in with Matthew's experiences.

A local newspaper article described Timothy Shirey as schizophrenic. Unable to live independently, he was cared for by adoptive parents. Shelly believed some of his friends were still in the area, and we were able to track a few down, including Mike and Lori Dopik.

The Dopiks described Timothy as withdrawn and childlike, making him, in a way, like Matthew. Another friend described how Timothy would come over to hang out, but would often just get up and leave without saying good-bye. He disappeared for days or even weeks at a time.

In his midthirties, Timothy's life changed drastically. One of his adoptive parents passed away and the surviving parent was moved to an assisted-care facility. The Shireys' eldest biological son decided to sell the house. Faced with fending for himself for the first time in his life, Timothy disappeared. According to a neighbor interviewed in the episode, when Timothy left, the only thing he took with him was a .22 caliber rifle.

Two months later, when Bryan and Shelly bought the house, Timothy hadn't been found. They remodeled so that Rachel could get around more easily in her wheelchair, and moved in, not knowing about Timothy. Matthew began seeing spirits a few months after moving in, and may have seen Timmy while he was still considered missing.

There was a big patch of overgrown land in the neighborhood. Six months later, workers began clearing it. People started walking their dogs and wandering around there. That's when a neighbor found Timothy's body, dead from a .22 caliber bullet wound.

Some of the locals we spoke with felt Timothy was murdered, but I tend to discount those stories. In many of the cases I've investigated, whenever suicide is the official explanation, some people just don't accept it. Given his situation and the fact he'd brought his rifle, suicide seems likely to me. Matthew was five at the time the body was found and his parents kept the news from him.

This history provided a direct explanation and an identity for one of the spirits. Spirits tend to be connected to location. Timothy would naturally feel attached to his former home, and possibly be as afraid to leave it in death as he had been in life. Spirits are also often disturbed when their environment is changed. The house renovations, the clearing of the field, and the discovery of the body may have contributed to the activity.

While interviewing Matthew, Adam asked if there was any specific place that the spirits appeared. Matthew led him down into the basement, pointed to a corner near the furnace and immediately started walking away.

"Over there?" Adam asked. "By the furnace? Right now or some other time?"

Matthew paused long enough to say "now," and then kept walking.

Did Matthew's reaction mean Timmy was actually there? Maybe.

Unless someone manages to videotape a full-body apparition, or something levitating in laboratory conditions, hard evidence of the paranormal is, to put it mildly, tough. In my own experience, even when something amazing seems to happen right in front of me, one of the hard lessons is that it's still very possible there's a natural explanation.

I can't stress that enough. There've been times when I've been certain something paranormal occurred only to wake up a few mornings later and say to myself, "Wait a minute, could there be another explanation?"

In Matthew's case, the simplest explanation may be that he was imagining things or making them up. After all, no one else sees Timmy or the mists. While we were there, he wouldn't even bring them up himself. He never said to us, for instance, "Oh my gosh, I'm seeing them right now!"

Are they there so often that Matthew just doesn't bother mentioning it? Despite the history, I had to wonder if at least some of his experiences *weren't* real. To go back to that basement scene a moment, first Adam *asked* if there was something there, which could have led to Matthew's answer. Then again, during the interview outside, Matthew is often looking over his shoulder, as if something's there. A close examination of that basement footage also reveals that he moves quickly away from the corner *before* Adam asks about it.

Matthew also spoke about things in a way that made more sense if he actually were in touch with Timmy. For instance, he described Timothy as wanting to find "the guy who cut down all the trees." Why? "Because when Timmy was alive, all the trees weren't cut down."

Other evidence began to mount. The Dopiks told us that Timothy constantly wore Walkman headphones, something I didn't know until we interviewed them. Yet, Matthew described Timmy as wearing something in his ears or around his neck. It's hard to imagine how Matthew would know that, or why he'd make up something so specific.

Mike and Lori Dopik also provided us with a great way to test Matthew's story. They had a group photo from their wedding, taken years ago, in which Timothy appeared. As far as we were able to determine, Matthew hadn't seen *any* photo of Timmy. All we had to do was show this picture to Matthew and ask if Timmy was in it.

In a pivotal sequence in the investigation, I brought the photo to Matthew in the Seighmans' backyard. As I walked down to the swing set, I prepared myself for a negative result. "He's not going to pick out Timmy," I told myself. "Don't hype this up. Don't let him see that you're disappointed when he can't do it."

It all happened very quickly, on-camera, without any cutting away. I took out the picture, a shot of about twenty people, one of whom was Timmy about ten years before his death. I showed it to Matthew. "One of these people here is your friend."

Without missing a beat, he pointed at Timothy and said, "That one?"

After the episode aired, some viewers pointed out that Matthew was asking, as if he weren't sure. But it was a photo of Timothy Shirey in his twenties. He was in his midthirties when he died, which is how I assume Matthew would see him. If you knew someone at a certain age, then saw a photo of them ten years younger, would you be immediately sure who they were, or would you ask, as Matthew did, "Is that him?" It seemed to me the natural response.

It's not absolute proof. Matthew could've somehow seen photos of Timothy, or been coached, but for me it comes down to what's easier to believe. It's much harder for me to think that this stressed-out family would use their son that way. To me, it strongly suggested that Matthew really saw Timothy, that he could well be the real deal, a clairvoyant.

Accepting that possibility also explained a number of other things. The mists may have been drawn to Matthew because of his ability to see them. Timmy and Matthew, meanwhile, shared a childlike quality. Matthew might be someone Timothy could relate to, and vice versa.

Having done all we could in terms of research, the next step was to try to communicate with any spirits. The best hours for psychic contact are generally considered to be between 9:00 P.M. and 6:00 A.M., in other words, in the dark. After being involved with demonic cases, I also learned that 3:00 A.M., specifically, was significant. It is considered the antihour—opposite the time Christ is believed to have died on the cross—as if an evil entity's presence on the earth at that time mocks that moment.

Due to those extreme cases we'd faced prior to the pilot, we were all very much in a *warrior* phase. I, in particular, still felt surrounded by what I'd call, for lack of a better word, malevolence. Some of that comes across in the episode, which I imagine is difficult to understand without knowing where we'd been.

But the situation also gave us reason for concern. Voices were telling Matthew to harm himself and others, and I was increasingly convinced his experiences were real. We all felt there might legitimately be a demonic layer to this case, so we decided to try to communicate at 3:00 A.M.

The funny thing is that at PRS we never called it Dead Time before the show. Back when I wrote that short outline, I'd jotted down "3 A.M. . . . Dead Time." It wasn't a reference to spirits. I just wanted the crew to turn off all their electronic equipment, to keep the house as dark and empty as possible. Dead meant *silent*.

When the producers saw "Dead Time," they loved it and it's been part of the language of the show ever since.

For our first "official" Dead Time, I split everyone into three teams. Serg was in the basement monitoring the walkie-talkies and cameras. Eilfie took a team to the field where Timothy's body was found. I stayed in the house with Shelly and Bryan.

Though Matthew was the key to the activity, we never considered having him present. If the spirits weren't real, seeing his parents confront them might be confusing. If they were real, it could be dangerous for him.

As a standard part of the process, we each took turns trying to speak to the spirits, hoping to elicit some response—an unexplained sound, a voice.

Shelly put out a lot of energy, warning any evil entities not to try to influence her son. After about forty minutes, she told me she sensed a presence. I asked what it was like.

"Nothing good."

She felt it move right in front of her. Several of us heard loud breathing.

When I'm in the presence of the paranormal, I'll sometimes get what we call "that feeling." It's not simply a sense of being watched, but more like an instinctive sensation that a predator is stalking you. When Adam announced that he saw something moving in the basement, I got "that feeling."

Full of energy, Shelly wanted to rush downstairs and confront whatever Adam had seen. I immediately stopped her. She said she wasn't afraid, but that wasn't my concern. With that predatory feeling overwhelming me, I worried something wanted to separate us. I've had that happen. Out of nowhere, everyone in the team decides to disperse. At times that's led to near accidents where people could have been badly hurt. So I very much wanted to keep everyone together.

The activity didn't stop. Adam heard his name called. I heard a voice, too, soft and male. It may have called out "Adam," but it was hard to tell. All the more reason to keep together. After a while, nothing further happened.

Despite the strong personal experiences, our equipment didn't catch anything. Attempts to record the paranormal can go either way. Sometimes the equipment won't pick up what we experienced clearly. Other times it'll pick up things none of us heard or saw at the time.

Whether the activity was paranormal or not, the family's suffering was real. Shelly and Bryan felt helpless. They feared that evil influences were hurting their son.

Some viewers have said that the show has a Catholic or Christian bias. That's definitely my background and personal belief system, so I do view the world through that prism, but PRS has no religious affiliation and I don't impose my beliefs on anyone. My relationship to Catholicism, which I discuss in detail later, is complex. Eilfie is pagan. Serg is agnostic. We remain open to all beliefs.

At the same time, it's our goal to empower our clients, to ease their sense of helplessness. I believe the best way to do that is by using whatever language they understand, spiritual or scientific. Along the way, when it's seemed the right thing to do, we've used everything from pagan chants to Native American rituals.

The Seighmans were Christian, so with their assent we performed a Christian cleansing ritual. Adam read from the Bible as we walked from room to room, projecting a protective energy. Upon entering Matthew's bedroom Adam felt woozy and sensed something trying to stop him. But we soldiered on until the ritual was complete.

By morning, though we were exhausted, it seemed there was an effect. The house felt lighter. The family, Matthew in particular, seemed relieved.

As a child, to ward off the things I saw in my bedroom, I'd sprinkle some holy water around. It helped me relax enough to get to sleep. So before we left, I gave Matthew a bottle of holy water.

There are often cases where I'd like to stay longer and try to do more, but we'd run out of time and exhausted the possibilities. Though the investigation was over, I stayed in touch to see how things were going.

In follow-up interviews, Shelly told me that before bed Matthew would go up to his doorway and sprinkle a few drops around. It seemed to make his evenings more peaceful.

Shelly had also always said that Matthew could be outgoing, but it was only during our follow-up visit that he appeared happy and playful to us, smiling in a way Shelly hadn't seen in years. Matthew even began sleeping in his own bed again.

Bryan remarked that his son finally felt understood, like he wasn't abnormal or alone, and that we had given him that. That was especially good to hear, not having been believed myself for so long. While I was pleased to think we'd helped, I was quick to point out that Shelly and Bryan had the real power to protect Matthew, even when it felt like they might not.

The concluding text of the episode says the Seighmans "continue to adjust" to Matthew's gifts. That's true, but as time passed, the family also went through a lot of personal changes. The episode was shot in March 2006. In September 2007, Matthew's sister, Rachel, after having lived quite a bit longer than doctors expected, passed away. After that, they moved out of the house.

We were last in touch with Shelly a few months before the time of this writing. Matthew was having trouble for a year or so after our investigation. During our last update, I was told that he no longer has experiences and doesn't recall anything about them. That isn't unusual; most children tend to lose their connection with the otherworldly as they approach puberty.

"Sixth Sense" was intended only as a demo, but A&E was so impressed we ended up expanding it into a full episode. In a way, it became our gold standard. Even looking back years later, I'm very proud of it. It really does get across what I wanted the show, and PRS, to be about—both by presenting an interesting haunting and taking a personal look at the clients.

It was also the last case I worked with Adam. But along with PRS I'd yet to face some of the biggest changes, like adjusting to shooting not just one episode but an entire series.

EILFIE MUSIC

What's your favorite first season episode and why?

"Asylum," which is interesting since I wasn't thrilled about doing the case. I have an interest in abandoned buildings, especially asylums and hospitals, because of the history behind the walls.

Such places seem not haunted by actual ghosts, but the memories and the emotions of the patients and workers. The cemetery had the biggest impact on me. It was a field the size of a football stadium, virtually empty besides a few numbered markers. Under that unmarked ground hundreds of people had been buried. Originally, I was worried the show would ramp up the spook factor and forget these were once real people.

What's the one thing you'd like people to know about you?

I'm also an artist. My work ranges from the strange and macabre to the symbolic and lovely, but it's always slightly dark.

What's the one thing you'd like people to know about PRS?

We're much more skeptical than we seem. We're open to new ideas, but we all have our own level of skepticism. Rather than taking anything at face value, we ask a million questions. I like the saying "Be open-minded, but don't be so open-minded that your brain falls out." Wish I knew who said that.

Has working with PRS influenced your beliefs in any way?

It's made me more aware of my own beliefs. Everyone in the group has their own ideas. It's a bigger benefit than if everyone believed the same thing.

How do you think you're different now than when the show began?

I used to hide under a hoodie and sunglasses. I'm much more open in front of the camera now, but only to an extent. Ryan still has trouble getting me to perform any type of ritual or talk about my beliefs on-camera.

SERG POBEREZHNY

What's your favorite first season episode and why?

"Vegas"! Why? Because we got to go to Vegas. The best part was that due to the weather conditions we had to spend an extra night. That was the best excuse I've ever given my teachers on why I missed class. Plus I made a few hundred bucks from craps. To this day, I have no idea how to play.

Has PRS been an influence on your photography?

Most definitely. Not only have I been fortunate enough to receive free camera gear, but we've gone to some really amazing locations. Production has a director of photography, so I not only study how they set up lighting; I use their lighting for my shots.

What's the one thing you'd like people to know about you?

I have a strong passion towards photography. Each season, not only do I improve, I also take more pictures. With all the other hectic things in my life, photography does a great job at keeping me grounded.

What's the one thing you'd like people to know about PRS?

Hmm . . . I think the show already depicts us as being pretty f-ing awesome.

How do you think you're different now than when the show began?

I believe if you work hard and are proud of what you do, you get wiser. I don't only mean in the paranormal arena. I feel as if I've learned and grown from all sorts of experiences: dealing with people, building business relationships, becoming more self-aware.

For me all this leads into my spirituality, which has definitely blossomed since the beginning of the show. I'm particularly fascinated by all the beliefs I'm confronted with, how those systems evolved and how they continue to change.

Which piece of equipment do you think has produced the best, most reliable results?

Bah! A tech question . . . It's hard to answer without overthinking. Who am I trying to produce the results for? Most of the time, I prefer paranormal phenomena that is meant for me. I'm not here to make skeptics into believers, or to prove to believers that they're not crazy.

But looking back, video surveillance allowed us to catch a chair that moved by itself. Then again our audio recording caught some pretty intense growls. Ahhhh . . . can't decide.

What's the biggest technical challenge in trying to record a spirit?

The fact that we don't know anything about the "other world." What if there aren't spirits? What if it's multiple dimensions crossing over? Honestly, I am glad that this area is still unknown. I feel like a Columbus or a Magellan of the spiritual realm. I love it.

Without considering it a "final word," what do you think a ghost is?

Part of my personal quest for discovery.

3

The Storm Before the Storm

Why don't you want to do PRS anymore?

After we shot the pilot, months passed without word from A&E about whether or not there would be a series. There was a lot for them to consider, I was told, beyond just a good pilot. Our show was very different from any other paranormal show out there, and they had to figure out if they could market it to advertisers and viewers.

After the first month, I decided to let it go and worry about the rest of my future. I'd just graduated with a degree in journalism. I'd also completed some credits for a second degree in forensic anthropology, a subject that always fascinated me. My mom had only been willing to pay for one degree, but now I hoped to complete a second. I planned to stay enrolled in the fall, but I needed money. It was time to look for a job. I applied to a few places, with no luck whatsoever.

With no job in sight, I headed down to South Carolina to get away for a couple of months and think. The biggest thing on my mind wasn't the show or even a job. It was the same question I'd asked myself since those extreme demonic cases: Should I quit being a paranormal investigator and start finally living a normal life?

Serg came with me that summer. He'd never been away from the Northeast, and found my family, as he called it, "interesting." Growing up as an only-child immigrant from Ukraine, I guess he'd never seen many family feuds or sibling rivalries.

We spent the majority of the time at my family's lake house, which was fine by me. Being near water, especially down South, always calms me. I tried to hide my struggle over my life quest, but one evening after a few games of cards, Monopoly, and Apples to Apples with my siblings, I couldn't shake the pressure. My insides were tired of being in limbo. They were begging me to choose. I had to take a walk.

I headed to the dock and watched the sun slowly fall into the water. People around the lake community were heading indoors. It was quiet everywhere but inside my skull.

I'd seen plenty of things that should've made me feel vindicated, that I was right all along. There *are* unexplained forces. Others *are* being affected. I wasn't alone! It wasn't just all in my head. Why didn't I want to go on?

"You look like you've got a lot on your mind," a familiar voice said. Down the dock, Serg was smiling as he walked toward me in his swim trunks and an open, button-down shirt.

Apparently, I wasn't as good at hiding things as I had hoped.

I looked back out at the lake. Storm clouds swept over the sinking sun.

I asked him, "What if we just stopped PRS or gave it to a new team of college students? We can move on and do something great. Something we really want to do."

Leaning over the dock beside me, he responded without hesitating. "But I want to do PRS. Why don't you want to do PRS anymore? You're just starting to see the organization grow. We have so much we can accomplish."

"Maybe" was all I said. I knew it looked like we were on the verge of expanding, that a lot of what we'd set out to do was finally happening. "I guess I'm just wondering if these are things I really want to do anymore."

"Look man," Serg said, "why don't you just tell me what's up?"

I tried to gather my thoughts. Why was I conflicted? When it came down to it, I was still thinking about the two demonic cases from 2005. I'd been warned I'd face something like that again. I knew if I kept investigating, sooner or later I'd have to. Could I? Did I want to?

Then there were the missed opportunities. I was the one who didn't show at parties, or had to leave suddenly because "something came up." I regularly lost close friends. We drifted apart because I wasn't there.

And where was I? Sitting in a dark room challenging a spirit (or the empty air) to come forward and face me, to leave a tormented family alone.

I looked at Serg. "I guess I can't make up my mind if I want to do something normal or something extraordinary."

He knew I was the one who had to make the decision, so we left the conversation at that. We stood on the dock, watching the waves rise and crash against the stone and cement that held the wooden structure together.

One thing I love about summers in the South are the sudden and unrelenting storms that roll through with no notice. That evening, we had one of the most extraordinary I'd seen in a while. A tornado, a weak one, touched down on the lake and traveled to the land, throwing chairs and other small structures all over. As it ripped through, I tried to get as close as I could, to watch the chaos.

I saw a streak of lightning and heard the thunder boom almost immediately. That meant it was only a few hundred feet from where I stood. Remembering how in high school I'd sneak away with my parents' car and go storm chasing, I laughed. I also remembered the looks on my peers' faces when I said I was going to hunt tornadoes. They thought I was utterly insane.

The thrill of being there, though, even if you don't get to see one, is extraordinary. Just the thought I might actually witness something, just the chance—however small—kept me going back again and again. And yes, to me, investigating the paranormal was a lot like that.

I spent the rest of the summer constructing a tree house for Roman, my youngest brother. It was a great distraction, a perfect way to not think about investigations or the looming possibility of a documentary show. The finished project was two stories, with a tire swing on the roof, and a rope pulley that let you swing off the tree house, all the way across the backyard to another tree. A week after I was done, it was nearly time to head back to Pennsylvania, get ready for school, hopefully find a job, or another passion, and continue to build PRS.

The day before we left, I received a phone call from Betsy. The decision had been made. A&E had given the series the green light for thirteen episodes. She congratulated me, but warned we'd have to start work very soon. They planned to start filming in October, which only gave us about five weeks to get everything in order.

The news should have been stunning, but I was sort of numb. Instead of any intense emotion, I had a million questions. When did she think we'd start? When was the show coming out? Did they have a name?

I broke the news to Serg and my family. There was no big celebration, partly because even I wasn't sure exactly what this meant. I'd talked to producers for years. I'd had interest from the Syfy Channel and MTV, but nothing had panned out. Was this different? Emotionally, I wasn't sure. I was in a kind of wait-and-see mode. But it did seem I had my life mission set, at least for the next year.

September consisted mostly of dialogue with production and the team. We usually recruited new members for PRS in early October. Each semester, I'd put up some flyers, attract interested people, and then accept new trainees. PRS held regular weekly meetings. At its most successful, we averaged about twenty members. We had the same meeting space for years—218 Thomas, a classroom that fit us all comfortably.

This year, production paid for newspaper ads, and that wasn't the only thing that would be different. The announcement that we'd be doing a TV series created a boom in attendance. We had to rent out a different room to hold the fifty-plus people that were showing up.

Most were just curious. Who were these students who were

getting a TV show? A lot of film and theater majors showed up, too, to ask if we were hiring. I had to explain it was a documentary show that would follow what we normally do within the club, so, no performances.

Because I wanted PRS to be as professional as possible, I'd established a club hierarchy long ago. Anyone could be a member, if you paid your dues, but to be an investigator, you had to take a semester-long training class that met once a week, take five exams (one each for vocabulary, psychology, applied theory, investigation rules and regulations, and a general overview of the history of paranormal investigation), write a ten-page research paper, and then go on three extensive paranormal investigations. You also had to go through a background check and take a psychological exam. If you were a student, you also had to let us see your grade point average in order to watch over your academic performance.

An investigator began as a candidate, and then moved up to trainee, assistant investigator, field investigator, field marshal, admiral marshal, and, last, director.

When I explained, the producers loved the idea of having trainees as part of the show. Audience members could get to know the paranormal world along with our newcomers, and see their progression to investigators. I agreed. A trainee could represent the casual viewer, someone who didn't know what an EVP (Electronic Voice Phenomena) or EMF (Electromagnetic Field) detector was. It would be a way to teach the audience, explain things.

On the flip side of that, while our producers expressed their confidence in our experience, with Adam gone, another more adult figure would lend an air of authority. I'd spoken to clients on the phone who assumed I was a forty-year-old professor, only to be surprised when a baby-faced twenty-two-year-old showed up on their doorstep.

Trainee recruiting wound up like a casting call. We met with hundreds of students of every type (jocks, frat boys, sorority sisters, athletes, etc.). It was terribly important we find people who had a genuine interest in the paranormal and weren't just interested in being on television. There weren't very many.

One of my favorite interviews was with an aspiring film student who said he really wanted to see a demon. When I asked what he'd do if that happened, he said he'd use the tools and camera equipment to defend himself.

"So," I said, "what you're saying is if you see a demon, one of the most powerful forces in the supernatural realm, you'd throw your camera at it?"

He didn't make the cut. Another interviewee, who looked a lot like Seth from the movie *Superbad*, said if he ever actually saw a ghost, he'd run screaming like a little girl. Another pass. I usually left the session feeling like I'd wasted my time.

While I'd been busy looking for trainees, the producers did the heavy lifting on finding an adviser. They knocked on every Penn State department door and for a long time, all we received—from people claiming to be educators and researchers—were insults. I found it hypocritical and disappointing. We weren't asking them to be believers, just to be what he or she were—a psychologist, a scientist, a researcher. If they felt that there was a natural explanation for something they witnessed, they'd be welcome to express that.

Looking back, I realize that there was a level of fear. Openly being a part of a paranormal investigation is perceived as career suicide. Even as a journalism student I'd encountered intense disdain from professors who felt that I had a lot of promise but should drop that "silly little paranormal hobby."

Joyce, with a PhD in neuroscience, was the only candidate who was open to the idea. At the time, she wasn't employed by the university, but she later became part of the neuroscience staff as a full-time researcher. She was also a complete atheist. By that I mean that she was not simply a skeptic. She didn't believe in God at all and likely never would.

I tried debating that with her. "If there were irrefutable proof that God existed, what would you feel? Happy? Sad?"

To her credit, she looked as if she was seriously entertaining the question. I couldn't help but feel there was a sting of panic, as if the idea that a God existed was frightening. After all, if there were absolute proof God didn't exist, it would shatter my world. Likewise I thought the opposite would shatter hers.

We didn't come to any agreement, but I liked Joyce as a person. We shared a major obsession with the Joss Whedon TV series, *Buffy the Vampire Slayer*, and we both enjoyed dive bars. It became clear quickly, though, that there was a wall between us. As Joyce traveled with us, scouting cases, she was quick to discount every paranormal claim. She was like Scully on steroids.

One day during the trainee interviews, a vaguely familiar woman walked in. She introduced herself as Katrina Weidman and said we'd met before. Years ago, at a PRS meeting, she'd told me how her young brother died at an early age. On his deathbed, he described heaven to his parents. The experience shook Katrina. She also claimed she grew up in a haunted house and felt she might have psychic/intuitive abilities. As she grew older, they seemed to be getting stronger.

When she started talking about psychic powers, I was turned off. At the same time, it was obvious Katrina knew the paranormal culture, and had her own experiences.

As we talked, she impressed me. She answered my questions honestly and questioned her own abilities. When I asked if she wanted to be a full-time psychic, she laughed. "And be a Miss Cleo? No, I don't think so."

Exploring her abilities wasn't even the main reason she wanted to join. She just wanted to learn more about the paranormal.

I also asked if she wanted to go on a demonic case (which seemed to be fascinating to a lot of people, as if they expected it to be an amusement park ride).

"I don't think I'm qualified to handle a demonic case. And, like, who would *want* to go on a demonic case? It doesn't sound like it'd be fun, you know?" she said.

My thoughts exactly.

As for why she'd originally dropped out of PRS, she explained that at the time her life got too complicated. She'd had a bad semester, sprained an ankle, had a bad breakup, and someone broke into her apartment. Now she was a senior, very excited about learning more, and ready to take on the responsibilities. As we wrapped up, Katrina added that she was fine to just be a part of the organization, with or without the documentary show, if we'd give her a chance. That also made an impression, and in the end I agreed to give her that chance.

Four others were admitted as trainees; one was a film student sophomore named Heather Taddy. Like Katrina, she'd attended a few PRS meetings, but was always in the background. She wore bright punk-rock kind of clothing, huge earrings, and hair all over the place. To my experience, the people who tended to stay with the club were more low-key. Heather's appearance screamed, "I'm crazy. I'm in a rock band!" She seemed like the kind of person who got involved with ghost hunting as a thrill.

Once we sat down, she seemed more interesting. She didn't have much of a paranormal background, aside from playing with a spirit board with her cousin, and occasionally ghost hunting for fun, but she was genuinely fascinated. She'd even kept a PRS flyer she saw in Altoona years back and brought it to the interview.

I remember the producers being very excited about her. She did have a personality unlike any other I'd encountered at Penn State. She was unique, which is exactly the kind of person we like in PRS. She was also an aspiring filmmaker interested in documenting the paranormal. That especially excited me. In the past, PRS had tried, unsuccessfully, to have a team documentarian record our findings for a future archive project. So, I agreed to let her in.

Training was to start in two weeks. Given that the program had an overall 70–80 percent dropout rate, if we started with ten, we expected two or three to stay. Most don't realize how tough we make the classes. They think they're joining a college club that will take them ghost busting. When they find out it's a serious effort to study the paranormal, most either lose interest or can't take the workload.

Once, a trainee wrote a scathing letter about how stupid our requirements were. He argued it should act like a *normal* college club. *Anyone* who was interested should go on investigations. Instead of requiring essays, we should focus on socials and fund-raisers. Needless to say, he dropped out to pursue something else.

I never understood that train of thought—to do things like everyone else. How can you do anything extraordinary by doing things the usual way?

Much as I had my biases about who wouldn't work out, I was wrong about Heather. Training began in conjunction with our fifth annual paranormal conference, UNIV-CON. Out of the five trainees, all of whom were expected to volunteer, only one showed up—Heather Taddy. I wonder if she remembers the look of shock on my face as I saw her guarding the entrance door to a lecture, wearing a UNIV-CON staff T-shirt. At that moment, I decided that I shouldn't underestimate Ms. Taddy. She showed up as needed and worked the entire four-day conference.

A PSYCHIC BIAS

Viewers of *Paranormal State* may think I have great faith in psychics, but the opposite is actually true. Succeed or fail, as an investigator I work to follow strict rules of evidence. Psychics trust their abilities, some to an unreasonable extreme. While their answers seem definite, they often can't be proven. That makes it too easy for a charlatan to take advantage of the vulnerable and emotionally distressed.

On principle, I have no problem with someone claiming to have an ability, but many of the psychics I've encountered also seem to have a huge ego, and an unwarranted influence over people.

In my experience, those who charge exorbitant fees tend to get belligerent if you question their abilities—even politely. My feeling is that if you walk around claiming to speak to the dead, you'd best be used to—and even welcome—some serious scrutiny. Doctors and lawyers are always under scrutiny. They have governing bodies that handle matters of training and malpractice. Psychics do not. Unfortunately, many people come to them baring their souls and ready to empty their pocketbooks just to hear what they want to hear.

To me, if someone has an ability, a gift, he or she has a responsibility to share it. It's not a right, but rather a privilege. I understand the need to make a living, but I've seen psychics charge upward of one thousand dollars for a reading, and, worse, to my mind, offer to cross loved ones over to the other side—for a price.

Overall, I don't believe in 99 percent of the psychic claims I hear. Since the show has come out, I've met many self-proclaimed psychics, or mothers hailing their children as the next Chip Coffey. In order for me to believe in their abilities, they have to drop hard, undeniable testimony, and prove without reasonable doubt, that they had no prior knowledge. I also refuse to let psychics perform readings for me.

That said, there are a rare few I do trust as human beings. Yet, even today, no matter how many times I walk through a house with a medium like Chip Coffey or Michelle Belanger, no matter how much I enjoy their company as friends, I question them *every time*. They have to prove themselves again and again. And any information they intuit is always taken with a grain of salt—until tangible evidence can be found to back their claims.

4

Triple-Time

Even my sister is haunted.

After UNIV-CON in mid-October, production went into full swing. I wasn't sure what to expect. Normally we'd spend two weeks preparing for a case. Club rules required that at least one or two secondary witnesses be screened before a case could even move forward. There'd be preliminary interviews, a psychological evaluation, and interviews with any medical and psychology experts the clients had been working with. Then our tech, research, and occult departments would evaluate the case. In the process, we'd come up with a battle plan. We'd even try to get photographs and blueprints of the house in advance.

Then, of course, we had to raise money for car rentals, gas, hotel rooms, and other supplies. Typically I'd work extra shifts at a restaurant. Much as I despised the work, it was fast cash.

Now I had a team of producers and filmmakers bringing back video of the clients and the location. Anything I needed, they provided. Plus, for the first time, PRS had a few thousand dollars for equipment. To an organization that operated with a few hundred dollars and rented university equipment, it was a huge sum.

The shooting date for our first episode was pushed back to mid-November, giving us ample time, I thought, to pick the first case. Previously, PRS received a few dozen inquiries a month. Among those, one or two piqued our interest. In the past, it was a sufficient case flow. We took our time working on one case. We could go back and revisit a site if need be. In some instances, we'd go back three or four times.

Now that was a problem. As much as production wanted to honor our work process, the network expected thirteen episodes by March. That gave us four months to do thirteen investigations, an average of three a month, tripling what we were used to covering. There was some definite pressure to find a pool of interesting cases.

Taking advantage of the Halloween spirit in October, we put out flyers and press releases all over Pennsylvania. Dozens of calls and e-mails came through. Suddenly PRS was operating full-time. Every member had to pull extra shifts to sift through the responses.

Meanwhile, coexecutive producer Alan LaGarde, along with other crew members, had moved to State College to get things prepared for the series. It was already strange knowing we were going to be followed around by a documentary crew. It was even more bizarre knowing that ten to fifteen people would be living nearby for four months because of us.

I first met Alan at a restaurant in downtown State College. He originally came from news broadcasting, which reassured me that they were looking for authenticity. I learned later that in his early twenties, he'd run an entire news station. That was something I could identify with. I've often found myself reminded how young I am to be an authority figure. After all, there I was, a twenty-three-year-old among seasoned filmmakers, producers, and crew in their forties. Alan had a professorial air and a genuine ability to listen. I felt like I had a mentor in him, someone I could go to for honest advice.

As for the cases, most didn't pan out, but we did find a few that seemed worth hitting the road to examine further. A scout team went out, consisting of: Alan; our "test" cameraman, David Miller, now a coexecutive producer; our new adviser, Joyce; and me.

At one point we thought we had our first case. It involved a woman and her dilapidated home near Harrisburg. When she called us, she was crying, really frightened. There was an empty apartment in her house, where she heard footsteps and voices. I think it was a blessing that she eventually got cold feet and dropped out. It was a pretty dull case. Looking back, we easily explained most of the phenomena. At the time, though, we were under the gun and really upset.

Next we scouted a case in Pittsburgh. The woman, who'd attended UNIV-CON, was very cool, but while the activity had been intense about ten years ago, the most recent was minor, and months old. During our last conversation, though, she said she felt her house was haunted because her entire family was cursed.

"Even my sister is haunted," she said.

I asked what she meant and she went on in incredible detail about what was taking place at her sister Helen's home. Helen Isenberg lived in Blairsville, near Pittsburgh, which was on the way back to State College. With nothing really to lose, we decided to pay her a visit.

Once I saw the location, I didn't need any further convincing. I know I'm blowing my own horn, but there's a certain gut instinct all good investigators have. Helen's house was down a lonely road in the middle of farmland. Across from it were several acres of corn stalks withering before the coming winter. The house itself stood on a large plot of land. The only other structure in sight was a neighboring house Helen also owned. I just knew we had a great investigation on our hands.

I also immediately recognized Helen. Like her sister, she'd attended UNIV-CON. Due to her experiences in the house, she had an avid interest in the paranormal. She and her son, Justin, had come to the conference to learn more.

Helen had a motherly quality. She seemed kindhearted, sincere, and loving, but her face was etched with pain. Her youngest son, Chris, had passed way six months earlier from a drug overdose, in May, on Mother's Day. The property also had a history: A man had once drowned in the pond there.

She claimed the second house was the epicenter of the activity, so we toured that first. The family had originally lived there, until she opened up an assisted-living business for the handicapped. When the business needed more space, they'd moved to the other house.

But here she said they'd seen shadow people, objects had levitated, and doors had slammed. The house was used for foster care. She'd taken on foster children from the state, providing a sort of halfway shelter until the kids found a home. Many refused to stay in the house alone because of their experiences. Some even claim to have been attacked.

Her late son Chris, in particular, had seen the shadow figure often and called him the Dark Man.

All this happened over the course of several years. Children came and went. The house would sit empty until a new group arrived. Helen felt that this proved it wasn't just the children passing down stories to scare the newcomers. She was convinced something evil was present, and worried it might have kept Chris from moving on. I wondered what made her think that, but she was very hesitant to elaborate.

After spending a few hours with her, I could tell she was withholding things. Having a client hold information back wasn't new. It's actually common. People are afraid they won't be believed about more extreme activity. There are also often big emotional issues involved that are tough to admit to, and family secrets as well. With Helen, I got the sense this went beyond a simple fear of being embarrassed. There was something more going on here, and the challenge of trying to find out what it was excited the hell out of me. Furthermore, I was convinced that Helen's belief that the house was haunted was genuine.

I was sympathetic to her pain, but as we left, I got in the car smiling. We had our first case.

STANDARD EQUIPMENT

Our producers use their own cameras and microphones, but PRS has always tried to document cases ourselves. Over time, the equipment available to us has become more sophisticated, but it generally consists of the following:

Camcorders: Team documentarian Heather Taddy always uses one for interviews and general coverage, but other team members sometimes use them during investigations, particularly in large sites where our stand-alone cameras can't cover everything.

Audio Recorders: Aside from interviews, phone conversations, and director's logs, audio records are used during EVP sessions, where we attempt to contact spirits. Sometimes what seem to be responses are only heard on playback, while other times, sounds we hear at the time don't appear to record at all.

Monitor System: To cover as much of a site as possible, PRS uses several stationary video cameras that are wired to a central set of monitors in whatever location has been established as our technical headquarters. The camera feeds are recorded via computer hard drive. Serg keeps track of these during Dead Time, but they generally run for the length of our investigation.

Walkie-talkies: During Dead Time, everyone is in communication using walkie-talkies.

Motion Detectors: These devices, often used in security systems, flash a light when something in range moves. We'll typically set these up in areas where there's been a lot of reported activity. In several episodes, during Dead Time, they've gone off when nothing visible (as documented by our cameras) was present.

Electromagnetic Field (EMF) Detectors: This handheld device measures levels of electromagnetic radiation. Common household items from radios to refrigerators always generate an EMF. Normally, these aren't dangerous, but high levels have been shown to influence the electrochemistry of the brain, causing disorientation and other feelings that can be mistaken for paranormal activity. If electrical causes are eliminated, it's a possible indication of a supernatural presence.

Thermal Cam: Rather than light waves, this visually records temperature differences. In an episode from a later season, "The Glove," the thermal cam revealed a handprint on the wall, even though we'd documented through surveillance that no one had placed their hand on that spot.

5

Finding My Footing in a Rocking Boat

So you're asking a pagan to cover for a Catholic?

In the days leading up to the first shoot, more and more people trickled in to State College. Aside from the crew, producers from NYC and LA arrived to oversee the production. With twenty or thirty extra people running around, it was overwhelming, not to mention crowded.

The first day of filming went by in a daze. The first official "scene" involved Sergey, my dog, Xander, and myself. Neighbors near the townhouse I rented on Marjorie Mae Street gathered to wonder why twenty filmmakers had descended to film us playing catch with the dog. Everyone was very good about the commotion, aside from an aspiring filmmaker neighbor, who suddenly stopped talking to me the moment the show was announced.

As they filmed, the producers asked about the upcoming investigation, and my thoughts on our trainees, Heather and Katrina. The footage didn't make it into the episode, but I did get to see it. It's interesting to see now how we looked back then.

Later that day, we filmed the briefing at the Penn State HUB building. Production wasn't the only group with a lot of people. Usually, PRS had five investigators for a case, but here we had eight. Several members of the "old" PRS crew were there, including Ryan Heiser and Lance Cooksing.

Lance was a well-liked, very social guy with a great sense of humor, who'd joined along with his best friend. He was going through his own spiritual evolution and eventually converted to Catholicism.

Ryan Heiser, who also appears in "The Devil in Syracuse," is titled in that episode by his last name to avoid confusion. He was well-rounded, and also very religious, part of the Newman Group, a Catholic organization. We weren't terribly close, but he asked my advice once, while he was debating whether to continue with his political science major, or to join the priesthood. He'd always struck me as someone keenly interested in a spiritual path, so that's what I suggested—and what he chose.

If, even in slight way, working with PRS or talking to me helped him make that decision, it makes me feel good. Being a priest was something I'd considered. I thought the priesthood could use someone who'd seen what I'd seen—and remained open-minded. Now, in a way, I didn't need to go that route, because Ryan would.

He also helped with a bad taste I had for religion when my friendship with Adam ended. I remember shortly before we got the green light for the pilot, investigating a haunted boat in Philly with Ryan. We got to talking about the fact that I couldn't accept that all paranormal activity was demonic. Because he was open, accepted my opinion, and still wanted to go into the priesthood, it helped me.

So I get very sentimental whenever I see "Dark Man" and "Sixth Sense." We were a great team, together for a long while, and I'm saddened by the lost opportunity. Had the series started six months earlier, I'd have had more experienced people to work with. By fall 2006, many were preparing to graduate and had to leave the group to focus on school. As we filmed that briefing, I realized PRS was changing. I was embarking on a new adventure with new faces.

I told everyone about Helen's late son, Chris, who reported seeing a dark man, or a dark shadow, and how she worried that his spirit was trapped by whatever was there. People didn't want to stay in this house, Helen said, and activity happened every night. She was also worried about her surviving son, Justin. Paranormal or not, she needed help moving on from her grief and fear.

The next day, bright and early, we headed to Blairsville. As usual, I called the client during the drive, only this time a cameraman was covering me. Apparently, when Helen told Justin we were coming, it freaked him out. I wasn't clear what upset him, but it seemed he was experiencing things he hadn't even shared with his mother.

As we reached the house, it was like arriving on a film set for a horror movie, creepy and isolated. As an investigator, that was exciting, but things were about to get very different in ways that weren't quite as interesting. For the pilot, the crew had just hung back. The process had suddenly become more earnest, and I had no idea what to expect.

Four Seasons International and Go Go Luckey were our production companies. They did *Laguna Beach* and *The Hills*. They were famous for changing the way documentary TV was made. Their work was very cinematic, but . . . they'd never done anything involving the paranormal before. We were totally new to each other, and things would have to be worked out along the way.

The second I got out of my car, a producer I didn't know rushed up to ask what I was doing.

"Going to see my client."

"We need you to wait until the cameras are rolling so we can film it."

About forty-five minutes later I was dozing off in the car when the same producer tapped at the window. I was taken to a production van, miked, then brought to a production meeting to discuss the day and the flow of shooting with the director.

"So . . . how long until we start investigating?"

"Ten, fifteen minutes tops?" another producer said.

At the first meeting, they wanted to hear my plan for the day so they could prepare to document the investigation. What would I do at 5:00 P.M., 5:15 P.M.? How would Dead Time be set up? Who would be where? They also had suggestions.

"Maybe you and Joyce should have a discussion about the case before going in?"

"What about having Katrina do an interview?"

I was used to working with a notepad and a gut instinct. Between all the comments, schedule charts, walkie-talkies, and monitors, I felt like screaming. How could I break down the day? You *can't* schedule the unknown. Glimpsing something paranormal is always a shot in the dark. Production, though, needed some idea of what to do so they could set up shots and figure out when to give their crew breaks.

I tried my best to give them what they needed. After all, it was as if we were starting together all over again. I think it was an hour before I was told to go to the front door and ring. Helen was waiting.

Once we were settled in the kitchen, I began the interview. She told me that Chris, born in 1987, started seeing what he called the Dark Man at five years old, but the experience lasted his entire life. She said that Justin would know more about that. As she explained that it was Justin who'd found Chris's body, she choked up.

I gently asked about the drug overdose.

"It was prom weekend," Helen said. "He was really tired and couldn't sleep, so someone had given him something. He went to his room, must have taken it, and just never woke up." On Mother's Day morning, she went in to wake him up, but didn't realize he was dead until Justin tried to rouse him.

I repeated my question for her from our first meeting. *Why* did she think he was still there?

She explained she'd had a dream where she saw him, and his eyes had gone all dark.

"That is not my son," she told herself. "That is not my son."

Helen wasn't convinced anything paranormal was going on. She just wanted to make sure her son *wasn't* there, that he was at rest. I had the sense there was more going on here, but I didn't know yet what it was.

After that interview, our new adviser, Joyce, asked Helen about Justin, why he was upset we were there. She explained he did believe in the paranormal, but didn't want to be involved. "He's afraid something might happen."

As I tried to get my bearings on the case, the producers asked Joyce and me to sit down to discuss the interview. As we did, they kept stopping us, asking us to talk about this or that, discussions they felt they'd need for the edit. I tried to stay focused, but I wasn't used to any of this. It got to a point where I wasn't saying anything that was on my mind.

I don't think for a minute they intended to be disorienting. Like me, they wanted a great investigation. But it was too much for me. My thinking was getting fuzzy.

Finally, Alan asked us to follow him out to the old front porch.

"I can tell all this input is distracting you," he said. "Just go back in there and do whatever it is you want to do. We're just here to follow you. All right?"

I couldn't describe how thankful I was. "Sounds great."

Things got easier for me after that. We split up into teams to tour the site and hear about the different phenomena reported over the years. Helen took me to a room with an old Victrola, explaining how one night it started playing by itself. Katrina and Heiser spoke with Ray, Helen's husband. The death must have been hard on him as well, but he didn't show us much emotion or care to interact, which of course we respected. He did describe hearing heavy breathing, and footsteps. Whenever he went to check out a strange sound, there'd be nothing there. "It's always like hide and seek," he said.

In the basement, Helen explained they'd had some activity

in a small room. Her friend Delores was grabbed around the arm there. Delores later told Joyce and Eilfie that the resulting mark started as a sort of hole, and then became a rash. She also reported that a man had drowned in the pond on the property.

I'd heard that story when we first spoke to Helen. Then she'd told me that a patient of hers, suffering from severe schizophrenia, committed suicide on the property. Repeating the story for us on-camera, Helen described him as quiet and a little intimidating. He also had a box he kept with him at all times. It was never out of his sight. What was in it? She had no idea. One night, he left his bed and drowned himself in the pond. His box went missing at the same time.

Ray described the weather at the time, saying it was a drought season, so someone wanting to drown himself would have had to walk to the center of the pond.

"And he wanted to take that walk," he said.

This was around the time Chris was five years old, the same age his experiences began, according to Helen. I asked if she felt if the entity was related to the suicide.

"I don't know. It seems to fit in, but I don't know."

I pushed for more information about this patient, but Helen was reluctant.

Originally, we planned to hire a diver to go down to the bottom of the pond and search for the box. That was a great investigatory opportunity that was now affordable thanks to the show. It was less than twenty feet deep, so I had high hopes we'd find it. At the last minute, though, Helen decided against it. She never gave us a reason.

I felt confident the clients were being truthful about their experiences, but there seemed to be something else going on.

There had to be something more to this Dark Man and its relationship with Chris. Could Helen's patient have abused Chris, either physically or mentally? Unfortunately, we never found out, but there were things we could research.

To verify the timing of Chris's experiences, I asked Eilfie if she'd found any records of the suicide. She had found one, a vague newspaper account, and the article did have a date. If it were correct, the death did occur when Chris was five—the same year he began seeing the Dark Man.

That connection seemed strong, but there wasn't much to go on. Maybe this man had been hostile to Chris in life and was continuing to be in death. Then again, it could all be psychological. I obviously couldn't ask Chris. I also couldn't look Helen in the eyes and tell her anything.

Hoping Dead Time would give us something more, we broke off into two teams. The first, led by Joyce, Eilfie, and Serg, was out by the pond. I was with Josh and Heather on the second floor, in Chris's room.

We'd all already decided that during Dead Time that everyone except necessary camera and sound people would leave the house to keep the investigation as pure as possible. Often, the crew and producers were outside in the cold or in cars for the hours of Dead Time. The crew, meanwhile, wanting the best possible picture, brought in a slew of lighting equipment. Two large crane lights were aimed at the house from outside. It was like the gods had gotten drunk and turned the moonlight switch to "wake the dead."

Realizing the conditions weren't perfect, I tried to get some response from the spirit.

"They say you bang on the walls all the time. Why can't you

do it for us now?" I said. "Either communicate with us, or we'll get rid of you."

Aside from walkie-talkie chatter and creaking floorboards from the crew, nothing happened. After nearly an hour, I decided to end it. Even under the best circumstances the paranormal won't show up on command. I did realize I'd have to be clearer and more vocal about what conditions we needed to conduct our investigations.

And then, as I turned off the recorders, and the film crew powered down, we had our first activity.

In the hall, a motion detector, hand-built by Sergey and Josh, went off. It was the first time we'd been using these, and I had a hunch about putting one in the hallway. What could have set it off? Reviewing the surveillance footage from our cameras, we saw that no one was there. Could the detector be defective? Serg walked near and around it, but couldn't trigger it until he stepped directly in front of it. It was working perfectly.

It wasn't a lot, but it was something.

It was customary for PRS to spend every night at the location, to embed ourselves and see if anything happened. The crew packed up, but we stayed. Serg and I spent the night in Chris's room, but there was no activity. In the morning, our eight investigators battled to use the one bathroom. With no water heater, we were greeted with ice-cold water. Serg, being of Russian descent, said he felt the shower was refreshing.

Despite the bumpy start, the second day was surprisingly more fluid. In less than 24 hours, we'd learned a lot about balancing the needs of production and our investigation.

Aside from the single article on the suicide, our historical research didn't turn up anything significant. Ultimately, I didn't think that mattered. My sense was that the information we needed to help resided with the family. As we delved into their personal lives, Helen seemed more and more emotional, increasingly somber. She apparently felt guilt, pain, and a deep-seated anger toward the supernatural force in the house.

Though she'd originally said she wasn't sure there was a connection, she slowly opened up and told us she was convinced the Dark Man was responsible for the death of her son. Still, I wasn't sure *how* the spirit could have anything to do with Chris's death until I finally spoke to Justin.

From the beginning he'd been avoiding us. There was no explanation, other than Helen telling us, "He's busy." He'd had two weeks' notice about when we'd be there, so that seemed suspect. Justin also wasn't answering any phone calls.

To my surprise, though, when the time came for his scheduled interview, Justin showed up. At first glance, he came across as a tough guy, the sort who'd volunteer to rough you up if you pushed him. At the same time, his eyes seemed locked in sorrow. He was reticent, but when he did speak, that tough guy demeanor disappeared.

Justin told me that Chris didn't just *see* the Dark Man since he was five. He claimed the thing had *tormented* him. That was news, and it made a lot of sense.

Justin described the first time Chris saw the Dark Man. They shared bunk beds and had a dog sleeping in the room. Late one night, it started howling. The sound woke Justin and he found Chris huddled in a fetal position. Chris was shaking, unable or unwilling to discuss what happened. All he would say was that he'd seen a dark figure. He wasn't just seeing it. He was tortured by it. Whatever it was terrified him beyond belief.

Justin handed me a photograph of Chris. He looked like a tough guy too. Justin said his brother lived "a lot of life" and no one dared to mess with him. He had a weak spot, though, since he was five, a chink in his armor: the Dark Man.

"There was a time when we couldn't even mention the name without him breaking down in tears," Justin said.

I never knew him, but I felt a connection to Chris. As a child, he'd had a life-altering paranormal experience that continued to eat away at him. His family believed it had resulted in his death. Part of me wondered if that could be my fate someday. Why not? I was only six years older than Chris was when he died.

"Why do you think he was so terrified of this figure?" I asked.

There was a pause. Justin seemed to have disappeared into a troubling thought, one that had bothered him deeply for years, deeper than the almost twenty-foot-deep pond out back. Ultimately, he couldn't say, or maybe he just didn't know. The full story of Chris would probably always remain out of reach.

And it wasn't over. Since his brother's death, Justin had seen the Dark Man himself. Hearing breathing one night, he looked in the corner of the room and saw the shadowy figure.

"It had like a head and shoulders. I jumped up and turned on the light and there was nothing there."

Like his mother, he'd been dreaming about Chris. One dream in particular upset him. "I asked him what heaven was like and he didn't say anything. So I said, 'Are you in hell?' He turned to me and his eyes were all black, as if his pupils had dilated completely. And his voice changed. It wasn't a demonic voice. It was a man's voice that I'd never heard before. It said, 'No, it's cold. It's very cold.'"

It's not unusual for a grieving family to dream about their loved one, but Helen and Justin both dreamt of Chris having dark eyes. Was he reaching out to them, or was something darker invading their sleep? It was as if the pain Chris had experienced was living on through them.

The reasons for Helen's concerns were clearer to me now. Whether Chris was trapped or not, it seemed she and Justin *were*. They were trapped in their grief for him, yes, but it was also possible that whatever had been victimizing Chris was now victimizing them.

Because Helen was so worried about Chris, she was adamant about asking a psychic to try to communicate with him. Given my concerns about psychics, I tried to point out the downside. "What if the psychic is wrong or tells you something that might convince you but isn't true?"

Helen listened politely, but her mind was made up. For her it must have felt like her one chance of finding out if the Dark Man was truly responsible for Chris's death. I tried to put myself in her shoes. A loved one of mine died suddenly, with no warning and no good reason. Now he may be trapped in a personal hell. Wouldn't I try anything to get at the truth?

I decided to contact CJ Sellers, a psychic who had come to UNIV-CON the month prior. She struck me as unusually trustworthy and I was comfortable that she was genuinely interested in helping people. Though she lived in Missouri, I hoped she'd be able to give a reading over the phone. A time was set for that evening.

Our adviser, Joyce, was even more skeptical about any psychic reading than I was. I agreed we should try to test CJ's accuracy. Joyce suggested that if we had to respond to questions at all, we should only give yes or no answers. I asked Helen not to spill any information, to be as discreet as possible.

As the time for the call grew closer, the atmosphere became intense. Helen really wanted that contact, that confirmation, so much so that I became concerned about what would happen. What answers would she get? What emotional state would that put her in? How would it affect the case?

"I do have Chris with me," CJ said over the phone. "What specifically do you want to know?"

I asked about the Dark Man. According to CJ, Chris spoke of him as someone who'd died but was still hanging around. She saw something on the property connected with water. There was a man there, silhouetted. CJ wasn't able to see him; she felt he wouldn't let her see him. He was covered in darkness.

"It has hands," she said. "Could it grab somebody? Could it push somebody? Yes."

I looked at Helen. She nodded. She seemed convinced this was the Dark Man.

CJ said Chris was concerned for their safety, but also felt his mother had the power to challenge this thing. While any one bit of information might not have swayed me, between the water, the darkness, and the concern, I felt our psychic had "hit" often enough to move on.

I asked her the big question. "Justin wants to know if the Dark Man had anything to do with Chris's death."

"Chris is telling me, yes," CJ said. "He's telling me he was pushed, to the limit. Whatever was going on, it happened again and again, time after time. His will was worn down. I feel like he just, he wanted it to be over . . . to be done."

It seemed like the stone walls "Tough" Justin and Helen

had put up crumbled. Justin's eyes filled with tears. Helen cried quietly.

I continued asking questions, but they'd stopped listening. Helen was staring off into space. I was worried, wondering what she was thinking.

After I ended the conversation with CJ, I tried to talk to Helen, to find out where her head was. Her responses didn't strike me as particularly coherent. She was upset, she needed time to think, so we all took a break.

I'd planned to invite her and Justin to the second Dead Time that night, but now thought it was a bad idea. They seemed too vulnerable. Helen wouldn't have it any other way, though. She insisted she be allowed to participate.

I'd have to proceed carefully. There was a balance to be struck. On the one hand, I wanted to be more aggressive in provoking the spirits. On the other hand, I was concerned about Helen.

I put her by my side during Dead Time, along with Eilfie and Katrina, in case I needed their support in tending to Helen. Serg would manage tech alone in the kitchen, while Justin would be with the others in the basement.

The harsh lights were gone, but we weren't a well-oiled machine yet. With us in Chris's room was the director, Brad, a cameraman, and a soundman. The basement was more crowded: Three producers, two cameramen, an audio guy, and a production assistant all sat against the wall, observing my team as they tried to communicate with a discarnate spirit.

As for Helen, for the first half of Dead Time she sat in silence. With all the feelings bubbling inside her, I felt it was only a matter of time.

Trying to goad whatever might be present, I told the spirit I didn't believe it was there. Helen played along, shaking her head in disappointment.

The minutes rolled by. Half an hour, three quarters of an hour passed and still nothing.

Then Helen found her voice. "He just wants the attention," she said derisively. "He wants to wait and then show off the moment the cameras are turned off. We're looking for something that's supposed to be so big and bad when there's just nothing."

She addressed the spirit directly, challenging it, as Chris—through CJ—suggested. "I'm going to give you a chance. Show me. If you are here, give me a sign that you're here. Do something!"

No response.

"Do you want me to walk into another room by myself?" Helen asked me.

My feeling was no, I didn't. But it seemed to me it would be important for her to gain some sense of control, so I also didn't want to stop her. Instead, I asked what room she wanted to walk into. Suddenly, she stood up. It dawned on me she probably hadn't been asking at all. Just as she had about inviting the psychic, she'd already made up her mind.

As she walked out, I asked if she at least wanted to take a flashlight.

"No!" she said defiantly. Then she exited the room. She was gone, out of sight.

My first thought was to go after her, but I also felt she wanted to be alone with it, as if she had to face it, to tell it something. There'd been no severe activity, or much activity to speak of, so I decided to wait and see what happened.

From down the pitch-black hallway, I heard her. "Okay, I'm by myself. This is where you scared my son the first time. This is where you made him afraid of you. And I have had it."

Hearing that, I looked at Eilfie and she nodded at me. We'd seen similar things on other cases where there was long-standing torment. The dam was about to break. The victim was about to stand up and take charge.

"If you had anything to do with my son's death, I want to know and I want to know now!" Helen said.

There was a reaction, sudden and strange. All at once, sounds came from different locations. It was as if one ball was bouncing down the stairs while another was thrown against a wall.

Helen called, "This light just went on."

The motion detector had gone off.

"You didn't stand in front of it or go into the room?" I asked.

"No," she said. "I stayed out here in the hallway the entire time."

"It's running away from you," I told her.

I examined the area. There was no evidence of anything being thrown.

Helen wasn't finished. She had a few more choice words to say. There was more banging. With the activity ramping up again, I asked her to return. I was a little surprised that she agreed so easily; she came back and sat down with us. But her anger, and her challenges to the dark, continued.

"How dare you come into my house and affect my children. I want you out. I want you out of my house and I want you out now!"

There was no further huge response, but we kept trying.

A few minutes later, I heard loud sounds and movement, but they weren't unearthly.

I radioed Serg. "Is there someone talking down there?"

The talking grew louder. I knew the voices. It was my team. Now I was annoyed. *They* knew how important it was to keep quiet during Dead Time. Why on earth were they making so much noise? And what took so long for Serg to respond?

"I think you should come down here," he finally said.

Helen looked at me, worried. I smiled. "My team is being a little rowdy and I need to tell them to be quiet. I'll be right back."

I signaled to Eilfie that she was in charge. She may be quiet and a little shy, but when necessary, if someone became hysterical for instance, I've seen her break into scolds that froze people on the spot.

Meanwhile, not knowing what was going on, I flew down the steps and met Serg in the kitchen. "Why the *hell* are they being so loud down there?"

"They said something happened."

Thinking Satan himself had better have appeared, I marched to the basement. There, the entire team was arguing with Joyce and production as they searched the basement.

Joyce spoke loudly and sternly. "We should get a camera to document every part of the basement. And *they* shouldn't have been down here. This should be a controlled environment."

By "they" she meant all the producers, assistants, and staff.

Still fuming myself, I looked at my team. "What happened?"

Josh explained that at first Dead Time had been completely quiet. He'd asked the spirit to make a sound and gotten nothing. As he explained, though, the activity occurred after Ryan

Heiser spoke some Latin. Due to his religious training, he knew enough Latin to ask, *"Es vos mortuus?"* or *"Are you dead?"*

As if in answer, there was a *very* loud bang. They described the sound as if something had exploded, then slammed up against something else.

"And you don't know what it was?" I asked.

"No," said Josh, continuing his search. "Not yet."

"How can we?" Joyce complained. "There are so many people here, we can't be sure it wasn't one of them."

"Excuse me," one of the producers said. "I haven't moved from this wall. None of us have."

It was a tense scene. I looked over at Justin, who sat there nervously, not knowing what to do.

"Everything's cool, man," one of my team said. "If it was supernatural, it was just making itself known."

I knew that wouldn't necessarily comfort him. This wasn't a harmless spirit to him. He believed that whatever it was had killed his brother.

With everyone hell-bent on investigating the sound, I stopped Dead Time. While the others continued, I grabbed Eilfie for a walk to the pond. It was cold, but I needed to talk to her. The activity left me convinced the haunting was real. I had an idea, and I knew she wouldn't like it.

"Elf, the family is suffering. Helen and Justin are frightened and angry. If there is something here, we have to try to do something about it."

She gave me a weary look. "What are you suggesting?"

"Can you do the banishment ritual thing?"

"Lesser Banishing Ritual of the Pentagram," she corrected. "And no, I won't."

I bit my lip. She'd made it clear previously that she was uncomfortable performing rituals on-camera. I hoped that after a few investigations with a camera crew, she'd ease into the idea, but I hadn't planned on asking so soon.

"Can't you do a Catholic prayer?" she asked.

I shrugged. "I don't have anything powerful enough memorized, and I didn't bring anything with us."

She eyed me. "So, you're asking a pagan to cover for a Catholic, is that right?"

Recognizing the trouble the clients were in, she reluctantly agreed. My next step was to ask if Helen was willing. She'd seemed to gravitate to Eilfie when they met and now gave a quick yes.

With the body having been found in the pond, we took an old boat and put it into the water. As we did, rain mixed with snow began to fall. It was already freezing. Now we were getting soaked. I wouldn't argue that the rain was paranormal, but there weren't clouds in the sky earlier.

Eilfie and I got into the boat. I would row while she did the ritual. It was a tiny boat, and every time we made the slightest movement it rocked as if a tidal wave slammed into it. So there we were, pagan and Catholic, rowing to the center of the pond.

I was concentrating on making sure the boat didn't tip over, but I could still see the crew running frantically from one side of the pond to the other as Eilfie chanted. I later learned they were barely able to get any sound. Until then, the film crew had no audio trouble to speak of. The *moment* Eilfie began chanting, they had major problems. The same equipment never had further problems, and to this day, they can't explain what happened.

Fortunately, Eilfie repeated the same chant to each of the

four corners, the cardinal points on the compass—north, east, south, west—so they were able to record enough for the show. Unfortunately, that also meant I had to turn the boat in the proper direction and keep it steady while she chanted.

The resulting scene is so powerful, the way it's shot is so cinematic, when I watch it, it's hard for me to remember that this is a documentary-based show.

Though the entire ritual is not Judeo-Christian, it does quote in part from a Talmudic prayer called Kriat Shema, which is recited before going to sleep, and mentions the archangels.

Before me stands Raphael
Behind me stands Gabriel
To my right, Michael,
To my left, Uriel . . .

Years and several seasons later, when people ask what my favorite episode of *Paranormal State* is, "Dark Man" is always near the top of the list. One of the reasons is I just love watching the banishment ritual scene. Another is what happened on the final day.

Once we ended Dead Time and moved on to the ritual, Helen went to bed. I didn't hear from her at all until the next day, when she appeared, in contrast to her former somber look, a bit sunnier. Despite my fears for Helen's emotional stability, she seemed fine. I think she was just angry, understandably so, and needed to say her piece.

Early that morning Heiser and Lance decided to go to a local church. I tagged along to say a prayer for Helen. As we walked out, the priest, as was the custom, greeted his parishioners. When we passed, he grabbed my hand.

"Wait," he said. "Who are you three?"

I was startled, but quickly figured it was easy for him to spot newcomers.

"Oh, we're just travelers."

"Traveling? For what?"

"Um, just trying to help a family here in town."

"Help a family? Is it charity work?"

"Well, Father, I'm not sure what you call it. We're just trying to help them overcome some grief and set things right."

"Then it *is* charity work. God bless you."

I tried to downplay what he said, reminding myself that while we were helping people, we were doing a TV show. That took the charity out of it, didn't it? As we walked to the car, I turned to see that he was still watching. Then again, I asked myself, who says TV has to be selfish?

Later that morning, CJ called Helen. "I have Chris with me. He says he's crossed over, that he's with his grandmother and he's happy. Never stop talking to him, never stop remembering him, but know that he's happy where he is," she said.

It was what Helen had been waiting so long to hear. But complex emotions, especially grief mixed with all that guilt and anger, don't vanish overnight. I knew we needed to bring in a therapist. Counseling is often a much-needed and powerful component of our work. Though the client may have only one session, we hope they'll consider continuing. In this case, production helped find Diane, a grief counselor, and while most of these sessions with clients are not recorded, this one was.

"Even though you know in your head you couldn't do anything, in your heart, you're a mom, and you think you should have saved him," Diane said. "And you know that Chris is safe now."

"Yes, I do," Helen said.

As I sat there watching, I couldn't help but feel that maybe we'd helped Helen move in a positive direction.

Our final sit-down is something I'll always remember. I was supposed to go over the investigation, summarize what we found, and suggest how Helen could handle the future. In this case, though, she did most of the talking.

"You opened me up to the fact that I'm a pretty strong person," she said. "And I can handle more than I thought I could."

Pleased, I told her that while we'd all been focusing on the Dark Man, Helen still had someone bright in her life—Justin. He was still alive, and together they needed to move on.

"I hope you understand that what you're doing is not just hauntings. You're helping people in a lot of different ways that maybe you don't even realize," she said.

That became a sort of motto for *Paranormal State*. It was intended to be a reality show about college students as ghost busters, but after that it was clear to everyone that something more was going on. It wasn't a new idea, and everyone contributed to making the show head in that direction, but it only became fully realized during Helen Isenberg's case.

I remind myself about that whenever I grow frustrated or tired. The work may be tedious and stressful, but there is good that comes out of it. At that moment, when I smiled at Helen, there wasn't a single bit of darkness in that house.

I wish I could say the happiness I experienced with Helen at the end of the investigation lasted for her, but she continued to struggle with Chris's death, and the activity did pick up from time to time. I saw her on occasion over the years and we kept in touch, until May 2009, when she passed away—three years after her son died.

I was in Iowa shooting the documentary feature *American Ghost Hunter* with investigator Chad Calek when I heard about it. Helen and her family had gone on a cross-country vacation, ghost hunting out west. She became ill suddenly, returned home, and died.

I wasn't able to attend the funeral because I was so far away, but Eilfie and Josh were there to represent PRS. We still keep in touch with Justin and the family and I think about Helen regularly. As much as she claimed we made a difference in her life, she made a difference in mine. She motivated me to keep going. With her gone, writing this chapter has been difficult, but despite the suffering she experienced, when I think of her she regularly brings light and motivation into my life. Although I'm sad that I never got to say good-bye, I'm also very happy because I know that she's with Chris.

A Brief History of Ghost Hunting

Nearly two thousand years ago, an ancient Roman author, Pliny the Younger, put down what may be the first written account of a paranormal investigation. In it, a philosopher named Athenodorus rented a house that was unusually cheap. That night a ghost tied in chains appeared and led him to the courtyard before vanishing. Athenodorus dug up the spot the next day and found a skeleton bound with chains. After it was buried properly, the ghost never appeared again.

In 1862, a paranormal research organization called the Ghost Club was founded in London. It boasted some famous members, including Charles Dickens and Harry Price, an early psychic investigator.

A few decades later, famous philosopher and psychologist William James founded the Society for Psychical Research, which attempted to use the scientific method in collecting evidence of apparitions, haunted houses, and other phenomena. It began in the United Kingdom but spread to other countries as well.

In the 1920s, Harry Price spearheaded investigations with the National Laboratory of Psychical Research. In the fifties and sixties, the work was continued by German and American independent researchers such as Hans Holzer, who first coined the phrase "ghost hunter," and the world-renowned Ed and Lorraine Warren. In the seventies and eighties, various independent investigators conducted field research and laboratory experiments.

The advent of the Internet, as well as movies and TV shows such as *Ghostbusters, Unsolved Mysteries, In Search of . . . ,* and *The X Files* led to a rise in the popularity of paranormal investigating. Reality shows such as *Ghost Hunters* on the Syfy Channel and, of course, *Paranormal State* continue to increase interest and feed an ongoing boom.

Today, scores of paranormal research groups exist across the world. Small businesses even sell ghost-hunting equipment, such as electromagnetic field detectors, white noise generators, and infrared motion sensors.

Unfortunately, the boom can also lead to inexperienced groups and people looking for a thrill to cause property damage, or worse, as in Ohio in 2007 when a group of teens decided to check out a "spooky" house. The reclusive owner feared he was being robbed and opened fire, permanently paralyzing a seventeen-year-old girl.

Shadow Men

Both fiction and paranormal literature are full of references to dark figures appearing in the night, most often as a quick movement in the corner of the eye that vanishes when you stare straight ahead. Sometimes it seems to move. Explanations range from the eyes playing tricks on a tired mind, pareidolia (explained in a sidebar on page 147) to ghosts, aliens, time travelers, or beings from another dimension. They have also been associated with the alien abduction experience.

With the popularity of investigating paranormal phenomena at a height, reports of shadow men (also known as shadow people) are on the increase. Some claim to have photographed these apparitions, while others say they see them clearly for long periods of time.

Stories about misty ephemeral figures go back thousands of years. The word "shade" is a synonym for ghost that goes back to ancient Greece and the Old Testament. The term in ancient Hebrew, *tsalmaveth*, means literally, death-shadow.

6

Loose Ends

I bury the dead, like the boatman who takes them
across the river Styx.

During "Dark Man" everyone was just getting to know one
another. We were all trying to figure out what did and didn't
work. As quickly as our next case though, which would come
to be called "The Cemetery," the relationships became more
relaxed. That was partly because the location, Clearfield, was
only thirty minutes from State College. The shorter travel time
helped our tight schedule.

Being college students, the shooting schedule had to work
around classes. By and large there was a two-and-a-half-day
shoot for each case. We'd leave Friday, then get back Sunday
night to be in class Monday. Here the extra time allowed for
some of our best investigatory work, most of which, unfortunately, didn't make it to the final cut.

It was November when we learned about Matt Franson, a

cemetery caretaker in his midthirties, and his bride, Chandra. As part of his job, Matt lived in a house with a barn adjoining the cemetery grounds. He'd lived there six and a half years and had experienced some activity on his own. He had felt paralyzed and seen a female apparition. But it was when Chandra moved there in June 2006 that their troubles really began.

Chandra began experiencing intense pains. Her back ached. At times her hands and feet became so inflamed she had trouble getting out of bed. Within two weeks of their wedding they started hearing noises, whispers, someone calling Chandra's name. Soon Chandra was hearing the voices every other day.

Matt, meanwhile, was having what he described as hallucinations. In the episode, he talks about lying in bed and seeing a woman climb out of a clothes basket, but he also described seeing the ceiling above him crack open. Tiny spiderlike creatures swarmed out and down the walls.

This couple was obviously in distress. Instead of enjoying their lives as newlyweds, they were feeling upset and threatened. The thought of investigating an entire cemetery for the first time was also very exciting to us. For the producers it made for a nice visual location, so the choice was easy.

We also decided to shoot a short sequence at a football game on campus. Originally the concept for *Paranormal State* was that it would include more details about our lives as students. Cameras followed us to parties, bars, Heather's band playing, that sort of thing. A reporter even quoted one of our producers as saying they hoped some of us would start relationships with each other. This episode has a sequence where Heather and Katrina ask Serg if he'd consider dating someone from PRS.

But with only twenty-two minutes and some great, detailed

cases, that concept didn't last. PRS pretty much was our lives, so it wasn't as if we had time for socializing. The early shows, though, make the effort, hence the football game.

We shot the game Saturday, which was fun, but complicated. It's hard not to get noticed when you're walking around with cameras pointed at you. The press passes the camera guys had also happened to be the same colors as the visiting team, Michigan State, so people razzed them.

We tried to get a shot of me walking down the steps, but as I went, everyone cheered and high-fived me like I was a big time celebrity. It was awkward trying to watch the game, but even with all that, I was happy to get to one before being wrapped up in production.

Next came the briefing. For the curious, the case file numbers I rattle off indicate the year, the month, the number of the case for that month, and a letter, *p* for parapsychological research and *f* for field investigation. All the cases on the show are field research, so this case number was 2006.11.26F, meaning we received the call and opened the file for a field case in November 2006.

Our Saturday briefing took place the day *after* I'd gone up to meet Matt and Chandra. By then, they told me a number of things about the case, including that an urn with unidentified ashes had been buried on the property, that the Fransons were born-again Christians, and that certain members of Matt's family apparently disapproved of their decision to contact us for social and religious reasons.

The clients also expressed strong feelings about not wanting to work outside their own beliefs. So during the briefing, I jokingly ask Eilfie not to bring her cauldron and Serg not to mention his agnosticism. When the episode aired, viewers gave me flak: How dare you say that to Eilfie?

I see how it might've come across, but Eilfie knew where I was coming from. We're being invited into intimate, usually very sensitive emotional situations. When the clients clearly tell me that they're not open to other beliefs, I don't see any sense in adding to their tension. It could easily get in the way of finding out what's going on and helping. Now that the show's been on the air for several years, more people know who we are and what we believe, so it's become less of an issue.

Looking back, it's also interesting that during the briefing I remind my team that spirits are human, and not all had happy-go-lucky deaths. In this case, there wound up being a different idea about the nature of the spirits involved between myself and the clients.

From my first meeting with them, Matt and Chandra came across as very reserved. I didn't feel they were hiding anything, just that they were quiet. I do remind myself that when a bunch of strangers come to your home with cameras, you can be anyone you want for a couple of hours. Usually, though, our clients are worried that they're crazy. Just showing up and expressing a willingness to believe them often gets people to open up. Here, though, it took time.

Matt did strike me as unhappy. There were things in life he said he enjoyed: rock, video games, and horror films, but he also said his family disapproved of that. It seemed his whole life revolved around maintaining that cemetery. When I asked what it was like, he joked that the customers never complained. He also said it was a special job. "I bury the dead, like the boatman who takes them across the river Styx."

It didn't seem to be a position he'd aspired to. He'd studied film at Penn State, but things didn't work out. My sense was that now he felt stuck there.

The cemetery opened in 1881 and Matt's family had been in charge ever since. His great-grandfather and his grandfather before that were caretakers. His father, Bill Franson, broke the tradition and became a successful banker and Matt's siblings since found different careers. Matt may have felt like he slipped backward.

Meanwhile, Matt and Chandra, who was about ten years younger, had married after two months of seeing each other. It was a big change that happened very quickly.

As I've said, I'm not a psychologist, but I'd spent time working with Adam, who'd been trying to figure out how psychology fit in with the paranormal. He shared his sense with me that wherever there's a trauma, dysfunction, or even ongoing unhappiness, the paranormal tends to parallel it, as if it finds a weak spot and fills it, or feeds off it.

Here there was potentially a lot going on emotionally.

To try to draw out Chandra, Katrina and another investigator sat down with her and went through their wedding photos. The few smiles she gave us turned out to be the biggest reaction we got from her.

As for their relationship, from what I saw, while Chandra had her say, she sometimes looked to Matt before answering my questions. It wasn't as if she were afraid, more like she looked up to him.

Between the emotional dynamic, the mysterious urn, and the hallucinations, there was a lot to look at, but the most urgent problem was Chandra's physical pain.

She told me she'd never experienced anything like it before moving in, but now it was constant. She'd been to a doctor, had blood tests and an MRI, but there were no conclusive results or even a theoretical explanation.

To try to figure out what was going on, I brought her for another exam, with Thad Diehl, a chiropractor at the university. He examined her thoroughly, and failed to find anything wrong. He did say that the types of pains she was having were more appropriate for an eighty-year-old.

Matt already had told me his own theory about what was happening. Feeling paralyzed and seeing a ghostly woman crawl out of his laundry basket made him think a female ghost had grown attached to him. Now she might be jealous of Chandra. He and Chandra both felt it was attached to the urn that had been buried on their property.

We also spoke with Matt's father, Bill, who said he believed what Matt was experiencing and agreed the activity was tied to Chandra's appearance. There was another family member, though, who came by while we were shooting, and seemed to have an affect on Matt.

Unwilling to appear on-camera, this relative made no bones about being unhappy about my presence. They were worried about the family's reputation, but also blamed the activity on demons. They felt Matt had opened himself up to it because of his interest in horror movies and video games.

They asked to speak with me directly, which was a tricky situation. On the one hand, here was someone doing what they felt was right. But Matt and Chandra were my clients, and I'd been asked to do a job for them. In situations like that, I try only to be reassuring, not to express any opinion.

It's difficult, though, especially in this case where I was being aggressively challenged. I was asked things like, "Do you even know what demons are?"

Inside I was thinking, "Man, if you only knew what I knew about demons." Instead, I calmly explained about my background and mentioned I'd worked directly with the Church. That gave them some respect for me. It was apparent, though, that Matt was getting flak for allowing us there at all.

Part of the issue went back to that belief I discussed earlier, that there's no such thing as earthbound ghosts, and therefore all preternatural activity *must* be demonic. It's a pretty widespread belief. To this day, I get letters insisting that no matter the evidence or the situation, it's always the devil deceiving us.

While I try to respect everyone's beliefs, I'd be doing my clients a disservice if I didn't trust in my own experiences. Here I just didn't see any evidence for a demonic presence. That led to some interesting situations not only with Matt and his family, but also some interesting conversations with the producers.

Prior to this person's visit, Matt rarely said the word "demon." He described his experiences as hallucinations, but also considered the possibility of a jealous spirit. He seemed open to entertaining whatever theory fit the facts. After the visit, though, Matt's demeanor changed. Suddenly, he was talking demon, demon, demon. And, while he'd originally agreed to bring in a psychic, now he refused.

It was a scenario I was familiar with. In my own life, growing up, I'd seen my mother's behavior change whenever my grandfather and his wife visited. When they weren't there, she'd take me to see the latest *Halloween* movie, for instance. When they were visiting, there were no movies for me beyond PG.

From watching Matt, I couldn't tell if he wanted his family's approval or felt as if he had to have it to avoid punishment.

As the others set up for Dead Time, I had a talk with Matt in the barn. I didn't think this was a demon case, but I spoke to him in those terms because I felt it'd be the most useful for him. There's also always an interpretive part to paranormal phenomena. If your beliefs don't allow for the existence of ghosts, you use other terms.

I pointed out that his identity as a "ferryman" put him in a good position to be attacked. Even so, he could take charge of the forces working on his life, no matter what he wanted to call them.

He seemed to open up a bit. He started talking about how he'd let his feelings stew, and then he would lash out. In a way, he reminded me of my father when he was younger, when he was feeling trapped in a job he hated. If my dad were in a bad mood back then, you'd stay out of his way.

Matt, though, described his pent-up feelings as a way for Satan to get through. I tried to convince him it was up to him to reclaim his home.

While our conversations before that were very matter-of-fact, now he said with some emotion, "I feel good. I'm ready to fight this son of a bitch."

During Dead Time, Matt remained committed. He asked if a demon was there to torment them, and condemned it back to hell.

At the time I heard nothing in response, but our recorders captured a very faint, almost electronic whistle. In terms of evidence, it was pretty light, but it felt as if things were starting to shift psychologically.

In the episode, the buried urn isn't brought up until about

halfway through, but it was during our preliminary talk Matt first told me about it. From the beginning, the Fransons considered it a possible source for their problems.

Years before, an unidentified urn containing ashes had been found by a police officer on the nearby banks of the Susquehanna River. The police thought someone might have thrown it off a bridge near the spot. According to Matt, on October 11, 2001, the chief of police brought it to him, asking if he'd bury it someplace.

Matt, concerned he'd have to dig it up again if someone claimed it, let it sit on a shelf in his barn. Almost five years later, on July 27, 2006, he decided it was finally time to bury it. He put it in his own yard, leaving a bit of cement on top to mark the spot. The burial roughly coincided with their marriage and, hence, the beginning of the activity.

Going into this case, one of our biggest concerns was whether or not our short schedule gave us the time to fully investigate the urn. As it turned out, I was particularly proud of what we were able to accomplish, and very disappointed that practically none of that investigative work made it into the episode.

One of the first things we did when we arrived was exhume the urn. There's a scene with Matt digging it up in the rain. It was a square metal box with a relief of praying hands, a Christian symbol, on one side. At first we didn't even know if the ashes were human.

We started by interviewing the policewoman who'd found it. Our first surprise came when she told us that at the time she found it, this "unidentified urn" had a metal ID tag. Whenever someone's cremated in Pennsylvania, the ashes are always given that sort of tag. Unfortunately, according to the police, before they took the urn to Matt, it was brought to a funeral parlor (this is not the same parlor shown in the episode). When it came back, the tag was missing.

It was incredibly frustrating. Not finding any lead at all is one thing, but in this case we were so close. There were only so many places in Pennsylvania that cremate remains. Based on the location, the ashes were likely from a crematorium very close to State College. With an ID tag, it would've been easy to find out who this was.

I called the parlor, but they denied there'd ever been any tag. In fact, they didn't seem to want to talk to me at all. Perhaps if they'd admitted to losing the tag, there may have been a legal or a public relations issue for them, but I found the attitude strange.

Our best chance gone, I took the ashes to the Penn State forensics department, hoping they could identify the remains through DNA. A technician there explained that not only would the results take weeks, there was only a very small chance of finding any DNA to begin with. It was likely all destroyed during the cremation. Then, even if they did beat those odds, the deceased would've had to have their DNA pattern stored in a database in order to get a match.

I was stumped. Not knowing when the person died, we couldn't just check hospital records. I figured someone must've thrown the urn into the river, but we didn't know when, how long after the date of death, or even how long after that the urn was in the river—two months or twenty years.

But that brought up another question. Why would someone throw an entire urn off a bridge? Maybe the deceased wanted their ashes scattered over the river, and someone tried, but dropped the urn. We'll never know.

The ashes did reveal a couple of things. I interviewed funeral director Bill William, and his examination of the ashes did make it into the episode. He poured them out on a plastic bag, and then sifted through them with his bare hands. I also put my fingers through the ashes. Unlike Mr. Williams, I wore latex gloves.

My career as an investigator sometimes involved sticking my head and hands into some very questionable places—including dead dogs, spirit vortices, and dusty attics. Here, I was actually touching what was once a human being. There's a quick cut in the episode with a look on my face expressing my feelings at the time.

During a modern cremation, the corpse is heated to around seventeen hundred degrees Fahrenheit, completely incinerating it. Even at that temperature, though, some personal items survive. Mr. Williams uncovered a bracelet and some surgical staples. The feminine bracelet led him to conclude it was definitely human, and likely a woman. The staples indicated she'd gone through a major surgery. Since these staples were of a type that is usually removed after the incision heals, it was likely she'd passed away before recovering.

This created an intriguing possibility that made me think Matt and Chandra were right in pinpointing the urn as the source of the haunting. Rather than a demon or a jealous spirit, I wondered if it was someone who'd been sick when they died. If they couldn't move on because they'd never been buried properly, they might be imposing their illness, their pains, on Chandra.

That fit, for the paranormal aspect, but I still felt that there were issues surrounding the emotional side of things. Chandra was experiencing the bulk of the phenomena, but Matt's notion of a demon or a jealous female put him at the center of the problem. He pictured this entity as wanting to take away the people closest to him. It sounded as if it wasn't so much about jealousy as punishment. I wondered if he might be using his theories to express feelings of guilt and being trapped.

At that early stage, I was very, very hesitant to bring a thought like that to a client's attention. I didn't think it was appropriate for me to tell people what I thought their personal problems were. But again and again those problems seem linked to the activity. These days, for better or worse, I try to be a lot more direct. If I believe it's true, I'll just say, for instance, "Hey, your menopause could be causing your poltergeist activity."

Whatever the explanation, I felt the best thing we could do was give the urn a proper burial. That would create the possibility for all three of them—the spirit, Matt, and Chandra—to move on.

Since the urn had a Christian symbol on the side, we assumed the deceased had been of that faith. Matt picked a spot in the cemetery and we made preparations. Once the decision was made, they both reported already feeling better, lighter. With that sense of impending relief, Matt opened up some more, revealing a sense of guilt.

"I had let my guard down over the years," he told me, "taken it for granted and let this demon come into my house and cause problems, but now this has been a rebirth for me, and I'm ready to fight."

He choked up. It was a very emotional moment for him. At the same time, though, I had to tell him what I thought. The complete conversation isn't in the episode, but I said, "I don't think you did anything wrong. I don't think you summoned a demon."

But I don't know if he ever believed me.

Because of the strength of his feelings at that moment, I wondered if there might be something he wasn't telling me. He definitely seemed to feel he was getting a resolution to something. What that something was, I don't think I'll ever fully understand.

Given his concerns regarding demons, I gave them a blessed Benedictine medal. It's the only medal that has an exorcism prayer on it rebuking Satan and evil spirits.

At the burial, I wound up performing the eulogy. I wasn't particularly comfortable with that. I felt it wasn't my place. I'm often seen performing Christian ceremonies, but I constantly worry that my faith isn't strong enough to make a difference for the clients. Unfortunately, though I ask, beg, and plead for spiritual leaders to come, many are adamantly against helping anyone who claims to be experiencing a haunting, which leaves it up to me.

Once we buried the urn, Chandra's pains really did go away, so far as she's told us. When we followed up a while later, for the first time, I heard happiness in Matt's voice. They'd bought themselves some cats, and he was going on and on about that. I was surprised, and thought, this does *not* sound like the Matt I'd met. It felt like I was talking to a new person, and I genuinely felt happy for him.

Was it the urn being buried? Did it mean that symbolically Matt was able to put something away and say to himself, "You know, I don't have to deal with that anymore?" Was it just timing? Who knows?

Just as showing up ready to believe can get someone to open up, sometimes doing *anything* can help bring about a change. The fact that a client is calling means they no longer want to keep their problems secret, and that often means they're ready to deal with it. It's almost like going to a marriage counselor for the first time. The issues come out. Then, once revealed, they sometimes resolve themselves.

As far as final thoughts, again, a paranormal investigation is usually based on theory and wild hunches that hopefully lead to some sort of answer. In this case, I don't doubt that the urn played a part. Though we captured no quantifiable evidence, the argument for that is solid. The forensic investigation gave us a strong indication, through the surgical staples, that the deceased went through a major surgery near the time of their death. The phenomena's escalation in July 2006 coincided with the urn's burial on the property. That was when Chandra began experiencing severe back pain and arthritis, symptoms that one medical examiner described as more appropriate to "an eighty-year-old." Chandra's illness could not otherwise be explained. Once the urn was removed and given a proper burial, not only did the haunting die down, but Chandra's health returned. Those are the facts.

How does an urn, carrying only the ashes of a human body, affect the physiology of another human being? I can give you theories, but they require that you take the giant leap that maybe the dead stay with us sometimes. The ashes in the urn in particular, lost from home, didn't seem at rest. History and mythology is full of tales of spirits lingering because of a lack of resolution. Maybe the deceased just wanted to be buried properly and given Christian rites (given the Christian symbol on the box containing the urn).

There are still unanswered questions. Matt claims he had a few experiences prior to the urn's arrival. But if we accept that the ashes could affect Chandra, what's not to say that the few thousand dead people buried in his backyard weren't occasionally poking their heads in?

Sometimes, despite all the technology ghost hunters carry or the plethora of testimony, the only answer amounts to a simple act of human decency: to honor the dead and let them pass on to the next world at peace.

As an interesting side note, when production heard Matt's original take about a jealous female spirit and a demon, they felt it would be a good idea to frame the episode around the concept of a "succubus," a female demon that drains the life force from a male victim.

"The Cemetery" remains one of my favorite episodes, for the emotional story, the creepy setting, the urn, and the resolution, but in terms of extra footage, it was a disappointment. We had so much good material left over that at paranormalstate. com online, there's an interactive game making use of some of the additional footage. Despite that, I think the heart of the story survives very well.

HYPNAGOGIC HALLUCINATIONS

When Matt originally described his visions as hallucinations, I was ready to consider the possibility he was experiencing what's called a *hypnagogic hallucination*. This is a well-documented experience that most people have at some point during their lives, though they may never realize what it is.

Hypnagogic hallucinations occur as the brain is falling asleep (another type can occur as the brain wakes, a *hypnopompic hallucination*).

During sleep, chemicals are released in the brain that tell it to stop paying attention to the outside world and start paying attention to dreams. In between, the brain can mix the two, reacting to the inner dream and the outer world at the same time. For instance, you'll see the bedroom you're in, but see a dream at the same time.

The brain also secretes a chemical that paralyzes you during sleep, so your body doesn't start reacting to your dreams.

Some people unknowingly enter that half-awake state, see dream images walking around their bedroom, and feel paralyzed at the same time.

Sleep paralysis combined with a hypnagogic hallucination is often offered as a possible explanation for stories not only of alien abductions, but also of vampire and demon attacks, such as the incubus and succubus.

Since people drift in and out of sleep, these hallucinations can happen anytime during the night. If someone's sleep deprived or otherwise prone, these hallucinations can even occur in the daytime, during short "microsleeps."

We regularly receive calls from people who wake up and feel something breathing on them, or see a spirit hovering over their bed, or some other startling image in their room. The experience is so vivid, so real, it's extremely difficult to convince people that what they're seeing isn't there. For this reason, it's vital for anyone having such experiences to get a professional sleep study to help determine the cause. PRS requires these studies and will not consider such claims paranormal until a formal sleep study has ruled out these hallucinations. Former Penn State professor David J. Hufford wrote a definitive book on the subject, *The Terror That Comes in the Night*, which I highly recommend.

INCUBUS AND SUCCUBUS

In folklore, a *succubus* is a demon who takes the form of an attractive woman in order to seduce a man. She drains his soul, usually by having sex with him, and then lives off that energy until her victim dies. Lilith, whom some folktales name as the first rebellious wife of Adam, and her daughters, the Lilin, are considered to be forms of succubi.

The *incubus* is a male version of the demon. It will lie atop sleeping women and force itself on them sexually. The earliest reference to these demons is from the Sumerian epic of Gilgamesh, which was written circa 2500 B.C.

CHARON, FERRYMAN OF THE DEAD

Cemetery caretaker Matt Franson likens himself to the boatman, who carries the dead across the river Styx. In Greek mythology, the ferryman is named Charon, or Kharon. It was a tradition to put a coin in the mouth or on the lips of the dead, to pay the ferryman. Charon would then take them across the river that divides the world of the living from Hades, the world of the dead. People buried without coins were believed to have to wait on the shores of the river Styx for a hundred years.

Roman poets called the river Styx, but the Greeks and later Dante in his *Divine Comedy*, refer to the river as Acheron.

7

The Best-Laid Plans

"I'm going to tell you something about me I've never told anyone before."

Once we finished with "The Cemetery," it was time for Thanksgiving. For the first time since we started, we had two weeks off from the show and school. I went to a great vacation in warm, sunny Puerto Rico and came back rested and relaxed. It turned out I'd need that extra calm for our next case. While it wasn't the most mysterious, it wound up being the biggest pain of the season. Ultimately, the investigation had to be abandoned. The episode sat on a shelf for months until we could figure out what to do with it.

It began with a lot of promise. Lauren, a Penn State freshman, had approached PRS about an apparition that she and her friends had seen in her dorm room. She'd been regularly playing a spirit game called 100 Candles that seemed related to the activity.

The game, which has a rich history, is played at night in a room lit by a hundred candles. Each player takes a turn telling a ghost story. After each story, the teller blows out a candle. After one hundred stories are told, the players are left in complete darkness, supposedly surrounded by one hundred spirits. Even though Lauren said she was really frightened, she didn't want to stop playing. For me, this should have been my first warning sign. Most clients, in my experience, who frighten themselves into a problem, then refuse to step away, aren't really taking the situation seriously.

I was on the lookout for special cases for the show, and this one sounded like it would provide a good opportunity to explore an issue that interested me: how certain games can open up doorways that people aren't prepared to deal with. I'd been interested in that ever since learning that the true story behind *The Exorcist* (book and film) involved such a game. There, a spirit board was at the center of a possession.

With Lauren on her own, away from home for the first time, there was also a strong emotional aspect. The fact that it was right there on campus was also appealing. I was thinking this would be another laid-back shoot, like "The Cemetery," where we could focus more on the case. Wrong.

The trouble began right after we shot the case briefing in the school library. Serg told me he wanted to drop out of the case to study for his midterms. He was one of our main cast members, so I didn't know what to do with that. Heather and Katrina weren't available in some of the later episodes, but Serg's absence was the first. And I felt it was way too early for someone to sit out.

Apparently it concerned the producers, too. They even

filmed Serg studying—which didn't make it into the final cut, for obvious reasons. Unless a ghost was looking over his shoulder, I don't imagine it was very interesting.

As it turned out, that issue was nothing. After one day, our client bailed out completely.

During my initial interview with Lauren, she did seem impressionable to me, that she was someone who frightened easily. She described how she woke up one night and saw a woman sitting on her roommate's bed. The woman shook her head, and then disappeared. About a month later, it was back, propped up on its elbows, looking at Lauren.

Some of her friends reported similar experiences. One said they saw a face in the window. Another, Matt, claimed he caught a glimpse of a white wispy form in the corner of his eye. It vanished as soon he turned to look at it. Lauren said she was at a point where she wanted to change to a new room.

Despite the descriptions, I had reason to think there might not be too much to this. Like many freshmen, Lauren had been on a haunted tour of the campus, which detailed all the purported ghosts and spooky locations at Penn State. Add to that the candle game, and they were creating a very spooky atmosphere for themselves. Still, her fear was real, and I related to the fact that her parents didn't believe her.

If this game was scaring her, why keep playing? Then again, lots of people who can't sleep for days after seeing a horror movie will go back and watch another. The rush of adrenaline is exciting. In this case, Lauren was also under social pressure in a new environment.

By now I was more accustomed to planning out the days with production. After the client interviews, we'd have a psychic visit.

This is actually the first time we used a psychic on the show in person. I was introduced to Shaurie by one of the producers, and although she seemed very nice, I didn't feel that she was the right fit for this case. To be honest, I don't think a psychic at all was the right fit for the case, which I'll explain later. That night we'd play the game ourselves, then go back to Lauren's room for Dead Time.

Before we took the case, one of our producers, Autumn, whom I trust very much, made it clear to Lauren that we'd need her for the entire weekend.

For some reason, though, once things got started, Lauren seemed to think we'd only talk to her once or twice, take a look at her room, and that'd be it. When we tried scheduling her for a particular time, she became upset. She complained that she wanted to go over to a friend's for a sleepover to watch a *Dexter* marathon. I was a little perplexed when I heard this. "Doesn't she say that this is a terrifying experience for her and that she can't sleep in her dorm? If that's the case, then why does it feel like she couldn't care less what we do?" I vented to Eilfie.

In my years running PRS, I've had similar experiences. I'm sure anyone who's put together a club or organization, especially in college, runs into the same sort of thing. Some people say they want to be involved, say they're serious, and then drop out.

To be fair, she was our youngest client to date. (We'd worked with children, like Matthew in "Sixth Sense," but there the clients were his parents.) I assume she was feeling social and emotional pressure and just really not equipped to handle the commitment. Obviously I no longer hold any grudge toward

Lauren and hope she's doing well, but I gotta tell you, at the time, man, I was pissed.

Though Lauren did not appear in the sequence, we went on with the psychic walk-through. It wasn't a standard part of the show yet. Our first nine episodes have no regular psychic. Shaurie came in from Pittsburgh and before the case, she gave me a reading that to be quite honest, was completely off. Nevertheless, I had agreed to try her out.

Concerning this case, Shaurie did have some hits. Eilfie took her to the second floor of the dormitory for a walk-through. With the cooperation of some students, there were five or six empty dorms. No one told her where Lauren's room was, but eventually she chose it. Inside the room, Shaurie sensed there'd been a death involving a female. That's not particularly impressive. It was a girl's dorm and she knew it was supposedly haunted. It's kind of like walking into a grocery store and sensing food.

More specifically, though, Shaurie "saw" a maroon car and two young men named Michael and John. The implication was that these guys had driven off with the girl and there'd been a car accident in which the girl died.

To follow up on that possibility, Heather, Katrina, and Eilfie headed to the local police station and did a computer search for any accident involving the names or the car color. Nothing came up. That doesn't mean it didn't happen, I suppose. The accident could have been older than the database—but for us it was likely a dead end.

By the time they returned, it was dark enough to play 100 Candles with the team. Our setting wasn't ideal—a forest near the campus, surrounded by cameramen—but it was still fun.

Katrina told how one night, as a child, her sister saw a girl on Katrina's bed who looked exactly like her. When she went downstairs, Katrina was already there. They went back to check, but the bed was empty.

Josh described a night when he was out driving—he tends to drive *fast*—and out of the corner of his eye saw an elderly woman crossing the street. She wasn't just any old woman; she was glowing blue. Seeing the apparition made him slow down. A few seconds later, he missed hitting a herd of deer that leapt across the road in front of him. If he hadn't slowed down, the crash could've killed him.

I shared two of my experiences. One was seeing a grinning monster at the foot of my bed. I began the second story by saying, "I'm going to tell you something about me I've never told anyone before." As a kid I had a bunk bed and my brother Jordan slept on the bottom. One night, I heard someone very clearly in the bed below, counting, "one . . . two . . . three . . ." When I looked, there was no one there.

Between us, we told ten to fifteen stories. They were all short, but each had shape: a beginning, a middle, and a surprising ending. Even in a few sentences, they got that spooky feeling across. It doesn't take much. The shortest ghost story in the world, well-known among horror writers, is only one sentence: The last living man in the world was sitting on his sofa when a knock came at the door.

Despite the cameras and the campus lights, the atmosphere did get a bit creepy. I could see the game's appeal, but nothing particularly unusual happened.

While we were playing our game, back in the dorms the case

was about to fall apart. Our psychic, Shaurie, sat down with Lauren and gave her a reading. She told her about the death she'd sensed in the room. In response, Lauren burst into tears. She was absolutely terrified.

I sat down to talk with Lauren. She still seemed very stressed out. Yes, she said, she was upset about the psychic, but she was also upset about school, her boyfriend, and all the things she wanted to do that weekend, which she felt we were taking her away from. At that moment, I wanted to yell at her, tell her that she was the one who invited us there in the first place. Before the investigation started, we explained the process in detail. But during the entire time we were there, it seemed as if she were expecting us to come in for an hour, use our proton packs to sweep up the ghosts and be out of her hair in time for her TV marathon sleepover.

I was in college very recently, so I got it. But college is also about taking responsibility for one's actions. In Lauren's case, she was spending time playing occult games for the thrill of being scared. The problem was, the game may have worked and she invited something in. She wanted it gone, but was hoping it would mean not having to face any consequences or hard work.

In thirteen years as a paranormal investigator, I have seen this type of client over and over. They want you to take care of their problems as quickly and as conveniently as possible. But they're not actually willing to put any work into correcting the mistake themselves. As we say in PRS, we can only help a client if they're willing to help themselves. She wasn't yet ready to tackle the problems, so I realized there was very little we could do to help her at that time.

We'd wanted to do a Dead Time with her in her room and

then play 100 Candles with her. The idea was that we could talk her through the process, maybe make it a little less creepy. But because it became such an issue, we decided the best thing to do was back off the case.

The next day, I did speak with Lauren once more. After a night's sleep, in the light of day, she said she felt better. In fact, she no longer wanted to switch rooms. When I asked why, she explained that she tended to run away from her problems and now decided to face them. So that was a positive result.

As far as the apparitions went, they could well have been caused by anxiety, but I didn't know for certain and wanted to err on the side of believing her. Since the game was the source of a lot of her fear, or at least that's where she was projecting it, I cautioned her to stay away from it.

Meanwhile, we'd decided to start working with Jamie Hernandez, a counselor whom I'd met at UNIV-CON. Rather than comment on the case, her role would be more to support the clients emotionally. So, after I spoke with Lauren, she met with Jamie.

There was some concern that Jamie looked too young to be our "older person," but I always felt she was amazing. We all did. She was very empathetic, very helpful to the clients. In the end, it didn't matter. After the first season, she became pregnant and moved on. I'm only sorry she's not in more episodes.

In a very short while, Jamie managed to talk Lauren through her feelings and help her feel more empowered and safe in her room. By way of good-bye, I gave Lauren a St. Benedictine medal and told her we'd be there if she ever needed us.

And that was it. Lauren dropped out of any further shooting. As of the time of this writing, I never saw nor heard from

Lauren again. One of my investigators did do a follow-up with her a couple years after the case. She reported that things were fine and that she had moved past that time in her life. That made me feel good. Wherever she is now, I hope she has a wonderful and haunting-free life.

At the time none of us had any idea what else to do, so we moved on to the next case. Two months later, in February, after I saw a rough cut of the episode, we realized there just wasn't enough to make it work. Fortunately, with all that time to think about it, I'd had an idea.

Since the case had taken place on campus, and had a ghost story theme, rather than focus on Lauren, why not open it up and make it about *all* the things students were afraid of? We could check out the truth behind campus ghost legends and even talk about some of my early cases with PRS.

As a result, we wound up shooting a lot more sequences. For example, the episode begins with me on a phone interview with the media talking about my motives for becoming a paranormal investigator.

To get more into the nature of ghost stories, I interviewed Penn State professor Simon Bronner, an expert in urban legends. He had an absolutely awesome house. I remember the basement had a huge library, with a big desk covered with old books.

He put our 100 Candle ghost stories in the context of urban legends, which are similar to myths and folklore, only modern-day. Basically, it's a local story told over and over and believed to be true. More often than not, they're complete fiction, but every now and then they have a germ of truth.

A university, he explained, is a perfect place for urban legends to thrive. Every year a new, large population moves in and has to figure out how to live in an environment that's basically unknown to them. The stories, mostly told by freshmen, give them a place to put their fears and concerns. Sharing them with other new people gives them an opportunity to bond.

I thought the whole idea of communally shared stories was a great opportunity to use Heather's documentary skills. She went out and interviewed all sorts of students about the campus ghost stories they'd heard. The same tales came up again and again, with small variations. Watching the collected clips really creates the sense that these legends are a strong part of the campus culture.

The most popular was, and is, the legend of Frances Atherton, wife of former university president, George Atherton. Mr. Atherton was buried on campus outside Schwab Auditorium. Since his wife isn't buried beside him, a rumor spread that her bones were kept in the attic of the building across from it, Old Botany. Stand by Atherton's grave at midnight, and look up at Old Botany, the story goes, and you'll see Mrs. Atherton peering down at him from the window.

I decided to check it out, and see if we could find those bones. Built in 1887, Old Botany is one of the oldest academic buildings on campus. These days it's an administration building. Part of the rumor is that there is no access to the attic, and that it was sealed off. At first this seemed true. The campus employees I spoke to had no idea how to get up there. There wasn't even an attic on their floor plans.

As we were filming, though, we caught a lucky break. Someone listening in came up and said, "No, the attic entrance is in one of the offices."

I followed him to the office and there it was, an entrance in the ceiling right above a bookshelf. We thought about getting permission, or at least help to move the shelf, but I said, "Screw this, I'm going up there to take a look!"

I climbed up on this professor's bookshelf, got into the attic and . . . nope, no bones. Scratch one part of that urban legend.

I thought it was the perfect place for Dead Time, though. It had a great atmosphere, and there were other stories about activity. While I don't think Frances Atherton was there, our experiences that night made me think somebody else was.

Early on, I felt blasted by heat. Shortly after, Josh, trying to speak to any spirits present, asked, "Can you make this lantern go out?"

And the lantern died.

Just as we're examining the lantern, my headset gave off some loud, wild static. Then it also died. We've had batteries drain in a few locations, but here, it seemed to happen in response to a direct question, making it pretty dramatic.

I've never found an explanation, but Old Botany remains a good source for activity. It's so "reliable" that at UNIV-CON the last few years we've held public sessions there with consistent success. Aside from inexplicable hot and cold spots and recorded voices, in September 2008 one of our guest investigators, Chad Calek, psychic Chip Coffey, and I were in the basement there with about twenty-five UNIV-CON attendees. Behind Chad was a narrow room, almost like a tunnel. It was empty, but all of us definitely heard something moving back there.

I sometimes wonder if it's an area where spirits congregate because they know we're trying to contact them.

The ghostly legends of Penn State provided the perfect backdrop to talk about the early PRS cases, since they took place on campus. I've already discussed the Cindy Song case, which first gave us national attention, and one of our very first investigations, involving Betsy Aardsma, who'd been killed in the Pattee Library.

When we went back for this episode, five years later, we asked if we could investigate again at the library, but the school turned us down. They'd let us film there, but only if we didn't mention Betsy Aardsma. For whatever reason the library didn't want the building to have the reputation of being haunted. Maybe it was the permanent marker those witches had drawn on the floor.

What I consider the first *full*, legitimate PRS investigation took place in March 2002, in Schwab Auditorium, the building where George Atherton was buried. The *Daily Collegian*'s Web site still has an article posted about it that was written at the time. Some people claim a woman haunts the auditorium, and there've been reports of people seeing a giant-sized Civil War soldier.

Back then, we locked down, stayed overnight, and had a couple of weird experiences. Mandy Bonavita—my cousin and a team member at the time—took a bathroom break and had the lights go out on her. She had enough wits about her to keep quiet during the blackout. She felt like she was being watched, but when she turned on her flashlight, the lights came back on.

In the attic, I and another early member heard some scraping against the concrete floor. Investigating behind some vents, we found a metal chair. It was so old it was covered with rust. A trail of clean scrapes on the floor indicated it had just moved.

It was good to have a chance to look back and think a little about what I've learned and how things have changed over five years. In the end, this episode, which would be called "Freshman Fear," was something of a hodgepodge, but it gave me a few surprises. Despite the problems, maybe because of those problems, we had an opportunity to do something different. There are so many ghost stories told, it kind of becomes *about* ghost stories, a 100 Candles game itself, which made it very atypical very early on. I honestly loved this episode because it tackles a large-scale issue: the power of an urban legend and fear. Both were covered in twenty-two minutes, along with a client case and bits of an origin story for PRS. Quite an accomplishment.

We did play 100 Candles again. While shooting our fifth episode, "Man of the House," after the crew left we stayed at the site and tried to tell all one hundred stories.

By about 5:30 A.M., we got too tired to continue, and called it a night.

Games and Ghosts:
The Original Exorcist

William Peter Blatty's famous novel *The Exorcist* was inspired by an actual case from 1949 involving a spirit board. Accounts of the story vary, but most agree that the trouble began when a thirteen-year-old boy named Robbie (sometimes called Roland) Doe was taught to use the board by his aunt Tillie. After she grew ill and passed away, he continued using the board to try to contact her spirit. It seems something else answered. The family began hearing scratching sounds in the attic. The noises grew worse whenever they tried to find the source. Soon objects were found moved. Eventually Robbie's bed started shaking. At one time it shook so hard he couldn't sleep and his covers were yanked away from him. If he tried to grab them, he'd be pulled onto the floor. Some accounts mention levitating chairs, horrible banging sounds, and words appearing scratched into Robbie's skin. Father Edward Albert Hughes was believed to have helped conduct the successful exorcism that allowed Robbie to lead a normal life thereafter, but to his death in 1980 Father Hughes never discussed the case. *Possessed*, by Thomas Allen and Thomas B. Allen (*iUniverse*, 2000), covers the complete story of this case.

Hyakumonogatari Kaidankai (A Gathering of One Hundred Supernatural Tales)

A hundred candles are lit in a sealed room. As each participant tells a story, a candle is blown out, until the room is in total darkness, summoning a supernatural entity.

It's believed the game originated among Samurai warriors as a way to put their bravery to the test. During the Edo period in Japan (1603–1868) it became a popular parlor game. The invention of an inexpensive printing process led to the production of scores of ghost story collections, or *kaidan*, in Japan and China. The popularity of the books continued long after the popularity of the game faded.

More recently the game formed the basis for a Japanese TV series that uses the game to retell classic Japanese ghost stories.

UNIV-CON

UNIV-CON is a national paranormal conference thrown by PRS and its affiliates every year in order to encourage education, diversity, networking, entertainment and new ideas when it comes to the world of the unexplained. The first seven conferences were held at Penn State. Attendance started out at about 300 and grew to over 3,000. Nowadays, attendees can expect to see world-famous talent in every avenue of the paranormal (previous guests include exorcist Father Lebar, psychic/demonologist Lorraine Warren,

Hellraiser actor Doug Bradley, *Amityville Horror*'s George Lutz and *Skeptic Magazine*'s Dr. Michael Shermer).

Over the course of four days, attendees are given access to dozens of daily workshops, including debates, technology workshops, meditation exercises, and a "paranormal congress," where paranormal experts debate in a senator-style chamber about protocols, ethics, and other issues. There are also ghost hunts, displays, vendors, ghost tours, parties, film screenings, masquerade balls, and lots more. Plus the entire cast of *Paranormal State* is in attendance, giving lectures and just roaming around to meet guests.

For more information, go to www.univcon.org.

8

If Only They All Went Like This

No one can tell me what I saw.

After the relatively laid-back schedule of the last two episodes, we were back on the road, this time not only to the suburbs of Pittsburgh, but also to and from the city for research. The shoot was a lot busier, but definitely worth it, because unlike our previous effort, "The Woman in the Window," it was solid and fascinating.

The clients came to us through another group of investigators. The Greater Pittsburgh Paranormal Society (GPPS) saw the ads placed back in October, and got in touch with us concerning what they felt was a genuine haunting in a house with a rich history.

While PRS is the first college-based paranormal group, there are lots of others throughout the country and the world with different degrees of skill and seriousness. I'd met some of the members of GPPS when they attended UNIV-CON, and they always appeared quite professional.

The case they told us about involved the Sokolowski family, who lived in an 1820s home that was likely part of the Underground Railroad, a network of "safe houses" that protected runaway slaves as they traveled north to free states before the Civil War. The house had a long history of activity. The tenants heard footsteps and the voices of a man and woman, objects were moved, and there'd been reports of full-body apparitions.

Specifically, my clients were Ally Sokolowski and her boyfriend, Larry Jones. Ally's stepfather, Peter, told us he'd inherited the house because his sisters were afraid of the ghosts. Ally and her mom, Kim, had lived in the house since 1980, most of Ally's life. There were other siblings and children living there as well.

Larry's experience was the most striking. Because Ally's parents disapproved of their underage relationship, they told us that she and Larry originally saw each other on the sly. The house was really spacious, and most of the bedrooms were situated toward the front. The back, though, had servants' quarters with stairs that led to Ally's room. To meet, Larry would sneak around back and Ally would let him in.

Larry told us that one night, he looked up and saw a woman in Ally's window. She was older, had long hair, and she was looking at him with great disapproval. To him, her expression seemed to be saying, "Who the hell are you to be coming here?"

Then she turned away.

At first Larry worried some family member had spotted him

and that the relationship had been discovered, but Ally told him there was no one else in the house. That night it was so cold in her room he could see his breath. Around a year later, after Ally had become pregnant, he saw the woman again one night. He was sleeping with Ally, and woke up to see the woman again looking at him with disapproval.

Ally and her mother, Kim, told me that sometime later, another friend of the family, a young African American named Brandon, walked into the same room and saw someone standing there. Thinking someone had broken in, he found the family and told them. He described the same woman Larry had seen.

Since the only two people who'd seen this woman were African American, Ally and Kim felt the spirit might be related to the Underground Railroad.

I arrived with the team and crew the first week of December 2006, about a year and a half after those incidents. Brandon was no longer around. Larry and Ally had a child together, a toddler name J. J., but Larry reported that he was *still* afraid to be alone in the house. And the activity was ongoing.

In our first interview, I learned that Ally and the baby had just had a bad night because of weird noises. Larry said he also woke up and heard a woman laughing. They were both very sincere. Larry was absolutely adamant, saying, "No one can tell me what I saw."

Next I wanted to talk to Larry alone. Before I did, the family pointedly asked me not to mention Brandon. Larry and Brandon apparently didn't get along, making it unlikely they'd make up a ghost story together.

I try to respect the clients' wishes, but here Brandon was a corroborating witness to an apparition, making him key to establishing the evidence. So, I brought him up anyway, with little result other than making Larry seem defensive.

Brandon aside, I felt as if there was much more awkwardness in the air whenever Larry was around. It seemed to me as if he felt like an outsider, so I asked him about that as well.

"At first they didn't know me," he said, talking about Ally's parents. "This is a white family and I'm African American, so . . ."

A racial or cultural gap may have been part of the issue, but my guess was there was more. Larry was also the guy their daughter had an underage relationship with, and he had wound up raising a child with her as a result. Whether you're black, white, or green, I assume that's not going to go over well with parents.

I don't say that to pass judgment. If Larry had been a lousy person, he would've left, but he didn't. It was clear he cared about Ally and the baby. In spite of the distance, I also got the feeling that Kim and Peter wanted to understand him. He was the father of their grandchild.

At the same time, Ally specifically commented that the ghosts came around more whenever they were fighting. So here again, the spirits seemed wrapped up in the emotional situation. It's important to note that the human emotion can indeed play an important role in a haunting. It can either be the genesis of a haunting or a contributing factor. A lot of ghost hunters look for evidence. PRS, on the other hand, looks for the who, what, when, where, why, and how. Building a theory about why a haunting might be taking place helps lay out the groundwork for collecting and presenting evidence that goes beyond grainy surveillance of moving doors. Evidence of levitation or moving objects is definitely cool, but is, in my opinion, nothing without a good theory. And that theory almost always comes back to the emotional makeup of the household.

In the case of Ally and Larry, they were raising a small child, which isn't always a calm, relaxing process. From what I understand, tensions between Larry and Ally's parents made him defensive, which made Ally defensive. So there were some arguments. All that tension and unresolved frustration could easily fuel the spiritual activity. If you think that's hard to believe, consider this analogy. Most everyone has experienced seeing a friend or relative, and without them saying a word or making a movement, knew they were angry or sad. That, in turn, affected the way you interacted with them. Maybe you became sympathetic and asked what was wrong, or decided to act like you didn't notice and tried to leave as quickly as possible.

The bottom line is the moods of others affect the way you act. If ghosts are the souls and personalities of the living, why wouldn't they have the same reactions? A spirit feeling family tension may have decided to put their two cents into the mix. A widely accepted belief among paranormal researchers is that a high amount of energy within a household is like one big battery to spirits.

I did wonder if there was any relationship between the night Larry saw the apparition and when their baby was conceived. Maybe the spirits were warning, "Hey, not tonight, unless you want a baby." I never did get an answer to that question.

With the emotional aspects clearer, I turned to a closer look at the phenomena. The most common activity was the sound of footsteps in the attic. The house was over two hundred years old, and no one had been up there in years. We decided to take a look.

When Peter opened up the entrance for us, insulation came down like snow. It was one of those places investigating takes you that you have to think twice about. The whole team put on masks, climbed on up, and found ourselves ankle-deep in dust and insulation. As we walked, it flew into the air, glowing in our flashlight beams. Even with the face mask, I ended up coughing pretty badly.

Serg spotted a little area of light in one corner, but it turned out to be a light shining up from Ally's room. There was no animal smell or evidence of nests, so we eliminated some possible explanations for the sounds. Otherwise, nothing.

Beneath the house, though, there were two sealed-up tunnels. One, mostly collapsed, ran under the kitchen all the way to an old barn. The other, short and filthy but more intact, ran beneath the parents' bedroom. It was a tricky, awkward space to investigate, but I felt there might be something in the tunnel that could connect us to the history of the house and possibly the haunting.

I'd seen robot cameras on television documentaries used for everything from exploring sealed rooms in the pyramids to hunting for alligators in sewer systems. PRS couldn't afford anything like that, but I thought we could do something similar by getting a remote-controlled toy car, sticking a camera on it, and sending it into the tunnel.

It didn't work. The car kept getting stuck, and the picture kept blanking out.

Instead, I went in myself. The tunnel was a crawl space,

the entrance about five feet off the basement floor. I stood on a chair and jumped in. The tunnel's floor was dirt, its ceiling the wooden floor of the house. It was a tight space, and, worse, there were enough spider webs to get my arachnophobia going. I did manage to stay long enough to find an old-fashioned hat, a tin cup, and some old newspapers.

Shortly afterward in the episode we examine an old photo. Over the years the families living there discovered these things, and collected what they found. The items were kept and passed along to the new owners. There was even a handwritten letter by someone who'd worked with Abraham Lincoln.

Most interesting was a very old photo of an unidentified couple. The image wasn't on paper; it was on thin metal, which meant it might have been what's called a daguerreotype—an early photographic process. Daguerreotypes were invented and used around the middle of the nineteenth century, the time of the Underground Railroad. So it was very possible that this was an image of whoever lived in the house back then. That meant it could be a photo of our apparition.

It was exciting to hold that kind of relic. Historical research has always been one of the best ways to uncover the reasons for a haunting and here was a situation begging for it. It was a great opportunity to inject that process into the show, and something we'd do much more in later episodes.

Attempting to identify the couple in the photo, we headed to Pittsburgh and visited John Ford at the Heinz History Center. An authority on the Underground Railroad, as well as a curator for an exhibit on the subject, he'd been collecting similar artifacts for years. With his help, some of the puzzle pieces began to fit together. He confirmed that the photo was mid–nineteenth century, and he shared some of the history from that period. Meanwhile, Eilfie, researching the clothing the couple wore, concluded that it was also consistent with the period.

The Underground Railroad, of course, wasn't an actual railroad. It was a series of safe houses and secret routes used to help escaped slaves. Some wanted to reach free states; others headed farther north to Canada, down south to Mexico, or overseas. Over the years of its existence, it helped roughly thirty thousand slaves reach freedom.

Pennsylvania had been a free state since 1780. At the time of the railroad's height, between 1810 and 1850, there were already a number of strong African American communities there, so it wasn't unusual for Pennsylvanians to be sympathetic to runaway slaves.

As for our case, things were opening up. With Mr. Ford's help, a search of the property records turned up the names of the home's original owners: Jacob and Jane Anne Witzel. With confirmed names to investigate, I quickly learned that Jane Anne Witzel had been active in the Highlands Presbyterian Church. According to Mr. Ford, that increased the likelihood that the Witzels were abolitionists involved in the railroad. Not only that, we confirmed that the house was near an Underground Railroad route coming up from West Virginia.

Given the location, the owners, the tunnels, and the timing, it seemed likely that not only was the house used to hide runaway slaves, but also that the photo was of the original owners, the Witzels. Frustratingly often, our research efforts lead nowhere, as was the case with the urn from "The Cemetery," but here the pieces fit. Historical evidence is an unbelievably useful method of paranormal investigation. If you can sift through the dust of yesterday to see how things evolved, you can look for signs, clues, or patterns. Finding out that there was an untimely death in the house, or a fire, gives us hints about where else to look. In this case, thanks to the Heinz Center, we had a lot of facts piling up that were very useful.

If this was a photo of the Witzels, we could use it to try to identify the apparition. Though the photo had been in the house, according to the Sokolowskis, Larry had never seen it. From what I saw, it hadn't been hanging on the wall or kept anywhere visible. It was stored in a tin box that they had some trouble digging out.

We gathered some other photos of people from the same time period, and showed them all to Larry. When I asked if he recognized anyone, in short order he pointed out the image we believed was Jane. This, he said, looked like the woman in the window. For us, this was very important evidence, just like the moment where Matthew picked out Timothy in a photo lineup in the "Sixth Sense" case. I can understand why some people don't see this as amazing as say, an EVP, but for us, this is just as big, if not bigger. If a client is able to pick out the photograph of a family they've never seen alive, that has been verified as having once lived in the house, and they're convinced "this is who I saw," it's a huge piece of evidence arguing for the existence of ghosts. This young man clearly saw something, and he said it looked exactly like Jane Anne Witzel.

From everything we gathered about the case, from historical investigation, testimony, paranormal investigation, and psychic walk-throughs, Jacob and Jane Anne Witzel fit the profile of the spiritual personalities to a T. It all seemed to add up.

Is this absolute proof? No. But, given the awkward relationship Ally's parents had with Larry, I don't envision them sitting around looking at antique pictures together. To me, it made more sense to believe he'd actually seen Jane Witzel.

Having taken the research as far as it could go, I agreed to bring in psychic CJ Sellers, whom I'd worked with in "Dark Man." In this episode you can see why she'd earned my respect.

To the best of my knowledge, CJ didn't know anything about the house. Yet when she entered, she didn't throw out millions of bits of information hoping to get something right. She was drawn immediately to Ally's bedroom. There, she sensed a couple, specifically a female who was old-fashioned, churchgoing, and proper. This spirit, she felt, disapproved of two people living together without being married. Even so, the energy didn't feel negative to CJ. It felt warm, protective.

Interestingly, the spirits didn't feel trapped or want to do any damage. According to CJ, they wanted to stay on in the house, and coexist peacefully with the new family.

At the end of the psychic walk-through, I showed CJ the photos we'd shown Larry. She likewise pointed out Jane Witzel, saying it felt like this was the spirit she was in touch with.

In a profession where hard proof is hard to come by, we were doing pretty well.

Afterward, CJ sat down with Larry and Ally. I thought she did a great job not coming across as judgmental while expressing the attitude she was getting from the spirits. For their part, Larry and Ally understood that the disapproval and concern from the spirits were based on hundred-and-fifty-year-old values.

I also want to briefly mention the "lives of the investigators" subplot for this episode. This one involved Katrina talking to Heather about intuitions and dreams she'd had that sometimes came true. The producers thought it'd be interesting to have her speak with CJ about them. CJ explains, basically, that like any muscle or talent, it was an aspect of her that could get stronger if Katrina decided to exercise it.

Katrina's interest in developing her psychic ability was something I kept a close watch on. To be honest, I had no desire to have a permanent psychic on my team. In the past, it's led to bad situations in PRS. Alleged psychic testimony can bias the rest of the team's viewpoint so much that we have a policy in place that does not allow any investigator to knowingly use any psychic talents on a case without written consent.

This isn't just my thought process. Sergey, Josh, and Eilfie also have hesitations about the use of psychics. As for the psychics we use on the show, they're called in, they give their reading and then they leave. Far be it for me to stop someone from pursuing a potential talent, but I didn't want that issue mitigating the team's objectivity. That said, I think Katrina did a great job trying to find that balance her first year in PRS.

Meanwhile, since the research had worked out so well, we went into Dead Time with a very solid theory. One aspect that didn't make it into the final cut was that, aside from Larry, two African Americans were present. To test the family's theory that the apparition only appeared to African Americans, I'd brought in John Ford and an old friend of mine, V. J. Cox, who lived in Pittsburgh at the time.

As we tried to contact the Witzels, just like back at Schwab Auditorium, we had battery problems. Flashlights were dying out for no apparent reason. Some people think this is hyped, but our crew is a group of seasoned TV production people. It's second nature to them to keep things charged and ready.

As far as it being evidence of a presence, part of the problem is that you never really know *when* the battery's being drained. If it's fully charged and some paranormal activity drains it to 80 percent, the battery still lasts thirty minutes. All we do know is that at certain times and in certain places, batteries don't last as long as they should. Why? One theory is that the spirits use the energy themselves, the same way they use the emotional energies of the clients.

I'm not saying that a bunch of nineteenth-century spirits are taking out their straws to sip on battery acid. They probably aren't even aware that they are affecting our machinery. Nonetheless, whatever elements make up a spirit, it seems that they pull from electrical currents in a big way. Think about it. The spirits don't have a body. How are they supposed to manifest and move objects? They need some sort of fuel just as we humans need to consume oxygen and food for energy. Perhaps spirits have unknowingly learned to adapt, now using our technology as a way to feed in order to manifest?

During Dead Time, V. J. became very emotional and claimed he felt a spirit move through him. John Ford, on the other hand, didn't have any unusual experiences.

There is a moment in the episode where I say, "I'm getting chills." It may seem that this is the result of some activity, but the truth is a bit embarrassing. It was late, it was really warm, and CJ has this incredibly soothing, nonconfrontational way. She was very relaxing to listen to. So, I closed my eyes and tried to concentrate on contacting the spirits, but fell asleep.

Everyone tells me my head just fell forward. To me it felt like I was out for a second, but apparently I was out for a good minute. To make matters even worse, apparently I started snoring. It was definitely not one of my finest moments. As I shook myself awake, I got chills from my sleepy limbs. Nothing paranormal there.

The most exciting thing about Dead Time nearly slipped by me completely. After a lack of activity in Ally's room, we relocated to the master bedroom. As CJ and I attempted communication, suddenly we heard an old-fashioned telephone ringing from somewhere in the dark house. At first I rolled my eyes. "Someone in production forgot to turn their cell phone off." As we continued to learn and adapt around each other, one thing I was trying to get them into the habit of was turning off their cell phones. This was only the fourth investigation; there was still a learning curve.

After we called off Dead Time, I walked down the stairs to meet Eilfie and one of the producers. "Hey, who left their cell phone on?" I asked the producer, Alan.

"No one. We thought maybe it was you guys. We were trying to look for that noise."

Eilfie and I looked at each other. "Well, I was with the other team and it wasn't us," she said. I obviously knew that it wasn't us. Suddenly, Eilfie and I ran off excitedly, trying to see if we could find the source of the telephone. Since we were on opposite locations of the house, we pinpointed it as directly above the first-floor kitchen. We tried calling their house phone and other cell phone numbers. The sound was not heard again. Despite all of us combing the house for an old-fashioned telephone, we didn't find one. Ironically, though, there is some significant decoration of an old-fashioned telephone throughout the house curve.

It was incredibly frustrating. The phone rang about five times, so if I'd realized at the time, it could've been tracked down. Everyone was disappointed that we'd missed a prime opportunity, so, between this case and the next, "Man of the House," we took a good hard look at how to be more careful during Dead Time.

We did come away with some evidence. The ring was captured on audio, so we compared it to the rings of all the other phones in the house. There was no match. I also asked the clients if they'd heard anything like it, but they hadn't.

It was a weird event in any case. Jacob and Jane Witzel were from the middle of the nineteenth century, and there were no phones at the time. It did raise the possibility that there were more spirits about. We had some indications of that. One night, for instance, Ally told us that she'd woken up in bed and saw not the older woman but a younger man looking at her. Since it didn't bear on the main story, it was left out of the episode.

During Dead Time, CJ also offered to carry any messages the spirits had to the family. She told us that they wanted to stay and coexist. As it turned out, the Sokolowskis felt the same way. When people watch this episode, some ask why we didn't perform a house blessing or ceremony to get rid of the spirit. My answer is this: If the spirit gives us any indication that it feels trapped or wants to move on, then we'd feel a personal obligation to do so. On the other hand, we also accept the possibility that some spiritual presences in a home are there by choice, for whatever reason. In that case, it's up to the homeowners, since it is now their space. If the spirit wishes to remain, we ask the homeowners if they have any objection. If they don't, then the spirit remains. If the clients do, then we have to have an intervention.

On the other hand, if the spirits give us an indication that they want to leave, but the clients don't want them to, then we will consider trying to remove the spirits even if it's against the clients' will. (Believe me, there are many instances of this happening. There are several ghost tourist locations that try to capitalize on the pain and suffering of the deceased, not even willing to entertain the possibility that they are there against their will. These owners will not allow anyone to go in there to remove the spirits because it would be bad for business.)

In this case, I talked it over with Eilfie, Sergey, and Josh, and we felt comfortable that we were dealing with a completely benevolent haunting, and therefore agreed to not interfere with the family's—and spirits'—wishes.

This brought us to an unusual resolution. It was sort of like the end of Tim Burton's film *Beetlejuice*, with dead and living getting along in harmony. Normally I'd be suspicious of that, but given everything else going on in the family, acceptance seemed the right way to go.

The next day, in a very moving moment for Larry, CJ conveyed that he did have Jane's approval. After that, we even managed to open up a dialogue between Larry and Ally's parents. For the first time, they talked things out. Larry had the opportunity to tell them how uncomfortable he was, not just from the spirits, but with them as well. By the end of it, they were laughing together.

Sometimes, whether it's paranormal or not, if we help remove the spirits or not, the shared experience is what matters the most. As Linkin Park put it in a song, "The journey is more important than the end or the start." In having shared this experience together, Larry and the Sokolowski family had something in common. This made the case feel, to me at least, very complete.

Very often in these investigations, threads are left hanging, mysteries unsolved, clients' problems unresolved. But this investigation was satisfying on many levels. On the one hand, I felt it was a genuine haunting. On the other, the emotional aspect had a satisfying conclusion. The ghost actually seemed to help unite the family.

Ally said she had less trouble sleeping in the house now that she felt she knew who the ghost was. Larry claimed he wasn't having any more problems. A couple of years later, we contacted the family to see how they were doing. They assured us that they were fine, that they still had some minor, harmless paranormal activity but it wasn't anything they couldn't handle. All around, aside from kicking myself over the ringing phone, for me this was energizing, one of the success stories.

PSYCHICS AND SUCH

Psychic is an umbrella term for someone with the ability to discover hidden information and/or influence the world through their minds alone. There are many subcategories, but the definitions tend to overlap and vary depending on the source and history. Here's a rough guide.

Mediums are people who communicate with the dead. The word gained popularity in the mid-nineteenth century, during the rise of modern spiritualism in the United States and Britain. *Mental mediums* sense spirits and communicate for them. *Physical mediums* act as conduits for spirit energies, allowing them to act physically on the world, either by speaking directly through the medium, causing objects to move or materialize, and even *transfiguring,* where the face of the spirit appears on the face of the medium.

Seers are able to see future events, through their own intuition or in combination with rituals or tools, such as crystal balls, tarot cards, runes, or the *I Ching*. This subcategory includes *prophets,* and span all the way from the ancient Greek Oracle of Delphi to the sixteenth-century Frenchman Nostradamus to today's tarot readers and astrologists.

Clairvoyance (meaning "clear vision" in French) is a general term that refers to the ability to gain information through means beyond the normal six senses. The subcategory *remote viewing* is more specifically the ability to visualize an unseen person or object and its location. Through the Stargate Project beginning in the 1970s, the United States military attempted to use so-called remotes to locate objects and other targets. The program was successful enough to continue operation through the 1990s.

Other types of psychics include the *telepath*, who has the ability to read minds, and the *telekinetic*, who has the ability to move objects.

True psychics are hard to come by. Amateurs, frauds, and the self-deluded abound. Because people under emotional duress tend to be vulnerable, it's crucial to proceed with extreme caution before placing faith in a psychic. Many of the effects are easy to fake through such things as *cold reading*, discussed elsewhere.

KATRINA WEIDMAN

Why the fascination with the paranormal?

The fact that my parents kept buying and moving into haunted houses probably had something to do with it. I was always the girl at sleepovers who brought the Ouija board. My friends, tears in their eyes, would call their parents to take them home.

I don't know what was worse for my parents, to have their

daughter say, "I want to be an actor" or "I want to be a paranormal investigator." In my case, neither took them by surprise. As I worked on my degrees in theater and integrative arts I also spent hours studying to be an investigator with PRS.

What was your most unusual interview?

During "Pet Cemetery," talking to Coley, a little girl. She was very hard to understand. All I could make out was her little voice saying, "I want to die; I don't want to die; I want to die." If you watch my face it pretty much sums up my feelings. Ryan does a lovely impersonation of my reaction.

What was it like handling your own case?

Loved it. I'll never forget the moment during "Beer, Wine & Spirits" when Ryan told Heather and me, "This is your investigation, girls." We just kind of stood there with blank expressions. I don't know how I didn't see it coming. The night before, Eilfie kept asking if I'd read my PRS handbook. "Did you bring it with you?" It was an odd question to ask at one A.M.

I made a lot of rookie mistakes, but in the end I felt like Heather and I stepped up. It was the first time I really felt like I was part of the team.

What was your most difficult interview?

Brian, the client from "Beer," just because it was my first time sitting down with a client without Ryan. I wound up forgetting a lot of key points and I don't think I did a very good job making Brian feel comfortable.

What's the one thing you'd like people to know about PRS?

What people see on TV is only a snapshot of what we do, and a fragment of who we are as people. We actually have personalities and know how to smile. People are always surprised to learn that when they meet us.

We also don't head home to sip martinis from diamond encrusted glasses poolside. That's what TV life's supposed to be like, right? We work extremely hard. We search for cases, do tons of interviews, plan new experiments, and do exhaustive historical research, all before we step foot on the property. Afterward, we spend hours reviewing the evidence and compiling a report.

How has working with PRS changed your views of the paranormal?

I used to be afraid of death. Now, I believe it's just the next stage. I used to think a ghost was someone who'd died and couldn't move on, but the word doesn't do justice to the possibilities. It could be from another dimension, an intelligence that attaches itself to human life, or echoes of moments of time. Maybe we're ghosts to the transparent figures we scream at and run from. That's what I find exciting about this field, the possibilities.

Sometimes I look back at the work I've done with my friends, who've become like brothers and sisters, and wonder what I'd be doing if my parents never bought that first haunted house. I didn't know it, but it was one of the best purchases they ever made.

9

The Client that Haunted the Ghosts

I asked how often she did the EVP recording. "Every day."

After "The Woman in the Window," we filmed "Man in the House," right up until a few days before Christmas. With that behind us, it was time for Penn State's winter break, giving us three weeks off from school. I'd always planned to take the show outside Pennsylvania, and without classes to worry about, this was the time to do it. Our producers were based in New York City, so they put out some press there and uncovered a few cases. We wound up shooting two in New York, which would become "Paranormal Intervention" and "Beer, Wine & Spirits," and a third in Massachusetts, "School House Haunting."

I spent the holiday back home in South Carolina, and then drove up to New York on January 2, 2007. Serg was from Queens, so it was a short drive for him. Eilfie took a bus from

State College, Heather from Altoona. Katrina didn't make the first case, but later trained in from Philly.

The night prior to the first shoot, we stayed in Queens near the first client's house, and had to get our asses out of bed at 6:00 A.M. to pick Heather up at Grand Central Station. We'd be seen reassembling there, and then hold the briefing in the café. Paranormal investigators are night owls, so for all of us, it was an unheard-of hour. Once we got there, the crew had trouble setting up. Worse, I was recovering from a bug and still feeling pretty sick, so I passed out on a bench.

The case itself would prove interesting, frustrating, and ultimately disheartening. It involved something we'd yet to explore deeply on the show: electronic voice phenomena, or EVPs.

Our client, an older woman named Carol Anne Crowley, lived in a beach house in Rockaway with her husband, Brian. They both claimed to hear bumps, footsteps, and voices. What made this different was the fact that Carol Anne told us she'd spent time researching the paranormal, found out about EVPs, and had produced a huge number of recordings of what she was convinced were spirit voices. She also told us she'd been experiencing bouts of depression that she blamed on the spirits.

My original goals were to investigate the house and the recordings, and if the phenomena seemed real, to try to resolve the haunting. But things wound up taking some surprising turns.

We were initially worried that Carol Anne was being victimized by the spirit(s). Just as in life people can have roommates or spouses who latch on and become draining and exhausting, in death it's possible for spirits to attach themselves the same way. Deliberately or not, spirits can affect the emotional and psychological state of the living in a sort of parasitic relationship. This intense spiritual attachment is almost never a good thing—I've yet to come across a situation where it is. Here, Carol Anne claimed that a woman who died in her house committed suicide. Now Carol Anne was depressed. Could it be that this spirit was now oppressing Carol Anne?

After we arrived, more of the story came out in our interviews. Carol Anne and Brian had moved into the house ten years ago. It was a very nice place in a really cool neighborhood. Retired, they said they were enjoying an active social life. In the basement, they had a finished club room with a pool table and bar. A sliding door opened out to their backyard, where there was a great view of the Manhattan skyline. They had a hot tub and grill, and a short walk to the dock where their boat was moored. Their friends were all neighbors, so they'd pull their boats together and hang out.

Apparently they were really enjoying life, until Carol Anne's involvement with spirits came into the picture. "My grandkids don't want to come here, so whatever's here, I'd like to clear it up and have it gone," she told me.

She also said the activity began within weeks of their moving in. There were noises in the hall. When her granddaughter stayed over with a friend one night, the friend said she'd heard someone walking up the stairs. Carol Anne heard breathing in her room, and voices.

According to Brian, they'd been living there about two years when a friend of his from the yacht club asked if he knew there'd been a suicide on their property. According to the friend, someone named Mary had hung herself in the garage. A neighbor told Brian that apparently, Mary's husband opened the door and found her. The neighbor heard the scream, went out to look, and saw Mary hanging.

Brian didn't mention the death to Carol Anne at first, but she said that once she found out, "We started asking around and people said, oh, yeah, someone really did hang themselves in your garage."

Carol Anne told us that she'd gone to a psychic. While she claimed she didn't tell this psychic anything in advance, when we later had our own psychic walk-through, Carol Anne added her own details to what the psychic said. It's possible the original psychic *was* hitting well, but based on what I saw, it was also possible Carol Anne provided a lot of the information herself. She seemed really eager to believe.

My understanding is that the psychic also suggested Carol Anne help Mary's spirit move on. In my experience, that's a big task, and it raises your sense of self-importance. You start to feel if you don't help this poor person *no one* will.

Either way, it seemed these experiences fueled her interest. Carol Anne told us that after that, she began going to more psychics, did more and more Internet research and joined online groups. About two years prior to our investigation, she said she learned about EVPs as a way to communicate with spirits and got into that very heavily.

Carol Anne told us that although she was afraid of the site of Mary's death, her interest was so strong, she went into the garage for an EVP session, using her cassette recorder. Alone, she asked, "If you're here, Mary, answer on the tape."

When she played the tape back, in response, she got a hissing sound, then a long, drawn-out "yessssss" and "Maaarrryyyyy."

"I just found it fascinating that you could pick up voices like that," she said.

I understood. Hearing what sounds like an actual answer to your question seems so much like solid proof, how can it not be exciting? I also knew EVP recordings weren't always as they seemed, and could be dangerous. As the case progressed to day two, Carol Anne's interest seemed, to me, to border on obsession. She said she'd record entire movies on VHS just so she could play them back and listen for hidden voices in the soundtrack.

According to Brian, he didn't believe in any of this until some of the tapes convinced him something was up. He also said he realized how important this was to Carol Anne and wanted to be supportive. At first it didn't strike him as a problem for her, but then voices took a darker turn, telling her to "get out of here." More recently he'd come home to find all the lights on. He had the impression his wife was too nervous to tell him how scared she was.

And the activity seemed to be escalating. Carol Anne's brother-in-law, Mario, told us he was staying there one night when he felt as if something was trying to get under his body and physically lift him.

"I'm going home. I'm wide awake now," he said to Carol Anne.

She filled in the details. "Two in the morning he got dressed, drove all the way home to Jersey, and hasn't slept here since."

There were a number of things to work on in short order. I wanted a closer examination of the tapes to learn more about Mary, and to figure out what the escalation meant.

Eilfie and Heather went out to interview the neighbors about

Mary, but that wasn't very fruitful. The only person willing to discuss her didn't want to appear on-camera. Claiming to be a relative of Mary, he did confirm that she had hung herself in the garage back in the sixties, but he did not know why.

As for the tapes, Carol Anne had amassed about fifty. I was eager to review them all, but our schedule didn't allow us to prepare for things like that in advance. Even though the analysis started right away, all of us could only listen to so many.

In a part of the investigation that doesn't appear in the episode, I also brought the tapes to an audio engineer. It was his impression that while a lot of the voices could be explained as originating from outside, or a television set, some could be legit.

The clips played in the episode were basically a "best of." You can clearly hear "Mary" and "get out of here" (for some reason that's been a catchphrase for malevolent spirits since *The Amityville Horror*).

There were also recordings where Carol Anne claimed to hear voices that we did not. I don't believe she was trying to trick anyone, but with EVPs, it's easy to trick yourself. Whenever dealing with faint sounds or blurry pictures, investigators have to be very careful of *pareidolia*, the tendency of the mind to see and hear patterns. The human brain is basically a machine that searches its environment for patterns. When it can't find one, it often tries to fill in the gap on its own, perceiving patterns that aren't there.

That's why, on many paranormal shows, certainly the better ones, investigators play captured sound for a client, and first ask what *they* hear before offering their own opinion. If someone is told what to listen for, it's more likely they'll hear it. Here it was very difficult to sort out what might be real or not necessarily imagined but at least misidentified. At the same time, there was enough on the tapes to make me believe something was going on.

With no luck research-wise, and a tight schedule, I hoped Dead Time would give us more. Since Carol Anne had recorded so much activity, it was logical to try to record our own EVPs. We set up audio equipment in the garage, the location of the suicide. We spent a lot of time trying to contact Mary, or any other spirit, but had no success. That made me wonder how much the activity might be centered on Carol Anne herself.

Another indication of that was Carol Anne's statement that over time, the spirits she felt she was in touch with changed. Some would pass over, she said, but others would show up. To me that meant she might not only be contacting spirits that were already present, but also attracting new ones, the same as a spirit board or the 100 Candles game.

Between the escalation and Carol Anne's depression, I was concerned that the problem could go beyond a standard haunting. As our focus shifted to Carol Anne, research on the spirit took a backseat. It's possible we could have found out more about Mary, but our time was limited and we had to deal with what I felt was most important.

Given my concerns, I was very pleased to be able to call on Lorraine Warren for help. A demonologist, paranormal investigator, and much more, she was someone I'd read about and admired for ages, making it a very special experience for me to work with her for the first time.

When I was sixteen and studying everything I could about the paranormal, the names Ed and Lorraine Warren popped up over and over. They'd been involved with prominent cases across the globe, from Amityville to the Smurl haunting. To me they were iconic.

Ever since we started UNIV-CON, I'd sought them out as guests, but the timing was never right. Sadly, Ed passed away on August 23, 2006. After his death, Lorraine attended and we did a video tribute to her husband. When the producers contacted her, I was touched to learn that she'd told them the only reason she agreed to do this episode was because of me. Lorraine is incredibly dedicated and professional. She'll take calls at 1:00 A.M., do whatever needs to be done to help someone. I could hardly contain my excitement when I heard that she had agreed. Little did I know at the time, but this episode's investigation was the beginning of a very close friendship.

Upon Lorraine's arrival, I played the tapes for her. She felt that some were spirits, and became concerned they could be malevolent.

With Lorraine and I both worried that the client might be drawing these things to herself, I asked Carol Anne how often she did the EVP recording.

"Every day," she answered. "I've actually gotten out of bed because I have to hear some of them, like two or three in the morning."

It really sounded like more of an addiction than a fascination—and a dangerous one. If you believe in spirits, it follows there are billions. Open a door, shine a light, and they'll start coming through. They're not all going to be warm and cuddly. The more recordings she did, the more frightening and damaging the haunting could become. And, according to her own statements, that's exactly what happened. It started out as harmless, but soon she was recording for over twelve hours a day, seven days a week. Her family started claiming to have frightening experiences while Carol Anne fell into isolation and depression as she became more obsessed with speaking to the dead.

Lorraine warned Carol Anne that because of her repeated efforts, something evil may have come through and been trying to oppress her. Oppression, in this sense, is one of the early stages of possession in which an entity makes it difficult for you to enjoy your life. That seemed to fit in with what Carol Anne was experiencing. As I explained earlier, spiritual oppression is like a parasite that latches on to you, slowly draining you, affecting you on every level: psychologically, physically, and emotionally. Whether or not you believe in ghosts, her twelve-hour a day EVP sessions were clearly affecting her lifestyle.

During this line of conversation, Carol Anne opened up to us more about her depression, and her feeling that it wasn't coming from within her, but somewhere outside. She told us that her friends had noticed the change in her. They'd visit on weekends to socialize as they had in the past, but Carol Anne said she would just stay upstairs, not even coming down to say hello!

There were other factors possibly making her vulnerable. Her voice choked with emotion as she told us how, in the last three years, she'd lost both her mother and a sister, and missed them terribly. Lorraine, having lost her own husband recently, was very sympathetic. She'd also come to a conclusion.

Taking me aside, she said, "This house isn't haunted, it's her."

Lorraine felt it was possible that Carol Anne wasn't letting some of the spirits, like Mary, pass on, because she was constantly trying to engage them. It made a lot of sense. I never heard Carol Anne say, "Mary, you've got to accept the fact that you're dead and move on." It was always, "Mary, Mary, speak to me." After all, how many times did she need to record Mary's voice? If she was trying to help her, there should have come a point where she'd ask Mary to depart. As far as we could see, that moment never came.

After this episode aired, I received a tiny bit of slack from some ghost hunters who thought it was absolutely ridiculous to think that one can be harmed trying to collect EVPs. I love ghost hunters, but sometimes they can be really thick and immature. Paranormal investigation, as well as ghost hunting, is not a game. It's not a toy board you can buy in a store, use to conjure up some spirits for "ooh's" and "ahh's" and then put underneath your bed until the next time you decide to get some kicks.

If you accept the possibility that there are spirits you can communicate with, then you have to accept that there are risks, negatives. In the case of Carol Anne, if she was indeed dealing with a spirit who committed suicide, then there must be some emotional and mental anguish still residing in that spirit's con- sciousness—unless you believe someone who commits suicide due to depression would decide to stick around the house for shits and giggles. There's clearly trauma and a lack of resolu- tion that needs to be cleared. The spirits do not need a bunch of overweight, fashionless ghost geeks walking in and asking for the spirit to do parlor tricks for their amusement.

In the past I'd seen the emotions of the client play in to the haunting in different ways, sometimes creating an *in* for the spirits. Here, for the first time, I thought it could be *causing* the activity.

While I don't think the haunting was completely demonic,

there may have been those elements present in some form. Due to the change of focus from the investigation to an intervention with Carol Anne, we didn't have time to conduct a full test to determine whether the phenomena were demonic. To be safe, however, we did arrange a formal Catholic blessing for Carol Anne. Ultimately, though, as long as that door stayed open and Carol Anne kept inviting things in, it could have gone that way. Regardless, the bottom line was that Carol Anne was, as she said, unhappy.

By now, Brian told us that he recognized a problem. While at first he wanted to be supportive, he confided in me and others that he was really kind of sick of this. It made sense to me. After all, they were in their retirement years. Instead of enjoying their life with family and friends, Carol Anne spent her time up in a room listening to dead people.

I don't like to tell people how to lead their lives, but in this case, I felt it was important to her for us not to hold back. Rather than continue with a standard investigation, I suggested we hold an intervention. Lorraine and I sat down with Carol Anne and tried to make it as clear as possible that regardless of whether the activity was genuinely paranormal or not, we felt that Carol Anne had an obsession, and that obsession was dragging her down. At the time, she seemed very receptive.

"There definitely was a change in me after I [moved into the house]," she said. When we pressed her to stop the recording, she agreed. "I really have to get out of it," she said.

As a symbolic gesture, I asked her to throw her recorder into the ocean, to tell herself she was really letting go of her EVPs. She did throw *a* recorder into the sea, but not the one she used.

That one belonged to her sister-in-law, so she said she couldn't destroy it. She did promise to return it to her sister-in-law, and she gave me all her tapes. Two bags full. That, I thought, was a big step.

Meanwhile, though it didn't make it into the edit, we did try to help Mary's spirit. Through Lorraine, we contacted a priest who said a mass for Mary, and prayed for her soul to move on. He also did a house blessing, asking for the spirit of Mary or any other spirits Carol Anne knew of, to move on.

Afterward, as happens with many cases, Carol Anne seemed lighter. When I called to check in a short while after we left, she told me her friends had come over. They all sat by the water, chatted, and she'd gone into the hot tub. Brian also seemed very grateful for the change.

In the closing director's log, I expressed confidence that Carol Anne would keep her promise. She said she was grateful we'd come and eager to change. If she followed through, I felt it would've been one of the best things we'd helped accomplish, more than removing a ghost or collecting some evidence.

Looking back, though, her apparent change of heart happened quickly. Just as she'd enthusiastically filled in details for our psychic walk-through, here she may have been filling in the blanks for the "recovery" story we presented. And, over time, things didn't go so well.

A few weeks after the priest did the house blessing, Carol Anne told me she was still having activity. "Don't try to contact it yourself," I said. "If you need help, contact the priest again."

A month later, she she told me she'd gone back to the psychic. She said there was a new spirit, a boy she felt very strongly she should help.

I urged her not to get involved. At the time, she still agreed she had a problem. But, when next we spoke, she said she'd visited three psychics and was recording EVPs again. I didn't know how to respond.

"Carol Anne," I said, "you're going down this path, and you're doing it at a bigger pace. By the time you get back to where you were, you're going to be three times more obsessive."

She didn't seem to listen.

I've since become more dubious about the psychological shifts our clients sometimes seem to go through immediately after an investigation. I said earlier that just bringing a problem to light could help fix it. We also bring a lot of energy. Suddenly, you've got all these people showing up with cameras. Someone believes you, tells you how you can help yourself, that things will be fine, great. Clients often want that help badly. They also sometimes want, in some sense, to appease us.

But I know that effect is limited. We're there for forty-eight hours. I can present possible solutions, but it's up to the clients to walk through those doors and deal with their lives. So, sometimes, if things *don't* get better right away, a client is devastated. "I did what you said and it's still here!" I try to explain that it takes time. "It's like a habit. It can't go away cold turkey."

Sometimes it works. Sometimes it doesn't.

A BRIEF HISTORY OF EVPS

EVPs, electronic voice phenomena, are recordings that many believe contain the voices of spirits or other paranormal entities. Importantly, the voices are not heard while the recording is made, only during playback.

With interest in speaking to the dead gaining popularity during the spiritualism movement (1840s–1920s), Thomas Edison was asked in the prestigious *Scientific American* if he believed it was possible. He didn't come down on either side, but said that if it were, the recording device would have to be extremely sensitive.

In the 1930s, Latvian photographer Attila von Szalay tried recording spirit voices. At first, he used a 78 rpm record, then a wire recorder, but achieved his best success in the 1950s using a reel-to-reel tape recorder. Some of his recordings include voices saying, "Help me!" the ever-popular "Get out!" and a young boy apparently saying, "Do you want to hear a fart?"

On September 15, 1952, two Catholic priests and music enthusiasts, Father Ernetti and Father Gemelli, were recording a Gregorian chant on an early device called a Magnetophon. When it kept breaking, a frustrated Father Gemelli called out to his dead father for help. He was shocked to hear an answer play back, "Of course I shall help you. I'm always with you."

In 1959, when Swedish painter and film producer Friedrich Jürgenson replayed a recording he'd made of bird songs, he heard what he thought were the voices of his dead father and wife calling his name. He made several more such recordings, including one he felt contained a message from his late mother.

Over the years hundreds of thousands of such recordings have been made, both friendly and malevolent, with varying clarity and integrity. The process of attempting to gather EVPs has become a staple of paranormal investigations. With high-quality recorders incorporating filters that can remove possible spirit voices, the best results are said to be obtained from poorer quality recorders that allow "noise" or "static" to be picked up, which, some believe, the spirits use to speak.

For more information on EVP research, I suggest visiting the Association TransCommunication group (formerly known as the American Association for EVP) at their Web site, www.atransc.org.

PAREIDOLIA

In some ways, the human brain is a machine geared to pick patterns from the mass of information provided by its senses. To think about it as a survival mechanism, the faster you recognize a predator running toward you, the better chance you have of living long enough to have children—even if sometimes you see or hear a tiger that isn't there.

When the brain gets it wrong, seeing a pattern where there isn't one, it's called *pareidolia*. Importantly, once the brain decides there is a pattern, it's extremely difficult to convince it there isn't one.

That's a big problem with EVPs and the reason why, on *Paranormal State* and other shows, investigators play the recording to a client *before* telling them what they think it sounds like. Otherwise, they'll listen for what they've been told is there, and then tend to hear it.

THE STAGES OF DEMONIC POSSESSION

Many demonologists believe that when a malevolent entity takes over a victim, it does so in stages. There are often other explanations for many of the stages, ranging from the psychological to biological, save the last.

Regression is when the victim returns to an earlier state, backsliding in his personal or spiritual progress. Typically the person begins to slowly loosen their grip on their faith and other strengths they'd previously enjoyed.

Repression happens as the victim loses the ability to express his feelings, be they joy or sadness. Here, the possessed always undergo a dislodging of their emotional self. The individual will often no longer feel happiness, but a hollow or paranoid sensation. This is where the demonic takes control of one's emotions, in itself a powerful form of attack.

Suppression occurs when the victim begins to purposefully hide information about himself, lying to friends and loved ones. This is confusing to the victim, for they have yet to make sense of what is actually happening.

Depression is when the victim experiences extreme and consistent sadness, even despair. Other signs include insomnia and an inability to concentrate. (Of course many people experience depression *without* any demonic influence.) The lack of sleep and constant depression creates a hole big enough for the demonic to begin their final rounds of attack.

Oppression is like depression, but the source feels more external, as if something outside the victim is weighing him down.

Obsession occurs when the victim is so preoccupied with an idea or habit that he begins to pursue it to the point of damaging the other parts of his life.

Possession is the final stage, where the demonic entity takes control of the victim, partly or completely.

My experience has convinced me that possession does take place, but there've also been many mislabeled situations, and attempts at driving away a nonextant entity that have led to tragedy—including the mental incapacitation or death of the victim. Anyone experiencing extreme emotional symptoms should first consult a doctor or other professional health practitioner.

A lot of people ask me if they're at risk of possession because they played with a Ouija board or watched a horror movie. I don't think it's that simple. You have to understand that there are rules to the demonic (if you already believe in the possibility of the demonic, is it so hard to believe that there are rules?!?). Free will, for example, is the gatekeeper to our soul. We can either make decisions that bring us closer to the divine, or the light, or to darkness. Some tend to think of the demonic as a bogeyman living under our beds. Closer to the truth is the idea that the demonic lives in the deep psyche of our minds. The attack is more psychological than physical. In the seven steps, the process to demonic possession is almost entirely mental.

Once I explain this, the next question is often, "Why would someone *allow* themselves to be possessed?" But that again pictures the demonic as a simple force of black-and-white. Millions of men and women subject themselves to abusive relationships. Often, they go through one abusive relationship after another. No one goes in consciously saying to themselves, "I want to be abused for the rest of my life," but for whatever unfortunate reasons, bad choices, attractions to bad people, they become trapped. Likewise, the process of the demonic is not as dramatic as *The Exorcist* plays it out to be.

For further information on the nature and psychology of the demonic, I recommend what is probably the most definitive book on the subject written in the twentieth century, *Hostage to the Devil* by Malachi Martin. Martin, a former Catholic exorcist, tells the tales of five real exorcisms that took place here in America. He unravels the full complexity of each case, showing just how each individual opened up the doorway.

10

Bored Until the Ghosts Show Up

I don't want to sound weird, but I don't think I want
to do this interview.

To be completely honest, after "Paranormal Intervention" I
didn't want to do the next case at all. I didn't know yet how
things would turn out with Carol Anne, but the schedule was
getting to me. After years of one investigation every month or
so, the once-a-week pace was exhausting. I'd been sick. I was
burnt out. On top of that, I just wasn't wild about investigating a haunted bar in Long Island. It didn't sound appealing, or
different. It also sounded small, like there wouldn't be enough
room for the crew. At the time I also thought we wouldn't even
be able to spend the night.

Tired and turned off though I was, we had a show to shoot.
The producers were sympathetic. They suggested I consider it

a fun break, something small, with a cool location, and apparently the client, Brian Karppinen, was a great guy. With no other possibilities, there I was, not in the best of moods.

Katrina had bused in from Philly to join us for the briefing at a diner in Smithtown. Brian, I explained, was having a pretty rough time. He'd been a motorcycle mechanic and bartender with a head for business, and bought a place called Katie's Bar—along with the debt from the previous owner—for a few hundred dollars. Interestingly, he never drank himself. As he later told our counselor, Jamie, his father had an alcohol-related death, and Brian never developed a liking for it. It might seem odd that he'd decide to open a bar, but he was a very social guy, so it made sense he'd want to do something with people around.

As he told the story, at first it was a dream fulfilled. He put his heart, soul, and life savings into the place, but things didn't go as planned. To pay for the remodeling, he wound up selling his house and motorcycle. Then his wife left him for a customer. With nowhere else to go, he wound up living at Katie's, which is when his experiences began.

His customers reported seeing apparitions. Not only that, wineglasses kept breaking. We would go in, gather evidence, and if possible, resolve the haunting.

Given my general glum outlook, and what seemed a simple scenario, I figured this would be a good opportunity to shake things up. I decided to hand the investigation over to our two trainees, Heather and Katrina. I'd done this sort of thing before the show, as part of the training process, and it had worked out well. I thought it would certainly make the episode different. Plus, the look on their faces was priceless.

Don't get me wrong. I didn't do this for TV entertainment.

Taking over a case with next to no warning is part of the PRS training process. The nature of the paranormal is to remain unpredictable, random, and uncontrollable. The reactions of the clients are also unpredictable. The reason for throwing our trainees into a leadership scenario is to see how well they deal with that pressure and unpredictability. A good investigator must always be able to handle the unpredictable nature of the supernatural. He/she must also be able to work under direct pressure. Weirdos like me thrive under pressure and impossible scenarios.

As trainees, before each investigation, they'd study how things worked. At the time of our fourth episode, "The Woman in the Window," they'd failed their first two quizzes. Now, after three months and six investigations, I planned to give them their own case. I also wanted to spring it on them, a surprise we could tape for the show. I gave our executive producer, Betsy Schechter, a heads-up, and told Eilfie, but everyone else was in the dark.

During the briefing, I thought I was giving it away. I pointedly asked, "So, do you think you know enough about how cases work?" I even said, "You guys are doing great. If you keep it up, maybe one day we'll give *you* an investigation." But they totally didn't get it. They were still in the dark as we headed to Katie's Bar for the walk-through.

The bar didn't seem to be in a great location to attract foot traffic, but the work Brian had done was fantastic. I'm used to Penn State's dive bars, but this place was gorgeous, with great lighting, woodwork, TVs, and karaoke. The main floor had a bar and stage area, booths and seating. Downstairs, there was a second bar. Impressive as it was, it was struggling. At the time,

Brian rented the basement space to psychics for readings. The experiences Brian told us about predated the appearance of the psychics, so I didn't consider them the cause.

During our initial interview, Brian described the activity in detail. His first encounter occurred during his renovation, as he stood on a staircase in the rear of the basement. Trying to remove a bar rail, he gave it a good slam, pulled, and all of a sudden, it came loose. It happened so quickly; he fell backward. He thought he'd fly down the steps, but something pushed against his shoulders and helped him regain his footing.

Whatever it was had saved him, so he said he was fine with it. But then he talked about some darker experiences. Wineglasses fell off the shelves and shattered. Patrons reported seeing ghostly images in a mirror. An oppressive feeling hung over the place.

In a sequence not in the show, Brian also spoke about something that happened while he was trying to sleep at the bar. He claimed to have seen one of his old dogs, from years ago. He was thrilled—he loved this dog—but suddenly felt that it wasn't really his dog.

"If you're my dog, you'll know the trick I taught you," he told it. When the dog didn't know the trick, he said, "You're not my dog." And the dog disappeared.

Brian said he believed that whatever spirit was in the bar was mimicking his dog to get at him. I wasn't so sure that was the case, and told him so.

I don't think of spirits as copying animals, except in the case of nature spirits. He'd also said he felt like he was out of his body at the time, that he wanted to move, but couldn't. Those are both symptoms of sleep paralysis. To explore that possibility, we brought in a sleep expert. Brian listened, but remained convinced what he'd seen was real. Which, of course, is the problem—when you're having a waking dream, it feels *exactly* like reality.

Regardless, Brian felt the presence of a dark energy. He thought it was keeping business down and he wanted it gone. It was an interesting case, but nothing I felt our trainees couldn't handle. Once the interview was over, I called for a group huddle.

"I'm going to turn it over to you," I said to Heather and Katrina. "We're going to leave."

They looked shocked. Neither said anything. Heather just smiled. I thought it was overconfidence, but since learned that she smiles like that when she's freaked. When it dawned on them, Katrina looked as if she was about to cry.

I took Eilfie and Serg with me, and left. As we walked out, Katrina still hadn't said anything. I heard later on that they both freaked out a bit.

Almost immediately following that, very interesting things starting happening on the boring case I didn't want to do. Serg, who never seemed to have any strange experiences no matter where we went, took me aside. "I felt something heavy on the chest area, definitely, the minute we walked into the basement," he said. "I've never felt anything like this when we've walked into a client's house before. It got progressively worse."

Given Serg's history, it was curious, but I hadn't felt anything at all myself, so I decided to let Heather and Katrina proceed. I didn't leave, though. For the first few hours, I hid and watched them through a portable monitor.

During their site tour on the first floor, they almost caught me, so before they came downstairs, I hid in a storage closet. I figured they'd never look in there, but they ended up walking in on me. After that I kept watch, but didn't interfere. The investigation was still all theirs.

Following the tour, they both interviewed Brian, who talked about the breaking wineglasses. Apparently this happened a *lot*. There was a two-week period when they couldn't keep a single wineglass intact. He said that one actually flew off the rack right in front of his workers.

"It went right past Jen's face," he said, "and landed between her and Debbie."

The fact that it was only wineglasses struck him as odd. Martini glasses, for instance, are more top heavy and would be, if anything, more prone to fall, but he hadn't lost any of those. Locals, and his customers, had also been telling him the place was cursed. "No one's made a nickel here in twenty years," he said.

Though their questions were good, Heather and Katrina had made their first mistake: They decided to talk to Brian together. It was understandable. Newcomers tend to think in terms of individual tasks. But with only a few days to cover all the bases, the work has to be split up or you fall behind fast. As they both interviewed Brian, tech wasn't being set up. While they both set up tech, their second interviewee, the bar's previous owner, Rich, was kept waiting.

When they got to him, their questions were again right on target. Rich said he'd owned Katie's for a few years and, like Brian, had a hard time businesswise. He didn't know any specifics about the building's history, but he also heard customers talk about a dark spirit. Interestingly, he'd *also* had a problem, specifically, with wineglasses. They didn't break. They just kept vanishing.

"I thought people were taking them," he said.

With nothing particularly exciting going on, I hung back and kept watching as Heather and Katrina met with Janet, a psychic who'd previously done a reading on the bar. Brian had already told us what she'd said to him and her information didn't change. Janet sensed a spirit named Charlie who wanted people to know he was still there, overseeing the place.

Katrina smartly asked if she had any sense of when Charlie lived.

"Nineteen thirty to nineteen forty," Janet said. She also felt that the steps where Brian nearly fell were the spot where Charlie hung out.

Given my bad experiences with psychics, I thought it would be interesting as an experiment to invite a lot of local psychics into the bar. We could record each reading, then do a montage showing if they contradicted each other or agreed. Unfortunately we couldn't schedule enough people.

At the end of the first day, I gave our trainees a little crit session. I was very happy with the way they handled Janet, but disappointed they hadn't tape-recorded any of their interviews. Serg pointed out that they should have asked Brian about his divorce, which was pretty traumatic. What was the relationship between that and the start of his paranormal experiences? Overall, though, they were doing well.

Splitting the team wound up being a little odd socially. At dinner, Heather and Katrina felt they had to stay apart, so they sat on their own and kept quiet. They did have an idea for a great experiment.

With all the breaking wineglasses, they decided to put baby powder under two for the night. Any movement by the wineglasses would show in the powder. Most important, setting up the experiment gave me the opportunity to whack Serg in the face with a rag full of baby powder. I immediately apologized, of course, but only to lure him around a corner where Eilfie happily whacked him again. He has yet to get back at us for that.

Many paranormal researchers have noted that when you set up this sort of experiment, it's as if the ghosts enjoy playing with you. Janet had also reported her sense that Charlie enjoyed messing with people. The next morning, the wineglasses were still in the same spot on the table where they'd started, but on one table there were streaks in the baby powder, as if the glass had moved one way, then moved back to its original spot.

Unfortunately, in another trainee oversight, there were no cameras pointed at that table. From the cameras we did have, I knew that no one entered or left, but any actual movement of the glasses was missed. To be fair to Heather and Katrina, placing our cameras has been a learning process. It's difficult, if not impossible, to eliminate all the blind spots, and we're always working for wider coverage. I think it's interesting to note, however, just how odd it is that the only area not covered by cameras is the area where the wineglasses moved. Coincidence?

There were those streaks in the baby powder, though, which we tried to explain naturally. We bumped the tables, stomped by, and so on, but the glasses didn't budge. There is a train station nearby, and some have theorized that the vibrations from a passing train caused the movement, but I've been at Katie's Bar four times now, spent the night, heard trains pass, and never felt a single vibration. And if there were vibrations, even on a minimal scale, we'd have seen the cameras shake. The trail in the powder also indicated that the glass moved forward and back to the same spot. That's an incredible coincidence if it were a natural force.

Given Janet's intuitions about Charlie, Heather contacted the local historical society. The next day, she and Katrina met with town historians Brad and George, and Cathy, a librarian, to piece together some of the building's history.

They had photos of the building from 1906, when it'd been a hotel, and they knew it hadn't become a bar until the seventies. When Katrina asked about the name Charlie, Brad nodded and told her the story of Charlie Klein, who'd worked at the hotel during Prohibition. His wife passed away and soon afterward an IRS agent walked in, undercover, and asked for a drink. Apparently, when Charlie pulled out the booze, he was arrested. According to the story, between his grief over his wife, humiliation, and a likely jail sentence, he shot himself dead while in the hotel.

Smartly, Katrina asked if the story was common knowledge. If it was, Janet the psychic could already have heard the name. But Brad and George felt certain it wasn't, and Cathy hadn't heard the name or the story before that day.

While Heather and Katrina were at the library, our counselor, Jamie Hernandez, interviewed Brian in the basement of Katie's in what turned out to be one of the most interesting and exciting sequences in the first season.

She asked, as a standard question, if Brian ever had violent thoughts.

"When my wife took off with a customer, I wanted to kill him," he said.

If you watch the sequence, that response brings an almost palpable tension into the air. Not that we felt Brian was dangerous. He struck me as a guy who could handle himself in a fight, but who also had heart. During one of our PRS Field Trips (where we go back to some of our more famous locations with fans for an educational and entertaining weekend), he let me hop up on his motorcycle with a girl who propped her legs up around me and put her boots on the bike, scratching the finish a little. Brian had to take a little walk, I assume, to blow off steam. It was perfectly understandable, but an indication his emotions might have the sort of excess energy that often plays into a haunting.

Shortly after, Jamie asked what his worst fear was.

"Losing everything."

At that moment, on the soundtrack, you can hear a wineglass break. It was an absolutely real moment. The breaking glass plays almost like the release of building emotional tension.

I didn't think this at the time, but looking back I see some parallels between Brian and Charlie. Charlie lost his wife, his business, and his life. Brian lost his wife, his house, his motorcycle, and with the bar doing badly, was on the verge of losing that, too. It's possible this was like "The Cemetery," where the spirit may have been re-creating its own situation before death. Or, maybe, as in "Sixth Sense," Charlie simply felt a kinship with Brian. But after the glass broke, the entire atmosphere changed.

Brian said, "Right now it feels a little creepy down here, so I hope you guys find something."

He wasn't alone. Jamie felt it too, big time. She couldn't breathe.

"I don't want to sound weird, but I don't think I want to do this interview," she said. Then she excused herself and quickly left the building. I'd never seen her react like that to anything.

This was more than interesting. Serg had already told me he'd experienced a heaviness. I soon learned that two production people, in the basement on separate occasions, felt something touching or squeezing them around their chest and back. That made four people from our group in one day.

I decided to do some investigating before Heather and Katrina got back from the library. Gas leaks can cause a variety of symptoms, but we ruled that out. Next, I took out the electromagnetic field detectors. We got some *very* high EMF readings. It may seem as if that's an indication of a ghostly presence, but in fact, excess EMF can actually cause hallucinations, dizziness, tightness in the chest and feelings of paranoia.

It is true that once you've eliminated those possibilities, a high EMF *can* indicate the presence of paranormal activity. In the basement, though, there was a DJ booth and a small dance floor with a lot of exposed wiring. Here, the high EMF was, without a doubt, electrical.

But, between the breaking glasses, the heavy feelings, and the historical information, things were much more complicated than I originally thought. While the experience during Jamie's interview with Brian seemed invoked by emotion, the others came and went without any pattern I could detect.

Deciding I didn't want to risk missing an opportunity to capture some real activity, when Heather and Katrina returned I took the reins back—much to their relief, it seemed.

That night's Dead Time was more of the same, only with the lights off. We heard creaks and rattles; a wineglass moved; the temperature dropped. As I investigated the stairs, another wineglass broke. Since the stairs seemed the center of the activity, we gathered there to try to flush Charlie out, calling to him, asking him to show his presence, but no luck.

As an investigator, I know I can't look for closure with every case—reality doesn't work that way. Here, on the final day, though I didn't feel it would resolve the activity, per se, I invited a priest to the bar to perform a general blessing. Jamie, feeling better, returned and spoke to Brian again. She advised him to take all his energy and feelings for the bar and try to exude a positive attitude, to tell himself he'd succeed no mater what.

My final voice-over for "Beer, Wine & Spirits" says something to the effect that we may have loosened the spirit's grip, but that wasn't everything. The bar remained haunted, but it wasn't necessarily a bad thing. "The Woman in the Window" was an instance where the clients were fine with the ghosts staying. Here, Brian turned his problem into a solution. Now people come to Katie's *because* it's haunted. His business is thriving. There are different ways things work out.

Unlike some of our other cases, there was no teary good-bye, no "Thank you for saving me!" Brian christened the bar and we toasted the place. It was a great time, a great adventure.

As for Heather and Katrina, having been with us for just two months, I think they were terrific. In the end, I was happy to promote them from candidates to senior trainees and give them our official PRS T-shirt.

Despite the fact that I felt uninterested in this case when I was first approached about it, by the time we left I felt that it was well worth our trip. It gave us a chance to investigate a location that was different from the family homes we were used to dealing with and allowed growth for Heather and Katrina. It also goes to show that even seasoned investigators such as myself can underestimate paranormal claims. I've been back to Katie's Bar three times now, and I can safely say that something strange is definitely going on inside the bar at night.

As for the high EMF, we suggested Brian contact an electrician immediately. The readings we got were off the charts, and prolonged exposure could be harmful. Whether it acted as a battery for the spirits, or was simply causing some of the phenomena (like the tightness of the chest and inability to breathe), we'll never know.

TYPES OF HAUNTINGS

It's believed that some places simply record old events, voices, apparitions, and play them back over and over, like a videotape. This is called a *residual haunting*. If true, in those cases where people report hearing their own voices, it's possible the current residents have been "recorded" and are actually haunting themselves.

An *intelligent haunting* is the more recognizable type, where the spirit seems to have a free will and intent, sometimes responding to the presence of others, and even answering questions. They are conscious entities that the living can interact with. Hauntings can be location-based, or spirits can become attached to specific objects. In rare cases, spirits become attached to a particular person and remain with them from location to location.

Portal hauntings are the most controversial, and to be honest, I'm not sure how much validity I give this phenomena. I believe it's possible, but that people use the term too loosely. In this type, or so some believe, a door has been opened between this world and the next, possibly through repeated human efforts at contacting spirits via EVPs, the spirit board, or the 100 Candles game. Once the portal is opened, various spirits can enter through the rift until it is sealed.

TYPES OF GHOSTS

Poltergeist, though sometimes translated as "playful ghost," is from the German for "rumbling" and "spirit." They make their presence known by moving, even hurling, objects. Poltergeist activity often occurs in the presence of adolescent girls. It's believed their excess emotional energy either causes the events or is borrowed by the spirits. The theory most widely accepted by paranormal researchers is that poltergeist phenomena is caused through psychokinesis. An individual, such as a teenage girl, acts as the conduit or agent, subconsciously causing the phenomena.

There have been several serious attempts to study poltergeists during the twentieth century, most concluding that unlike ghost phenomena, this activity is chaotic, meaningless. Furniture may be knocked over at random, as opposed to a ghost haunting, where a moving object usually has some connection to a spirit, like a photograph, or a rocking chair that used to belong to them in life. Those who suffer from poltergeist phenomena are also usually experiencing deep personal trauma, emotional duress, abuse and/or a psychological disorder. Once they receive proper care and treatment, and the trauma is taken care of, the phenomena stops.

Orbs are usually small spheres that appear on video or still photography, but can very often be easily explained. Modern digital cameras tend to resolve blurry shapes into geometric objects, refining things like dust, rain or small passing insects into spheres or rods that many people mistake for evidence of the paranormal. I can't begin to tell you how many times someone has run over to me with their orb photos, only to have me disappointingly say it's a reflection, dust, or some other natural occurrence. The bottom line is, take enough photos with your digital camera and you will capture an orb. Does that mean it's a spirit? No. There are some small, rare cases of true orb phenomena, glowing, spherical objects that float in midair and have no explainable source (such as a car passing by), but they are seen with the naked eye. If you capture a little gray orb in your photo, don't get excited, and please don't send us any more orb photos.

Shadow people are popular as urban legends as well as in ghost hunting. These types of spirits, generally considered malevolent, appear as humanoid shadows, usually just in the periphery of vision, only to vanish when the person turns to face them. There have been instances of shadow people caught on video.

Demons, which appear in various religions throughout history, are powerful, malevolent spirits who seek to do harm, sometimes possessing victims to do even more damage, or to drain their energy for their own purposes. Some Christians believe that since the human spirit winds up in heaven or hell after death, any earthbound spirit must be a demon acting on behalf of Satan (see additional sidebar on page 148).

HEATHER TADDY

What's your favorite first season episode?

"Mothman," which dealt with a legendary creature I'd read about as a child. Searching through the woods for a six-foot-tall bird-man was definitely my idea of adventure. I enjoyed trying to figure out why it was attached to that particular town. Was it the Cornstalk Curse or was Mothman some weird accidental creation? I also had a great time filming the townspeople and hearing their stories.

What's the one thing you'd like people to know about you?

I laugh and am a total goofball. On the show I come across as being superserious and shy. I'd also like them to know I have other interests, such as music, film, and fashion.

What's the one thing you'd like people to know about PRS?

I don't think our personalities come across. We love to laugh and make jokes.

When you started working with PRS what interested you most about the paranormal? Has that perception changed since?

It started when I was a teenager with a Ouija board and kept expanding since. I still have a strong interest in Ouija boards, especially the way things can change for some people if they use it.

Life on other planets is something I've also been reading about lately. When I was in third grade and first reading about UFOs, I told people I was an alien. I think I still believe that a bit. In this crazy world, anything's possible.

What was it like taking over for the "Beer, Wine & Spirits" case?

When Buell broke the news, I thought it was one of his clever jokes. Then I realized it was the real deal and started scrambling to remember everything I'd observed.

It was tricky completing an investigation with two people. We did forget some key points, but overall I think Katrina and I did all right.

What's the one unanswered question from the first season episodes you'd most like to have the solution to?

There are many unanswered questions and I like it that way. If every question had an answer, the mind couldn't wander. If I had to pick, I would like to know why some see and experience things that others don't. Why did Savannah, from "Vegas" or Matthew in "Sixth Sense"? It just seems so crazy that only some individuals have that ability.

Eilfie Music on
"Beer, Wine & Spirits"

When Heather and Katrina took over the case, I observed them as they did tech (which took forever) and conducted interviews. It was a great case, but I was bored since I couldn't really do much other than watch their joined-at-the-hip investigating.

The one thing that I regret, which seems to happen often, is that we had a camera on one of the wineglasses set out for the spirit to move. At the last moment, we moved the camera to a different wineglass. Of course, the wineglass that originally had had the camera on it was the one that moved. It sometimes seems like the ghosts know where the cameras are and stay out of range on purpose.

11

Our First Controversy

"I sense there was a girl that recently walked away?"

"No."

"Watch for it."

After "Beer, Wine & Spirits," we were due for one final case on our road trip. On a cold, snowy January day, exhausted from having investigated for eight straight days, we drove for six hours up to Leominster, Massachusetts. We were all drained and not feeling at our best. Our "break" off for Christmas had been just one week. For me, that meant a twelve-hour drive to South Carolina to visit my family, and then another twelve hours to New York City for shooting. Looking back, I think what kept us going was that we were on the final stretch. After this case, we'd get a week off in State College to relax and prepare for the final five cases.

This case, "School House Haunting," wound up being surprisingly controversial when the client, Shannon Sylvia, later became a trainee investigator on another show, *Ghost Hunters International*. I also had a chance to debunk a psychic in this one.

Throughout the first season initial contact with clients often came from our producers' efforts. It wasn't like the days before the show, or even more recently, when we'll receive an e-mail saying, "Please help us." More often production worked hard on following up leads, handed us the client name, e-mail, and address and asked if we were interested. That's how we met Shannon.

She lived with her husband, Jeff, in Leominster, Massachusetts, in an old schoolhouse that'd been converted into condos. They reported hearing children playing, as if inside their apartment, though there were no children in the building. One evening Shannon said she heard the wall creaking. The bathroom door hammered open and hit the wall behind it so hard, it put a hole in it. She also said she was having disturbing dreams but did not want to discuss them on-camera.

She said that half of her thought her home was truly haunted and half of her wondered if it was stress. She was in the process of opening up her own health spa, and talked about having trouble with the business as well as tough times with her personal life.

From the beginning, she was also open about the fact she'd had psychics and paranormal teams investigate her home before us, and that she wanted to be a paranormal investigator. We knew she'd worked with New England Paranormal and helped TAPS (The Atlantic Paranormal Society, the organization behind Syfy Channel's *Ghost Hunters*) in Rhode Island. Her take at the time was well, the phenomena are still happening, why not get a different perspective?

The trip from Long Island to Massachusetts took six hours. By the time we arrived, we didn't have a lot of energy. But, when I'm in a new town, I like to check out the local papers to get a sense of the community, so, the day we arrived, I looked at the *Leominster Champion*. On the front page was a picture of Shannon next to a headline about her being featured on a new A&E TV series, *Paranormal U*, the shooting title of our show.

At first I thought production was doing promotion, though typically we like to keep a low profile while shooting. When I found out they weren't, I contacted the paper, trying to figure out how the story could have been leaked. One of the staff members told me, matter-of-factly, that Shannon contacted them. This did, of course, raise a red flag about Shannon's motives, but it wasn't enough to make me feel that Shannon was *only* doing this for publicity.

Beyond that, we had big problems with the size of the space. The site was an old schoolhouse broken up into twelve apartments. Shannon's home was nice for a one-bedroom living space, but tiny for a TV crew. The crew had to stay out in the apartment complex hallway, which wound up angering the other residents. Production-wise, it was so difficult we promised ourselves we'd never do an episode in a space like that again.

During the primary interview, Shannon said her experiences began immediately after moving in. In a loft area, she'd once felt something flick her ear. On a few occasions, lightbulbs were found completely unscrewed. At night, she and her husband sometimes heard voices in the hallway that sounded like their own.

The fact that they were hearing their own voices was interesting, but not uncommon. Some theorize that certain places can record events. I understand that Shannon and Jeff sometimes had arguments, and the excess emotional energy may have been captured and played back.

While others had investigated this case, a psychic named Trish was key to the clients' beliefs about the haunting. I don't remember how Shannon came in contact with Trish. I do know Shannon told us she'd been to psychics she'd seen advertised along the road, but Trish may have been referred to her by friends. In either case, when Shannon first wanted to contact Trish, Jeff was skeptical and worried about the cost.

"But," he said, "she identified four spirits by name and never charged a dime."

After that Jeff felt he couldn't discount the possibility there was something going on. In fact, they told us they based a lot of their beliefs about the haunting on the information that psychic gave them. Trish claimed to have seen apparitions, a little boy and a little girl, and told them she'd "seen" a murder-suicide that took place in their apartment before the building was a school.

With that possibility in mind, Katrina and Eilfie spent a lot of time researching the building, but rather than confirm what Trish sensed, the information they found contradicted it. Most of the structure dated back to the 1880s, but the section with Shannon's condo wasn't added until 1919–20, after it was no longer a school. They also spoke to a librarian who'd never heard or read anything about any murders or accidents at the location. That in itself didn't mean a murder-suicide didn't take place, but it's likely that if something that dramatic had happened, the newspapers would have covered it.

Despite the residents being unhappy with our crew in the hallway, I asked around about any activity others may have experienced. One young couple didn't want to appear on-camera, but said they had an attic in their apartment and would hear things up there. When they went to check, they found it empty. We'd heard another resident had experiences, but no one answered the door.

I know this will shock some of our fans, but hey, I want to make sure you get your money's worth for this book, so I'll now reveal, at great personal risk, that there is a moment in the final version of this episode in which we look very weird. It's the sequence where Heather "catches" Serg playing with some plastic toy ponies. In our off moments, we like to have fun. Here, without many leads to follow, Heather and Serg were bored, so they taped a "skit" where Heather pretends to catch him playing with toy ponies. When we saw that production actually used it in the episode, it surprised us all in a funny sort of way. I did say they included some of our weirder moments. When it aired, people thought it was real, as if maybe Serg had secret toy-pony issues.

Anyway, after the pony incident, we regrouped for an EVP session and did encounter some activity. As we tried to contact the spirits, Katrina heard heavy breathing in one ear. I, meanwhile, heard a woman's voice. It was the first clearly audible voice I'd heard in a long while. It said something that sounded like "Katie" but it was so soft it might have been "eighty" or "Haiti."

Neither the voice nor the breathing were recorded, which left us little to analyze. There wasn't enough historical information to piece together anything about the haunting, but I did want to interview the psychic, Trish. From what I understand, she'd visited a few times, as far back as three years prior to our investigation, and Shannon seemed to swear by her.

After arriving, Trish assured me the place was haunted. "There's a little boy; his name is Billy. He comes up to me and wants to play." She also felt the presence of a woman, Elizabeth, and was certain a male had hung himself in the apartment in the year 1856.

When the team met to discuss the interview, Katrina pointed out that what Trish told us had apparently changed drastically from what she'd told Shannon. Originally, according to Shannon, the children were Jacob and Elizabeth; now they were Jenny and Billy. Aside from that, we knew that the section of the building where Trish sensed that a suicide occurred in 1856 hadn't been built until sixty years later.

Given the other questionable psychic experiences I'd been having, and the lack of anything else to investigate, I decided this would be an opportunity for the show to take a good hard look at the psychic process. So, we asked Trish to do a reading with Serg, to test her accuracy.

"I sense there was a girl that recently walked away?" she asked him.

"No," Serg says with a shrug.

"Watch for it," Trish assures him.

It went on like that for twenty minutes, one miss after another. Despite getting everything wrong, Trish walked away seemingly convinced it wasn't her abilities, that the problem was with Serg, that even though he didn't know what she was talking about right now, one day he would.

I'd been wanting to do some debunking like this and I was pleased to be able to.

Shannon had apparently put a lot of faith in this woman, but to her credit, admitted she was still learning. When I pointed out the variations in what Trish said about the ghosts, and the historical inaccuracies, Shannon said, "I've known those stories for three years and just repeated those facts over and over again in my mind so often I believed them."

We did have our own experiences now, though, and that night, during Dead Time, we tried to contact whatever spirit may have said "Katie." While the size of the apartment made it tough for production, it was much easier for us to set up our monitoring cameras. There were fewer places to cover, but nothing was picked up on video. A motion detector went off and there were a few knocking sounds, but nothing noteworthy.

To be honest, this episode aside, Dead Time can be very uneventful. The method of paranormal investigating where you take a bunch of gizmos and walk around looking for ghosts is not, in my opinion, always the best. Our original investigations weren't one-hour efforts; they were long, drawn-out experiences. When things did happen, it was almost at random, while I was talking to someone, or asleep, not when I was walking around looking for it.

The next day something did happen, not activity per se so much as a strange coincidence, a synchronicity. Jeff told us he'd been talking to a friend at work who mentioned his wife knew someone who used to live in the apartment and heard they'd had similar experiences. Jeff didn't know the woman's name at first, but while arranging for us to speak to her, was surprised to learn it was Katie, Katie Gahl.

I was tired and eager to get home. If I hadn't heard that voice, we might not have gotten in touch with Katie at all. As it was, arranging the interview was a crazed, last-minute thing. On the phone, Katie told me she'd lived in the condo starting in August 1986. She said she'd hear children playing, and wake up in the morning to find everything in her home messed up, as if twenty kids had just run through. Here was some apparently independent confirmation of the activity, and it seemed related to my own experience. I invited her over to share more details.

Katie was a very pleasant woman who'd lived with her elderly mother in the apartment. She told us she remembered the sound of the children, clear conversations they were having, but not what was actually said. Things were always being tampered with, she reported, the toilet seat left up, the refrigerator door open, the doors locked. Her mother was bedridden, but Katie would come home from work and find everything changed.

Why did I hear her name? It's possible I'd heard a spirit calling her. There've been cases where spirits have memories, and this one may have been comfortable with her. Or, maybe her mother called her name repeatedly while they lived there, and that was recorded as a residual haunting.

Having confirmed some activity, but debunked the background story, there wasn't much more I felt we could do. Shannon did feel uncomfortable in her home, so I contacted Keith and Sandra Johnson, a team of demonologists, to perform a blessing. Keith had appeared previously on *Ghost Hunters*, but wasn't with the show any longer, and I thought it'd be cool for paranormal enthusiasts to see him.

Brian told us he felt more comfortable after the blessing and Shannon said it was a great experience.

That was it . . . until about a year later.

We'd filmed with the Sylvias in January 2007. That summer, casting began for *Ghost Hunters International*. As I mentioned, Shannon wanted to be a paranormal investigator and had already worked with TAPS. She tried out for the show and got in as a trainee.

GHI premiered January 9, 2008, as a big hit for Syfy. There was a strong buzz about the show in the paranormal community. Our episode, "School House Haunting," originally aired later that same month, January 28. So Shannon was first seen as an investigator for *GHI*, then as a client on *Paranormal State*. To anyone who didn't know the shooting dates, it appeared as if she'd gone from being an investigator to a client.

For some, the timing of Shannon's dual appearance raised the question: Why not have your own team investigate your home unless you have something to hide?

These were early episodes for both series, and when you're new, your credibility is questioned very heavily in the paranormal community. Worse, since, honestly, this wasn't our best investigation, one of the biggest thing viewers took away was, "Hey, that's the girl from *Ghost Hunters International*. What's she doing here?"

Shannon tried to explain it, get the truth out, but she was pereceived as a sellout. A huge online storm started. Ultimately, Shannon left the show.

She didn't expect a problem, and neither did we. When we advertised our episode, we said up front that our client was Shannon Sylvia from *Ghost Hunters International*. Still, she seemed angry at us for a little while. She sent me an e-mail questioning why we hadn't mentioned in the episode itself that she'd wanted to be a paranormal investigator or had been involved with TAPS.

Frankly I'm not the editor, but I could see how Shannon's paranormal background wasn't relevant to the story. Had it been mentioned in passing, the thread would've had to be picked up, followed through, and resolved.

In the end, I don't think there was anything Shannon, or the rest of us, should've done differently. I've no doubt that if *Paranormal State* had aired first, it would've been less of an issue. It does go to show how incredibly important credibility is in the field. There's a dedicated group of people who watch paranormal shows and try to prove that they're faked.

Some of them try to argue that all paranormal reality shows, including *Paranormal State*, are staged. I can't speak for the other shows, but other than some honest mistakes, and time-crunched editing, which I discuss in this book, it's not true so, in our case, no one's able to back up that accusation. In fact, an employee of James Randi, the world's best-known debunker, told me they tried to debunk our show but couldn't. We present people's experiences, the factual evidence and research we have, and offer theories. As the employee put it, "How can you debunk someone's testimony? It's just a he-said, she-said argument. So we just gave up on your show!" I laughed. I do enjoy being difficult.

I hate to say it, but in the end, the scandal was actually good for our show. Any publicity at that point was good. It got people talking about *Paranormal State*. And hey, I'm all for having controversy on the show, as long as we do our best.

Past that, I do want to say that while I remain proud and excited about a number of first season episodes, in all honesty, this wasn't one of them. It lacked a compelling psychological story, the evidence was weak, and I don't feel as if I gave it my best effort.

Normally, we did some research and interviews beforehand. Here, we were just stumbling in. I also don't mind winging it, but only when my gut feels right, after I've planned things in advance. We'd done three cases in eleven days, our system wasn't set up for that, and I was disappointed. I knew then we'd have to seriously rethink our scheduling if we were going to do more good work.

I didn't realize it yet, but this was actually a rest break, compared with what came next.

COLD READINGS

Cold reading is a series of techniques used by psychics and other fortune-tellers to convince clients they can see hidden knowledge, when in fact they're using nonparanormal methods that can be learned by anyone and have been demonstrated in numerous documentaries. With a little practice, you can tell a lot about someone just by paying attention to their clothing, their body language, and their tone of voice, a process closer to what a detective does than someone with extrasensory perception.

These techniques result in a lot of "hits" or correct statements about the subject that can convince the unwary that the information was gleaned through psychic means. There are a variety of examples:

Shotgunning is a technique in which the psychic will rattle off a lot of vague information hoping they'll hit on something specific to the client. Every hit a psychic makes allows him to narrow things down and appear more specific.

While shotgunning, psychics rely on *Barnum statements* (named after famous huckster P. T. Barnum, also referred to as the *Forer effect*). In an effort to gain trust, they'll say very general things that are true about most people, such as "You're having a problem with a friend or family member" or "You tend to be a bit insecure around people you don't know."

The *rainbow ruse* is another way to elicit trust, by saying that the client has two contradictory characteristics, such as "Sometimes you're happy, but sometimes you're sad" or "You can be friendly, but like to keep to yourself at times." The purpose of the process is to glean more and more accurate details by watching the subject's reactions, their agreement and disagreement. Ultimately, they leave the impression that the information was achieved through extrasensory means.

While in a cold reading the fortune-teller genuinely doesn't know anything about the client, in a *hot reading*, they've researched their subject beforehand and then pretend to "see" what they already know.

People tend to bring personal, sometimes traumatic issues to psychics, making them vulnerable. That's why I'm often more concerned with what sort of person the psychic is rather than whether their abilities are genuine. Some false psychics use these techniques to try to bring their clients help and closure. Others may be inexperienced, or more interested in money, and may do psychological harm. While I've been very impressed by a few psychics and consider it possible their abilities are genuine, others may honestly believe themselves to be psychic, but use these methods subconsciously.

BUYER BEWARE: WARNING SIGNS ON WHAT TYPES OF PSYCHICS TO AVOID

They charge . . . a lot!

I understand the argument that psychics, who are so in demand for their talents that they've decided to quit their day job at Walmart in order to devote their time to the profession on a full-time basis, need to charge to earn a living. But $500.00 an hour?!? That's more than some hotshot lawyers or doctors get paid!

They charge to remove a spirit.

I get e-mails from sobbing women who say they've emptied their bank accounts to a psychic who promised to remove a haunting but it didn't work. They ask me how much I charge and if they can work on a payment plan. When I tell them I never charge, I think it sinks in that they were taken advantage of by their psychic. Again, I understand a psychic charging for a general reading, but if they have "add-ons" like spirit removal, or to offer their assistance in passing a loved one on, that's pretty much psychic fraud in my book. There's no governing body determining who can and can't actually remove spirits, so for psychics to take advantage of the pain and desperation of others is a little concerning. Why not pass on the loved one as a free bonus to the reading? It seems heartless not to. You can walk down to a priest and he'll say an entire mass for your loved one with no financial expectation.

They ask too many questions.

As explained in the cold reading sidebar, some psychics ask a ton of questions, such as "Is your grandmother well?" That opens the door for them to make comments without being completely wrong. If you say, "No, my grandmother isn't doing so well," the psychic can nod and say, "I thought so." Whenever a psychic tries to read me, or if I'm using a psychic on a case, if they ask me a question, I usually throw it back at them without giving them any answer. If they ask, "Is your grandmother well?" instead of answering, ask, "Why do you ask?" If you're paying $500, they should be doing all the talking and answering, not you. Please don't fall in to that trap. They bait you to try to get you to pour open your heart so they can make comments about things they know you want to hear.

The best psychics in the world . . . don't charge!

Psychics like Michelle Belanger and Lorraine Warren do not charge for their services, which is why I respect them so much. I believe psychic ability is a privilege that should be used to help mankind; 99.9% of the psychics out there are frauds, so beware!

12

Demons Inside and Out

You amuse it.

After the draining, frustrating experience of "School House Haunting," the biggest thing on my mind was that we were almost done. We had just five investigations left to complete our season. We were over the hump, or so I thought.

As things turned out, the next two cases, which would become "The Name" and "The Devil in Syracuse," would be the most complicated, frustrating, and dangerous investigations of the season. I'd soon be dealing with the fulfillment of a demonic promise, people I felt I couldn't trust, the return of some deep personal issues, a surprising run-in with production that at first I worried would undermine the show's integrity, and a situation grave enough for me to send our trainees away for safety's sake.

The threads of these stories are tough to unravel. Not only was my faith in myself as an investigator and a human challenged and changed, the cases overlap in subject and timing. For the first time, we had to leave before returning to complete each investigation. So it seems appropriate to set the stage here, discuss how my involvement began, and then talk about the relevant parts of my own background that came into play. In the next two chapters, I'll discuss the details of each case as they unfolded.

Things began in January 2007, while we were still in Massachusetts. A producer told me about a case that looked pretty good. Teena, a woman in Syracuse, New York, had sent a couple of e-mails talking about some dark activity she and her family had been experiencing. She lived in a trailer home with her husband, Raymond, and their two small children, Katie, four, and Charlie, who was a little over one year old.

I remember giving her a call while we were filming "Schoolhouse Haunting." I took a break to sit outside Shannon Sylvia's apartment in the hallway so I could have some privacy while I spoke with her. Among other things, Teena described an incident where the phenomena had gotten so bad she and her children fled their home. Raymond stayed behind, though, later telling Teena that he'd tried communicating with whatever was plaguing them.

"Who are you?" he asked.

In response, he claimed that a deep, scratchy voice announced a very unusual name. Though demon names no longer frighten me, out of respect for the damage I've seen these entities create, I still do not use the actual names while discussing demonic cases, and will refer to it here as B—.

These cases are particularly complex, and while the editing is a valiant effort to convey the story, some things are collapsed by time constraints. In this case, for instance viewers might think B– is the same demon I'd encountered in 2005, before the show began. I'm eager to clear that up. That demon went under a different name. I'd never heard the name B— before I spoke with Teena. By the end of things, that wouldn't be the most confusing thing going on.

At the same time, as I've mentioned, in 2005 I *had* been told demonic forces were aware of me, and that I'd encounter them again.

When I first spoke to Teena, I wasn't thinking about any of this. I was only aware of how compelling her story was. Something about it struck me in a way I can't explain. I've had lots of these conversations, but it felt as if her telling of the story gave me the experience. Either it was a complete lie, or she might actually be dealing with a demonic entity.

I didn't expect a full-blown demonic case for the show. We'd had inklings; Matt, in "Cemetery," felt he'd summoned a demon, but I disagreed, and there may have been a nascent demonic layer in "Paranormal Intervention."

Here, though, I felt I'd be dealing with the issue directly. Compelled as I was, this wasn't something I was eager to do. The 2005 cases in Pittsburgh affected everyone involved. The clients claimed objects were levitating, and I saw the aftermath of some incredible events, including bent crucifixes and walls that seeped a brownish liquid. The liquid we recovered from the wall was analyzed and found to be blood containing fleshlike matter.

As I said earlier, these cases also left me drained and deeply depressed, to the point where I'd considered dropping my investigations completely. I still didn't know if I was strong enough to go through something like that again.

In 2005, the activity centered on someone who seemed invaded. A malicious personality came through, one whose rage was targeted against religious symbols and beliefs. I believe I witnessed full possession of this individual, as well as a partial possession of another. I wasn't eager to face that again.

With part of me already convinced there was truth to what Teena was saying, I told my producer this was the case I wanted to work on, but I didn't really say why. I had decided to keep this case confidential, hardly sharing any detail whatsoever. Whatever drew me in when I listened to her also made me decide I would do this case no matter what, even if it meant they didn't cover it for the show. It didn't come to that. They gave me the go-ahead.

I do try to maintain an objective investigator's viewpoint and I'm proud to work within the context of a variety of traditions and belief systems. Yet *Paranormal State* has been described as having a Catholic bias, and a lot of that sense comes from the episodes that deal with the demonic. Unable to come up with any other appropriate term to fully explain what I was witnessing, I go back to one with religious connotations—demon.

There are other explanations, but they fall short. Some parapsychologists feel possession can be explained by mental illness, a delusional secondary personality, coupled with the sort of psychokinesis seen in poltergeist cases. But in the case of mental illnesses, the afflicted person doesn't always believe that they're a demon. They're just as likely to believe themselves Jesus, Moses, or Napoleon.

The distinction between schizophrenia and possession isn't

simple. But I have to ask what form of dementia specifically targets a person's loved ones and religion? It doesn't seem as if that would be part of nature.

Well-known parapsychologist Ian Stevenson* has distinguished poltergeist phenomena from possession by theorizing that the source of a poltergeist resides entirely in the mind. That the activity is caused by internal anguish. Deal with the psychological problem and the activity stops. In possession, the activity doesn't stop even after the psychological issue is addressed. It won't stop until someone goes through the ritual of driving out the external force.

Christianity isn't the only religion with a belief in demons. Pagans, for instance, believe in negative natural forces, but my experiences have involved households with a Christian background. My view is always evolving. Importantly, though, when I'm involved in these cases—in the heat of the moment—I don't really stop to think about all the theory, I just worry about what's going on in front of me, and think in terms of my faith.

Since I do fall back on that religious explanation, and my faith is a big part of who I am, I think it's important to talk more specifically about my own beliefs. Though my relationship with it has been anything but easy, Roman Catholicism runs in my family, not just as a religion, but also as a way of life.

My parents divorced when I was four years old, my mother remarried, and we moved from Corey, Pennsylvania, to Sumter,

---

* "Are Poltergeists Living or Are They Dead?" by Dr. Ian Stevenson. 1972. *The Journal of the American Society for Psychical Research* 66:233–252

South Carolina. There aren't a lot of Catholics down South, but eventually, we found a church and joined. Every Sunday my mom would force us to go. My stepfather was a believer but not a churchgoing man. He eventually stopped and with my little brother too young, that left Mom and me.

Like many kids, church was the last place I wanted to be and as I got older, I fought with her more. She insisted I go through confirmation, the process in which you're recognized as an adult in the church and allowed to take the sacrament. To do so, you had to take classes, which I hated, but I went through with it.

In part, I think my mother wanted the approval of her dad and his wife, who were Italian and very strictly Catholic. At the same time, though, my mother was actually great at exposing me to different cultures. I think she recognized early on that I had a deep fascination for films, so we had regular trips to the theater, where we'd see anything from family comedies to horror films like *Hellraiser 3*. My mom definitely didn't shelter me; she let me go out there and explore the world. I think that played a large part in my development and appreciation for diversity, education, and adventure.

When my maternal grandfather and his wife would come to visit, however, suddenly I wasn't allowed to watch anything over PG. Even when I was seventeen, if I wanted to go out past 8:00 P.M. when they visited, my grandfather and step-grandfather would give my mother a look as if she were allowing me to run around doing drugs. Worse, whenever they'd come to visit, it usually meant I'd have to endure their criticism and passive ways of demeaning me. I used to be angry at my mom for wondering why all of a sudden we had to change our lifestyle once they came over. As I grew older, I understood the position she was in, wanting to impress her father and step-mother.

When I was nearly grown, I heard things about my grand-father that, if true, were seriously at odds with the talks he'd given me. It's not my place to go into detail about it here, out of respect to my family, but the bottom line is that it left me won-dering: Who was this guy who was judging me and my family? What doctrine was *he* following?

My paternal grandfather, also a devout Catholic, and part Native American, is a different case. As a child, I spent summers with my father. He worked days and went to a tech school at night, so my grandparents often babysat me. I definitely looked up to my paternal grandparents. They had always been in my life and I feel they played a large part in raising me.

My grandfather can sometimes be a strong-headed man (probably where I get it from). At the same time, though, I know he had, and has, respect for me. I can respect his unwavering beliefs, until those beliefs hurt people. Sometimes I feel like he came down a little hard on the family for not sharing his view-point, but then again, through my life, there have definitely been times where I've been guilty of doing the same thing to others.

At thirteen, I tried to share some of my beliefs with him. We got into a discussion about faith through the expression of music. He played some old Christian radio, and I thought I should play a song that I heard on my own radio stations. I played him Joan Osborne's new song, "One of Us," with the lyric, *What if God were one of us?* He'd probably have slammed anyone else for bringing up a song that almost tries to humanize God, but instead he respected my effort. He at least always had a discussion with me. He helped me get through college, too. He's supported me and still brags about me.

Overall, though, between the judgment and the hypocrisy of some of the members of my family, my relationship with religion was difficult. It became more difficult when I discovered that I was bisexual, attracted to both sexes, something the Church still considers a mortal sin. I've been open about my sexual orientation in confession, and with my close friends, but it hasn't been general knowledge.

The feeling was probably always there, but for the longest time I didn't know what it was. I was attracted to females, but every so often I was also attracted to males. Growing up I didn't think it was unusual. In South Carolina, I still felt like a kid at eleven or twelve. I was very innocent, and didn't even know what a bisexual or homosexual was. We never talked about it, and so I never knew I was "different" or in the minority.

That changed a bit when I was thirteen and lived with my dad for a year. In the small Pennsylvania town the kids threw around terms like "fag" or "homo" and it was clear that a fag was something you didn't want to be. I knew it was derogatory, but it didn't click with my own feelings.

When my grandfather, the one I looked up to, found out a cousin of mine was gay, he refused to let him into their house. I remember my dad saying, "No son of mine will ever be gay. He'd be out the door and I'd never talk to him again." He said it loudly and proudly to the rest of the family. I remember freezing, because in my teens I began to realize that my heart and hormones didn't really discriminate a gender when it came to attraction. It was only then that I began to wonder if there was something wrong with me.

I also asked myself what kind of world are we living in where your son could be a murderer, and *that's* more acceptable?

Even as I reached fourteen, I didn't label myself. I just went with the flow. If I liked someone I liked someone. It was only when I started seeing things on the news that I really started to understand the social implications. I saw my fellow Christians waving "God hates fags" banners around. Then I saw the grotesque photos of Matthew Shepard, a gay teen who was beaten up and left for dead tied to a fence. I didn't understand it, and I still don't.

I'm out to my parents now. Telling them was awkward, not so much because of my orientation, but more because I had to talk about my feelings at all. My social life, romances, were never something I discussed.

As I write this, my paternal grandfather still doesn't know. Part of me still wants his respect, perhaps in part because of the sense of isolation I felt after my childhood paranormal experiences. But so many people struggle against this kind of prejudice that I've decided life is too short to hide who I am for anybody.

I'm tired of turning on the news and seeing another teenager commit suicide because they were afraid of the social implications. I'm tired of seeing third-world, backward countries like Uganda impose death penalty laws for gay people. I'm tired of American politicians turning down gay rights but then getting caught at a gay bathhouse, unbeknownst to their wives and children. Most important, I'm tired of gays, lesbians, and bisexuals being told that they're going to hell and that God hates them for who they are.

So many gay, lesbian, and bisexual people turn away from

their faith because they have been told by bigots that God has already turned his back on them. I received an e-mail from a young man who told me that he was gay, and wondered if he was going to hell. "Since you deal with spirits, have you ever come across evidence that suggests that they do go to hell or they are in torment?" This broke my heart. We humans can be so cruel to one another, but the teachings of Jesus Christ are that of love and compassion. I've decided to share my sexuality and struggle over faith in hopes that others will no longer feel as though they are alone or that they can't be religious.

I don't bring it up here as a political point, though. My bisexuality brings me back, in a roundabout way, to the demonic. I had a close friend and investigator I'd been open with. At first, he seemed accepting of me, but around the same time I was dealing with the aftermath of those cases in 2005, he started telling me that I was committing a mortal sin and that because of it I was detrimental to my clients.

It's my understanding that he also began warning several priests I'd looked up to about me. Apparently he told them not only about my orientation, but also that I was too accepting of other people's beliefs in things like paganism, and that I was open to psychics. Whatever the case, several priests suddenly shut their doors and stopped talking to me. When I asked them about it, I was essentially told that although I was trying to help these families, *I* was really the problem. I was going to hell. I was doing the devil's work just by being who I was, and I was in denial about it. One of these priests even suggested I go to a sort of straight boot camp to be purged of my sickness.

At best, these priests felt I was flawed and that I had an illness that would allow the devil to attack me. Since I was refusing to accept that I was damned, since I wasn't treating bisexuality as a spiritual disease, I was, in the eyes of God, perverting and desecrating his work. They didn't seem able to tolerate any viewpoint other than their own and spent a long time trying to make me feel very guilty.

That sense of betrayal lived in the back of my mind for a very long time. It was a big part of the fallout from those demonic cases, which brought me to the dark crossroads in my life that eventually put me on a path toward *Paranormal State*.

Consciously, I never felt that I was serving the devil. I did worry that the drumbeat of guilt could be used against me, though. After hearing it so often, it was as if a lying voice in the back of my head said, "How can you expect God to answer your prayers for these people when you're a sinner?"

Though I knew what I believed in my heart, it took a very long time for me to fully accept they were wrong. There was even a moment when it finally dawned on me, but that wouldn't happen until we were in the middle of shooting season 1.5.

I'd invited Father James LeBar, an exorcism consultant on several films, including *Constantine*, to appear at UNIV-CON. After agreeing, he suddenly backed out. Surprised, I asked Lorraine Warren, who knew him, to ask what happened.

Apparently Father LeBar told her he'd been approached with disturbing information about my sexual practices and my acceptance of paganism. When Lorraine heard that these stories had come from my former friend, she contacted him. It seemed that during that conversation, he not only revealed every confidence I'd shared with him as a friend, but also told her a series of sexually graphic lies.

I remember Lorraine calling and saying, "He told me the most horrible things about you. Are they true?"

I was shaken. I hadn't told her about my sexual orientation because I'd thought of her as an old-fashioned Catholic. She'd been married to one man for fifty years, and worked very closely with the Church. Plus, she was an icon to me and had she judged me that probably would have been it for me. I felt at that moment that I was about to lose her in my life. But I knew I couldn't lie to her.

"Lorraine, yes, I'm bisexual," I confessed. "If I was ever asked by a priest, I told them. I know you may think it's a sin, but I can't change who I am. I didn't ask to be this way . . ."

"Honey," she interrupted, "I don't care that you're bisexual. Tony (her son-in-law) doesn't care. It doesn't make you any less of a person in the eyes of God or in my eyes. I love and respect you just the same."

My eyes watered as I heard her say this. It wasn't what I was expecting to hear, least of all from someone very steep in her Catholic faith.

"I can't believe this man is going around saying these things about you," she shouted, "and to priests? That is not his place. That is between you, the father, and in confession. How dare he, as a Christian?"

At that moment, Lorraine made me realize there was no need to feel guilty about who I am. In a way, it was instant closure to a part of my life. So, I spoke with Father LeBar myself. Apparently, my sexuality hadn't been an issue for him, or my working with pagans. It seemed the people who spoke to him about me made it sound more like I worked with devil worshippers.

He told me, though, that he'd once shared a stage with Anton LaVey, the Satanist, to debate him.

I remember him saying, "Not everyone's Catholic. How are you supposed to teach others unless you work with them? You know what, I'll come to your conference. To hell with what they think!"

He did appear at UNIV-CON. Sadly, he passed away in 2008.

In the end, I learned what I should have realized all along: I shouldn't be ashamed of who I am. The people who mattered most, like Lorraine, stood up for me.

So, yes, I've had a complex relationship with religion, but a funny thing happened along the way. Instead of becoming anti-religious, I found my faith. I stayed with the Church. Yes, there are prejudices within it, but if I leave, what good am I doing? I don't need to leave my faith. The prejudice needs to leave my faith.

I'm not saying it's perfect. I continue to go through cycles of doubt and frustration, but I'm going to continue to do what I do, and if I influence anybody spiritually, I'll say I'm a Catholic.

In January 2007, as I spoke to Teena, though, I'd yet to have had that final revelation about myself, and her story had an effect on me that carried strongly into the days ahead. I had deep concerns about engaging in a demonic case, yes, but B— meant nothing to me, yet.

Prior to shooting our three out-of-state cases, I'd found a new house. I'd been living with Serg and a third roommate in a low-rent townhouse, but because of the show we now had an office, we'd gotten a dog, and had run out of space. The new place had an in-ground pool, front and back yards, a screened-in deck, a fireplace, and from the first-floor windows you could see the mountains.

The point is that when we returned from shooting "School House," it was moving time. I dumped my luggage off at the new place, and then went to the townhouse to pack. As I worked, the radio was on. I don't remember the details. But out of nowhere the announcer—talking about some weird thing that happened—said something like "Hey, maybe it's the demon B—."

If I hadn't had that conversation with Teena, I wouldn't have thought anything of it at all. As it was, I dismissed it as a coincidence. But, a few days after the move, I was watching TV and heard the name again. Again, I don't remember the context—it was a news program referencing something religious—but the name was clearly mentioned. This second occurrence of the name didn't set bells off, either, but I did think it strange.

I hadn't mentioned the name to anyone. Other than the e-mails our producer read, which didn't mention B—, I was the only one who'd spoken with Teena. I wasn't trying to hide it. I just didn't think to bring it up.

I was also having more conversations with Teena. She was opening up more, revealing more frightening details about her experiences. I don't like to reveal personal details about clients, and never will when asked not to, but in this instance it's important to understand the extreme nature of the situation. Teena told me she'd been raped by an unseen entity. She said she'd even woken up one night and found blisters on her genitals. Apparently, she went to a doctor, whose sole advice was for her to stop masturbating with a hair iron, which he insisted was the only thing that could have caused the blisters. Teena was obviously shocked and embarrassed by this accusation from her doctor.

As we spoke more, she reported that the activity was getting worse, saying that her husband, Raymond, had also been physically attacked. These days it's not unusual for clients to claim things are getting worse. Some just want to get on the show, but this was before we were even on the air. I took it as another sign there was something legitimate going on.

Compelled as I was to pursue the investigation, I knew this wasn't something we could rush into. We needed to spend time researching the situation, especially if it wound up being demonic. As part of that, we decided that Jamie, our counselor, should interview the family first to try to understand what might be going on.

This was after the rush of winter break, so there was some time to develop cases. My request to delay was easily accepted, but, meanwhile, we did have to shoot something.

We'd gotten another e-mail, this one from Jodi, a single mother in Elizabethtown with a teen son, Nate. They'd responded to a newspaper article about us. Among the activity they reported experiencing was the behavior of a doll they thought was haunted. I don't recall the exact details, but it'd been given to Jodi by her husband or boyfriend as an anniversary present. When they pulled the string, it supposedly sometimes said things like "I'm going to kill you, bitch."

The doll was also based on the main character from an extremely popular, long-running animated series. I thought it was great, certainly less complicated than what I'd been hearing from Teena. We agreed to do this case next and had the doll shipped to us ahead of time.

Serg and Josh took it to an Applied Research Lab at Penn State. Everyone there thought it was a hoot; the engineers were totally stoked. They analyzed the chip and found no defects or defaults. As far as they could tell, it was a normal, healthy doll.

Without that, the case didn't seem particularly interesting. I'd never say this to a client, but the other activity, as Jodi described it—a child's voice, an imprint on a couch—sounded mundane. We'd go in, maybe get some almost-interesting evidence, and then help the family cope with their fear. Big deal. I'd already had problems with "Schoolhouse Haunting." But I'd already agreed.

Recently a mutual friend had suggested a psychic named Chip Coffey, so before the shoot, I gave him a call. As I spoke with Chip for the first time, I was standing in the new house, looking out the windows at the mountains and feeling pretty relaxed. I didn't ask for a reading so he could "prove himself." My goal was to try to find out if he was a good human being. The rest would come out in the wash. He sounded like a nice guy, very sincere. If anything, he seemed pretty down-to-earth, different from my usual impression of a psychic. He also had a background in psychology. I particularly appreciated the fact that, like me, he was a paranormal investigator, not a TV psychic. So I said, "Okay, let's give it a try."

Production arranged to fly him up from Atlanta to Elizabethtown, being careful to keep him in the dark about what I thought was a simple little case.

My conversations with Teena were ongoing, so my mind was focused on Syracuse as the next exciting thing. Even so, hearing that demon name on radio and television was still, to my mind, likely in the realm of coincidence. It did remind me though, that back in 2005, on the same day, three people experienced the name of the force we dealt with then, much in the same way I was experiencing B—.

As we drove to Elizabethtown, I remained comfortable it was random, a fluke. That is, until I happened to be reading an article in a local newspaper—and in it was the name.

THE MORNING STAR

While many cultures have stories of evil spirits, the Catholic viewpoint is that a demon was once an angel. This belief doesn't appear in the Bible, but it does turn up in other ancient sources, such as the apocryphal Book of Enoch, which mentions a figure known as Lucifer—the morning star, brightest in the sky—who led a war in the heavens.

Many believe that Lucifer is the same as Satan, the Adversary, who appears in the Old Testament, but some believe they're different beings.

Seventeenth-century poet John Milton details the battle, the creation of the world, and the Fall of Mankind in his epic work, *Paradise Lost*, famous partly for the well-known line uttered by Satan: "Better to rule in Hell than serve in Heaven."

The basic story is that before the world was made, God's favored angel, Lucifer, decided to challenge him for his throne, resulting in a civil war. Some claim Milton made Satan too sympathetic, but the poem makes it clear Satan is doomed to fail, and exists in eternal torment.

According to this story, the rebel angels, banished to hell, are what we now refer to as demons. They retain their angelic powers,

and follow a hierarchy, with Satan at the top, or, rather, bottom. As a way to avenge themselves against what they see as their conqueror, they seek to corrupt the works of God. Their goal is the ruin of souls, the destruction of Creation.

Some see the existence of demons as part of a necessary step in our spiritual evolution. Eating the fruit of the forbidden tree gave Adam and Eve the knowledge of good and evil, and the ability to choose between them. As opposed to already accepting God, we each must find our way back to the divine.

13

Blindsided in Elizabethtown

I'll get them all.

To restate the obvious from the previous chapter, I didn't consider the Elizabethtown haunting demonic in any way. Everything the client, Jodi, described sounded light. She and her son heard footsteps and voices at night. They'd seen a couch pillow that rose as if someone had been sitting on it. Jodi sometimes felt as if she were being touched by an unseen presence. She'd also seen a purple x hanging in the air. It all seemed easily explainable. The footsteps could be the house settling, the voices could mean anything, pillows sometimes pop up like that when the heat goes on, and the x could have been some sort of optical quirk. Once I knew we couldn't use the trademarked doll, I was concerned that the episode wouldn't be very good. Production agreed.

But nothing in Elizabethtown turned out the way any of us expected.

"The Name" wound up being one of the most frenetic, convoluted investigations I'd ever been on. The time line is jumbled, partly due to a heroically impressive effort on the part of the editors to squeeze more than forty-two hours of video into twenty-two minutes and still tell an engaging, coherent story, and partly because the case was completed in two sessions. I'll try to sort it all out as we go along.

Our first shoot was the briefing, done in the PRS office. Ryan Heiser was there as well as our regulars. I ran through the few details I knew at the time. Single mother, Jodi, and her teen son, Nate, had moved into a house in Elizabethtown, Pennsylvania, and said they instantly started having experiences. Jodi described herself as being raised Catholic, but no longer practiced. She worked as a forensic accountant, someone who prepares books for use in court cases. She was very tight-lipped about her work for legal reasons.

During the drive, after I'd seen the name B— in the local paper, I received a call from Jodi. She said she was having a fight with Nate. In the past she'd ended communication with both his biological and then his adoptive father, which had been difficult for him. Out of necessity the episode abbreviates these factors, making it seem as if these were the only two men in their lives recently, but Jodi also had a boyfriend. She told us that it was her recent problems with him that left Jodi and Nate at odds. Because the full story would have been too complicated to explain, the boyfriend appears only briefly in the episode, sitting around the dining room table. Blink and you'll miss him.

Once we arrived, Jamie and I interviewed the clients separately to give us a better sense of the family situation. First I spoke with her boyfriend, who felt that the paranormal phenomena were making Jodi erratic, affecting their relationship. He said she'd kick him out, and then invite him back, leaving him feeling used. At first I felt sympathetic, but Jodi later told a different story, saying she'd asked him to leave for other reasons. I don't know what was true, but it did point to the sort of excess emotional energy that so often surrounds activity.

Meanwhile, Jodi spoke with Jamie about her divorce five years prior, and how difficult it was being a single parent. She talked more specifically about the activity, too, stressing how often they heard footsteps.

We also learned that her grandmother, who was in her eighties, had lived in the house the first week and seemed to have some encounters of her own. According to Jodi, she claimed to see two small children, girls, who would pull at her. Jodi said the activity upset her grandmother. In fact, it was one of the reasons the grandmother left to live in a home. When asked, Jodi explained that her greatest fear now was that if what was going on was real, it might hurt her son.

Nate was fourteen, but well-spoken and forthcoming with his feelings. "I don't really have a father figure right now," he said. "Even if it's not [my mother's] fault, I feel like there's something inside me blaming her."

I don't usually get involved with these situations; it's not why we're there, or what we do, but I felt like I understood where Nate was coming from. Though my father stayed in my life, my parents' marriage ended very, very badly and I'd grown up feeling stuck in the middle of someone else's failed relationship. There were times I'd have a fairly normal fight with my mother over something stupid, but it would boil over, and I'd end up accusing her of driving my father away. The feelings were bottled up, and when I was younger they erupted at inappropriate moments. Nate reminded me of that. He said he would get angry and punch walls, or claim his mom drove his father away, that sort of thing.

I remember trying to give him some advice, but I have no idea if it helped any.

Nate also talked about his paranormal experiences. "I'll just be looking out the front door, and I'll feel like someone is standing behind me, or has a hand on my shoulder."

I still considered the activity light, but during my interview with Jodi I began to notice things. At one point, she became visibly uncomfortable and said she was feeling cold. Since she'd reported feeling touched, I asked if she felt that way at that moment.

She nodded vigorously. "On my back."

At that moment, I felt that something strange was going on. The touching and the cold were signs there might be a connection between her and whatever was going on in the house, especially if this thing was bold enough to be doing it during an interview. There was something about the way she carried herself that made me worry she had experienced more than she was saying. At the same time, I was aware that I'd been thinking so much about Teena's problems in Syracuse my interest in that case could have been biasing me.

I did try to follow up by pointedly asking if the spirit had done anything else. She didn't answer. She just looked at me kind of funny.

"Okay, we'll come back to that," I said.

Then she showed me some crystals she'd found on the property, thinking they were peculiar and possibly related. I had Eilfie take a look at them, but nothing came of it. Some may have been broken glass, the sort found in cheap landfills used in construction. I also asked about the previous owner of the house, but at that point, she didn't answer.

By the end of the interview, my sense that there was something she wasn't saying was stronger. So I asked again if there was anything else.

"No, no," she insisted. "That's it."

Right after we ended, though, she suddenly said, "I have something I forgot to show you . . ."

She pulled out a copy of a newspaper article, said the previous owner had given it to her, and handed it to me. The headline read:

Six silenced by slayer, one of classic murder stories.
Parents and four of eight children wiped out 52 years ago.

At that moment, despite whatever else Jodi may have been afraid to discuss, I was convinced I'd been set up. A paranormal investigator is at her home and she *forgot* about a mass murder? How was that possible? The only thing I could think of was that she'd been coached, that production, worried the episode might be boring, had stepped over the line and asked her to spring this on me while the cameras were running, to create some drama.

"This happened here?" I asked. Instead of fascinated, I was angry. I didn't say anything else. I just walked away. If this was true, it was big. I had to understand what was going on. So I headed over to production.

"I'm trying to do a real investigation. If you coached my client, that's against everything we stand for. If they're not going to be truthful, we can't help them."

Worse, I didn't know if Jodi had been coached about anything else. I actually threatened to leave.

I remember the director being apologetic because a producer did know about the information and hadn't told me, but there was nothing else any of them was aware of.

The producers and our crew work tirelessly, following us at all hours of the day into some deeply bizarre places, then crafting a great show. I appreciate that enormously, but the integrity of the investigation is more personal to me and my life. Over the years, my reaction to this sort of issue has given me a reputation for being difficult.

I didn't fully appreciate it at the time, but the surprise distracted me from pursuing my hunch that there were things Jodi had yet to be open about. For now, I had to figure out how to deal with this article. The mass murder, after all, was something PRS hadn't uncovered about the case ourselves, so I was blindsided.

Regarding that article about the murders, there's another misconception about the details of this case, partly caused by my initial question, "This happened here?"

The victims, members of the Kreider family, were originally from the area but had moved to and were murdered in North Dakota. Their bodies were transported back to Elizabethtown, and buried in a cemetery literally across the street from Jodi's house.

Once I'd calmed down about the sudden appearance of the article, I began to wonder why Jodi never called the previous owner to ask about them. "You don't think he was trying to tell you something?" I asked her.

When I contacted Brian, the former owner, he was very forthcoming. "I've been waiting for *someone* to call about that," he said. He definitely believed the house was haunted. He said that he and his ex-wife heard children laughing in the basement. According to Brian, she even claimed to have seen them, corroborating what Jodi's grandmother saw. Brian's wife had also gone to the state library, found out about the murders, and learned the family was buried across the street.

Brian explained that he hadn't told Jodi outright, fearing she'd think he was crazy. "I felt so guilty about not telling her that when I realized I hadn't given her the ownership title, I gave her that article, too. I was hoping she'd ask questions, but she didn't."

Jodi's reticence about certain things was becoming more curious.

Meanwhile, I asked Eilfie to find out if there were any surviving family members of the victims still in the area. She managed to track down a grandson, Robert Greiner.

Our first psychic walk-through with Chip Coffey came next. When he walked in, that was literally the first moment I physically met him, a moment captured on the show. Our first phone call aside, my initial impressions weren't positive, but as viewers know, my impression changed radically and he became a staple of the show for the first three seasons.

After talking about how "hard" the cemetery struck him as he drove in, he almost immediately started talking demons, which sent up warning bells for me about his accuracy. There'd been no indication of that kind of activity at all, but Chip felt that not only might one be present, but that Jodi was drawing it in. He didn't offer any details, making it sound even more unconnected to what I'd seen. I became more and more skeptical about him by the second.

We walked through the house, then into a bedroom with a painted mural. Jodi had painted the mural as a sort of bonding experience.

There, Chip became even more dramatic. "There's definitely residual energy with a little girl in the house but there's also that male energy. There's something that tells me it's demonic. Interestingly enough, I have to tell you something about you. You amuse it. It feels like it knows what you know inside your head. Can I be real honest with you about what I just got in my head? I just got 'I'll get them all.' So be careful."

Under other conditions, this would have been frightening news, but based on what I believed about the case at the time, I was thinking, "This guy is full of shit. This is the last time I work with him."

That night, along with Jodi and Nate, we visited the graveyard and located the tombstones of the murdered Kreider family. Jodi and Nate seemed very moved. Nate even teared up. There were a lot of emotions floating around.

Since Chip was already here, I felt obliged to give him another chance and invited him to sit in on Dead Time. Usually we don't have minors at Dead Time, but Nate wanted to watch, and Jodi wanted him present, so we had him sit in with Serg in tech. The house wasn't that big, tech HQ was downstairs, and we couldn't really move around a lot.

Despite my hunches about Jodi, I still wasn't expecting anything. But I swear, as we tried to contact the child spirits, I heard *very* clear footsteps down the hallway. Everyone heard them, even the cameramen. I looked down the hall, wondering what was making the noise, and saw nothing.

Since we'd been trying to contact the child when the footsteps started, I said, "Okay, let's have the child move away and let this male figure come through."

Jodi seemed to react. She said she was feeling a presence, then reported that she was being touched.

"Who are you?" I asked. "What is your name?"

B—, the name of the Syracuse demon, popped into my head. *Ryan,* I told myself, *you're going overboard. That's next week's case. Stay focused.*

But then Chip announced, "I've got a name. It's a strange one."

For some reason I couldn't explain, I asked him not to say it, but to write it. As he wrote, my intuition was telling me, *It's going to be the name. It's going to be the name.* But, my mind said, *Nah, couldn't be.*

I opened the paper. There it was: B—.

My own emotions had been running a gamut that day. Now, I was floored. I felt like my breath had been stolen from me. The room started to spin. My heart started to race. I became hyperaware of every single noise in the house. I make no exaggeration about this incident. It was the biggest physical reaction I ever had on *Paranormal State.* I stared at it for about thirty seconds. Finally I looked up at Chip. "Why did you write this name down?"

"That's what I got. Do you know that?"

"Yes, I do. It's the same name that I've been . . ."

"Picking up? You knew that was what was going to be on the paper, didn't you?"

"You've never come across this name before?" I asked, ignoring the question.

"No. Does that have great significance to you or something?"

"Yes."

At first, the name startled me, but suddenly the rational part of the brain kicked in. *This has to be a trick*, I thought, still believing Jodi had been coached, that someone had told Chip the name.

"I think we should take a break," I announced.

The producers were in the garage, so I stormed out and yanked open the door so suddenly that everyone inside looked like deer caught in the headlights. I told the director I had to speak to him immediately.

"Did you give Chip that name?"

I don't remember the exact phrasing of the conversations that followed, but he said something like, "I don't know what you're talking about. I don't even know what was on the paper. It wasn't on-camera."

"You didn't tell him about next week's case?"

"How could I? I'm a director. I don't know anything about a case until a day or two before we get there. I'm not involved in those conversations."

I found one of the producers. "What did you tell Chip about next week's case?"

"Nothing. I'm not even involved in it. Segment producers alternate. Autumn's handling the next one."

They were adamant, but I simply did not believe them. I remember saying loudly, to anyone who was listening, "If I find out anyone is lying to me, so help me God!" They all looked at me as if they thought I lost my mind.

I went back to Chip. He looked very confused as I dragged him into the bathroom to talk. "Did the producers tell you *anything* about next week's case? Did Autumn talk to you?"

He was pretty shaken, looking at me like I was about to snap. "No, Ryan. I know nothing about any other case. I don't know who Autumn is. All I got was this name in my head. Are you angry with me? What did I do wrong?"

I was sure it *had* to be a setup. I realized Autumn did know about the Syracuse case, so I called her. It was one in the morning, but I kept calling and calling until she answered.

"Did you tell anyone about next week's case?"

"What?"

"The name. Did you tell anyone about the name?"

"What name?"

"You didn't talk to Chip?"

"Who's Chip?"

I started to pace the bathroom, not even realizing one of the camera guys was filming me through a crack in the doorway. It had to be a trick, I thought. But then I started to analyze it in detail. It came down to two possible scenarios—1) the film crew had set this up and people were lying to me or 2) Chip was either very crazily lucky or was truly psychic. I remember being terrified of both possibilities. If production was lying, then it meant I couldn't trust anyone. After all, this would be one intricate and elaborate setup. The question appeared in my mind: *How far would they go? Have I been manipulated this entire time? Is Jodi even really having any experiences, or was she hired?* Looking back, my feelings at that moment were probably similar to what Jim Carrey's character went through in *The Truman Show* felt when he realized everything around him was a stage.

Paranoia set in. The fear became overwhelming. I leaned up against the sink and tried to take another crack at analyzing this logically. As I took emotion out of it, the possibility of production setting this up just didn't make any sense.

Then I finally realized something—they *couldn't* have given Chip the name. Teena had only discussed the name with me over the phone. It wasn't in her e-mails and I'd kept our conversations private. I hadn't even told the team. Then I thought about the way production was reacting to things. They were hoping that my team and I would feel that the Kreider murders had something to do with Jodi's haunting and were pretty bummed when we felt it wasn't a strong enough connection. If they were hoping it was the Kreiders, why suddenly throw out a demonic name?

It was like a dream, and not a good one. I was rattled. I'd been shouting at people. Now I knew that things had gone way beyond coincidence. Why had that name been bugging me? Was the promise from that old case that the demonic would find me again coming true? It felt as if this thing was announcing itself to me. I had the sick feeling I'd walked into a trap.

I had to talk to someone. I called a priest I'd been working with, and left a message. I started pacing, not knowing what to do. I thought of Eilfie and asked where she was. Everyone could see I was freaking out, so they scattered to find her.

At first she figured it wasn't a big deal. "Okay, I'll be there in a minute."

"No, he needs to see you *right away.*"

She came rushing back and we took a walk outside. I told her everything I knew about Syracuse.

"It sounds demonic," I said. "And there's a name associated with it that's been popping up." I handed her the paper Chip gave me. "Do you recognize the name?"

"Possibly. So you think we've got something tagging along?"

It was freezing out, so we headed back in. Everyone sat around confused. On every case before this, I'd been pretty calm. Now I was raising my voice, short with everyone, glaring.

Eilfie and I went to Jodi's bedroom to talk some more.

"I knew this was going to happen," I told her.

She'd been part of those earlier cases, so she knew what I was talking about. I'd hoped that if there were going to be another demonic case that at least I'd have time to prepare for it. I was half-expecting a confrontation in Syracuse, but not here.

Whether or not you believe in demons, those cases in 2005 really hurt my team, to the point where some still have trouble coping. Serg and Eilfie were both affected, but theirs isn't my story to tell. I also knew they could make their own decisions about staying with this case. I did become concerned about our trainees, Heather and Katrina.

"You know, Ryan," Eilfie said, "we don't know what's going on. We need to think about what we're getting into. Send them home."

PRS has a term, "friendly evacuation," where unnecessary people are removed if the activity gets out of hand. That's what I did here. I asked Heather and Katrina to head back to the hotel. They asked how soon I wanted them to go. "Right now. Right this second."

They hopped into the car and left.

If I hadn't confused production earlier, it seemed I had now. "What's going on? Are you going to investigate more?"

"No. I need time to think about this," I told everyone. "We're shutting down for now."

I tried to calm myself down, then, of course, attempted to do the same for Jodi. "Were going to stay and keep watch," I told her. "Please, try to go to sleep and we'll talk in the morning." She'd seen how upset I was when I saw the name, but I tried to downplay it. "I'm thinking about another case that the paper reminded me of, that's all."

I doubt she believed me.

Serg, Eilfie, and I stayed awhile, chilling. Nothing happened. There was no crazy paranormal stuff. At 3:00 A.M. we tried communication. Nothing. So we called it a night.

The next day was kind of a "we don't know what to do" day. I woke up and got a call from one of our producers, who wasn't at the shoot due to a family emergency. He'd heard shooting had ground to a halt and was concerned.

We'd talked about demonic cases before, so I tried to explain. Understanding the difficulty, he suggested I go back and focus on the murders instead, but I refused.

"I can't shift gears. This is real. I have to do what I have to, to help the family."

Had we all known about the demonic aspect from the beginning, I'm sure production would've been open to it, but having it show up in the middle was as much a curveball to them as it was to me.

It was during these conversations, though, that I became

truly convinced they *hadn't* given Chip the name. If they had, they'd expect me to see the significance and follow it. Instead, they were advising I shift the focus away from it. They were saying it was too complicated a subject.

After the phone calls, I sat down with Heather and Katrina at the hotel and tried to explain what was going on and discussed the 2005 cases. When Heather asked about that name, I cautioned her not to mention it. "Never mention the name unless you want to go into full confrontation with it."

For the sake of the show, the team, and our client, I pushed aside my personal issues and tried to focus on doing what I could for now. That day, I went on to interview Robert Greiner, whose grandmother was Eva Kreider, who'd survived the murders, and he recounted the story of the killings.

Production understood we'd be coming back, but still wanted some sort of closure before we left, just in case. I felt a house blessing would be a good idea, so I contacted some parishes and a local priest invited me in. Since I was talking with him about some sensitive issues, the film crew waited outside.

I gave the priest my background, the details of the case, and explained my reasons for believing the problems at Jodi's house were demonic. He heard me out, then said, "If you hadn't told me about the demonic aspect, I could've done a house blessing. But for an exorcism, you have to petition to the bishop. This family needs help, but if what you're saying is real, they need the *right* kind of help. Unfortunately, you'll have to be patient."

Frustrated, I called Lorraine Warren for advice. She agreed with the priest. I remember her saying, "I know you want to give them help, honey, but you have to take the proper steps."

While the father wouldn't do a blessing himself, he'd given

me some signs to hang in the house as part of a more informal blessing. It wasn't a solution, but I agreed to do it.

I went back to Jodi and told her what I thought was happening. Again I pointedly asked her if there was anything she hadn't told me, anything at all. She opened up a little, and admitted to me that she felt not just touched, but physically attacked by the presence. But I still sensed she was holding back. I decided that it could wait. I remember telling her, "I know there's probably more to the story, and that you're reluctant to tell me some things, maybe because it's humiliating, and that's okay. I understand. I hope you know that it's crucial for us to know these things so we can help you. You don't need to tell us on camera if you're not comfortable. It can be a private matter. Let's just talk about it when we return. I promise we will."

Before she shared the information about the physical attack, I didn't know if the demon had just appeared when we arrived with the team. Now I was certain we'd been on a demonic case the whole time. Jodi just hadn't told us everything.

Then I conducted the house blessing. With that, we left for a few weeks, during which time I had my first encounter with the situation in Syracuse. Meanwhile, I'd been in contact with the diocese. Arranging an authentic exorcism isn't the easiest thing. I also spoke to Lorraine again, and she agreed to consult on the case.

When we returned to Elizabethtown, the Syracuse case was far from resolved. Heather and Katrina stayed behind this time, but Serg and Eilfie came back. Lorraine brought her son-in-law, Tony Spera, who was personally trained by Ed Warren and was his favorite student. He's been described as a demonologist, but he does not go by that title.

I shared what I knew and showed Lorraine the name. Though I didn't know the name, she recognized it as that of a powerful demon. "But you have to understand. They're all liars. This may not be its name, but it's using it against you."

As for Chip, ever since I'd become convinced production hadn't given him that name, and that we were on a demonic case, I'd been more impressed with him. Now Lorraine, who I trusted, echoed a lot of what he'd said.

"You have to be so careful," she said. "The anger in this house . . . There's a lot going on here. I'm surprised the roof doesn't blow off the place."

Afterward the three of us sat down with Jodi. Lorraine confronted her with what she'd sensed about Nate. "His room is sad. He's a very sad boy. Your son is a victim."

Hearing that, Jodi became very choked up. Between everything that had happened and our efforts, it seemed as if we blew open a door for her, exposing things, letting them air out. "I know he does not have a male figure in his life, and I tried so hard to be everything for him," she said.

She'd kept quiet about much more, revealing some things I vowed we would not repeat, including a violent assault from the entity which paralleled what was going on in Syracuse. Jodi was also, in her words, very angry with God for the problems in her life.

"There are so many underlying causes here," Lorraine said afterward. "Through the law of attraction, she's brought a great deal of phenomena to this home that's manifesting in all different types of ways."

Demons, I knew, feed on shame and secrecy. Their victims

often believe they can't talk about certain things because they feel inside that they're bad people.

Lorraine and I petitioned the diocese again, flexing what political influence we had, promising we wouldn't stop calling. At last we got through. They heard us out and agreed to allow an exorcism, provided it would not be filmed. I was fine with that. "Please, just help these people," I said.

It's possible the spirits of the children were present in addition to the demon, but after the exorcism, all the activity and the attacks stopped. As time passed, Jodi's relationship with her boyfriend ended, but she was getting along better with Nate.

The text at the end of the episode mentions Jodi miraculously surviving an accident in a fire. Months after our investigation, she had a barbecue and there was a flash fire. Her hair, eyelashes, and eyebrows were suddenly burning. She felt as if she might die. After having been so angry with God, now she prayed. "Please, help me. I don't want Nate to go through life without a mom."

Scary as the fire was, she was saved. She believed it was because of the protective energy that the exorcism had evoked. She'd found her faith again, and a sense of peace.

Looking back, even if in some crazy way it had *still* been production setting me up, at least it led to some good. Had that not happened, I might've left that case thinking it was a simple haunting. Had I not freaked out, maybe Jodi wouldn't have opened up.

Happy as I was for Jodi and Nate, though, I was not at peace when we left. As we made the drive back to State College, shame hit me. Even if it was for a short time, I'd lost my defenses and allowed my rational thinking to be replaced with fear and hysteria. I started thinking about the warning I was given two years ago. Why did the demonic show itself but not deliver an attack when we lost our footing? It didn't make any sense. I couldn't believe that the demonic popped in to Jodi's case just because of Syracuse. Jodi, I believe, was suffering from a mild demonic attack for a year or so. Were we chosen then, set up by some intangible intelligence, to pick two demonic cases back-to-back? No longer fearing I'd been manipulated by production, I began to fear that I was being manipulated by an unseen, malevolent force.

If that were true, it meant this consciousness had superior intelligence and cunning. I felt like I was a pawn on a chess board, maneuvered without even realizing it. Where was I going, and what would happen next week in Syracuse? For those who've never been in a truly demonic scenario, I know it sounds crazy. Trust me, there've been many nights when I think it is crazy. But ask yourself, what if it's true? What if there are two opposing forces out there, *in* this world but not *of* this world, one of pure good and light, the other of hate and destruction, both conscious, both always watching? Despite thousands of years of theological study from every different form of religion, the duality of nature, light and dark, remains unfathomable.

I decided I needed a break from the two cases, to get my bearings. If Syracuse was truly going to be a worse situation, then we needed to be ready.

WHAT'S IN A NAME?

Two years prior to the start of shooting *Paranormal State*, I'd been contacted by a Roman Catholic diocese to help on a demonic case. During that case, through intuition and other methods, a name came to us, M——. That name appears in the Old Testament and is associated with a pagan god that requires a costly sacrifice, often a child, involving fire.

Within a few days, three of our investigators encountered that name in odd places: dreams, radio, newspapers, and television. It was then we started referring to demons as "bunnies," to undermine their power by making fun of them.

Once the name B—— from the Syracuse case began popping up, it reminded me of that initial encounter. From what I could research, B—— has an older history, translating as "without worth" or "never to rise," which could be a reference to a fallen angel. Interestingly, Edgar Cayce, a famed trance channeler from the late nineteenth and early twentieth century, claimed this demon was worshipped in Atlantis.

In "The Name," a jumble of letters appears as a montage in which the name is fairly easy to pick out. I want to make it clear that I was against that. I felt it was inappropriate and disrespectful, but from a documentary standpoint, I understood. I respected the fact that they were trying to document things.

My own concerns about the name at that time, at that moment, are captured on film. Things have changed for me since. The significance has lost all value to me. It doesn't frighten me. If the names come up in other contexts, I say them freely and don't believe that doing so will conjure them.

At the same time, I'm not going to say demon names just to make fun of them. There are those who disrespect the power behind the names, and use them in a taunting fashion, daring themselves to say the names out loud. Because of that, whenever I'm discussing these cases, I do not use the full names.

THE KREIDER FAMILY MURDERS*

On July 7, 1893, Daniel Kreider and five members of his family were killed in what may have been North Dakota's first recorded serial killing. The murderer was Albert F. Bromberger, a twenty-two-year-old farmhand. During a card game the night before, Bromberger had told Kreider of his interest in his elder daughter, Annie. In response, Kreider made it clear his advances were unwanted and told Bromberger he should leave the farm.

The next morning Bromberger used a rifle and possibly a knife to kill Kreider, his wife, and four of their children: Bernice 15, Melby 12, Mary 9, and David 7. The other children, Aaron 13, Eva 5, and Henry 3, hid while Bromberger forced Annie to make him lunch. He stole what money he could find at the property, fifty dollars, raped the girl, and ran. Annie then had to walk into town for help.

Bromberger was captured, sentenced, and executed. The surviving Kreider children were brought to the former family home in Elizabethtown, Pennsylvania, where the victims were buried.

At the time the murders hit a big chord in the country. There was a lot of press, sort of a media circus. I just have to mention a weird part of the headline in the article I was handed about the murders, since it seems so out of keeping with the tragedy: 15,000 AT BIGGEST FUNERAL ATE 400 PIES. Go figure.

---

* Details from www.ndcourts.com/court/news/executend.htm.

14
Bearing Witness

This thing really was here, wasn't it?

After leaving "The Name" unfinished, I was convinced Syracuse would be the big one, the return demonic attack promised two years ago. Back then, I'd felt personally at risk, that my team was at risk, and I'd always known that if I kept working, something similar would happen. The resulting depression slowed me down and made me question whether I should continue my investigations, but it ultimately didn't stop me.

But thinking something *might* happen and being convinced it was *about* to happen are two different things. I hoped I'd grown and that I was more confident, maybe even wiser, but I had no way of being sure.

The episode documenting this case, "The Devil in Syracuse," opens with a shot of me praying in church. I'd gone to mass on campus, but only from time to time. It was very crowded there, and, to me, impersonal. The church here is one I'd found about a mile from my new house. Anxious, I decided to go, register, and give confession. Afterward I met with a priest.

"I know you might think I'm crazy," I told him. "You may not believe in the personification of evil, but I do." I described what I'd been going through.

He listened, but didn't say whether or not he believed in the demonic. You might think all Catholic priests believe in demons, but I'd read an anonymous survey saying that more than 50 percent of American priests don't believe in the devil, let alone demons. Many think it's entirely a metaphor. Regardless, the father didn't reject or judge me; he respected me. When the producers asked to film in the church, he agreed, as long as we didn't disturb the other parishioners.

Before making a final decision about shooting this case, I also spoke with our client Teena's husband, Raymond. His responses were short, and from the beginning, he seemed to be concealing something. At that point, though, I decided to take the risk.

As we prepared, weird things happened to the production team. They heard knocking and rapping in their hotel rooms. As she researched the case, Autumn, the segment producer, had odd bouts of depression that were very unusual for her. When a production assistant looked up B— and said it aloud, she started having nightmares. She was told to let me know, but was afraid of looking unprofessional, so before we left I met with them all.

"If anything happens, I need to know," I said. "It could be part of what's going on in this case. If you're having experiences, don't just tell each other and not tell me." I gave them all blessed medals.

As for the team, Heather asked to stay behind, but Katrina wanted to go. I agreed with the understanding that she wouldn't be allowed in the home without supervision and couldn't take part in Dead Time. I also asked Ryan Heiser along, because of his religious background. Eilfie and Serg came, too, but don't appear much on-camera. It was a trailer home, so there wasn't much to do in terms of tech and research. Serg was trying to find his voice at this point, and tended to hang back.

In the briefing, as usual, I rattled off the details, some of which I've already mentioned. Jodi and Raymond claimed they heard growling and scratching. They saw black shadows. Objects moved. Teena said she felt cold presences and regularly saw a dark red figure in her doorway. She also believed that Raymond's personality had changed, and that whatever this thing was had made him darker, more distant.

Teena, Raymond, and Katie all claimed something had attacked them. Raymond, a three-hundred-pound man, said an unseen presence had thrashed and thrown him around. They'd provided a photo of scratches on his body, though these didn't seem as dramatic as the clawing they'd described.

In the episode, as we prepared to leave, you'll see me pack an antique box. I used to bring it on any demonic cases, but these days I usually leave it in the office as a memento. It was a gift from a former investigator. By some coincidence, it happened to have my initials on it, RB, so they bought it and refitted it to hold a crucifix, Bible, holy medals, and holy water. Eilfie became a kind of "keeper" of that box. She hangs on to it until I need it, makes sure it's taken care of, packed properly. So I feel her energy from it.

The eight-hour drive to Syracuse, New York, was long, and colder and colder as we headed north. By the time we'd arrived at the trailer park, there'd been a huge snowstorm.

Teena and Raymond's home wasn't particularly small, but it definitely wasn't cared for. Raymond had been laid off from a factory some time ago and Teena was working at McDonald's to pay the bills. Apparently, Raymond would sit around all day as the house fell apart around him.

Teena said they'd tried cleaning before our arrival. I can't imagine what it was like before she cleaned. In some locations, you can sense a presence or heaviness in the air, but this was such a mess, it wasn't possible to sense anything. The smell was pretty overpowering, too.

The front door led to a living room. To the left was a kitchen, a bathroom, a side section with washer and dryer, and then the master bedroom. To the right were two smaller bedrooms belonging to the children, Katie and Charlie, and a second bathroom. Debris was everywhere. In the master bedroom, where Teena claimed the bed had been lifted and dropped, there were so many clothes piled all over you couldn't get to the dresser without crawling across the bed.

Convinced the presence was demonic, Teena and Raymond had hung crosses all over, some of which were just two pieces of wood screwed together. These had been blessed, but the family wasn't sure what denomination the pastor was. It may seem odd, but I've met a number of people who identify themselves as Christian, but don't know the denomination of their church.

As part of the walk-through, Teena took us to Katie's bedroom, where she said the activity started. Apparently it had begun around the time of Charlie's birth, intensifying after Ray lost his job. The hormones of childbirth can play havoc with the mother, which meant there were psychological concerns. To be clear, as things progressed, I thought there was hysteria, but couldn't write it all off that way.

"My daughter has been sleeping with us because she won't sleep in her room anymore," Teena told us. "Last night I think she was harassed because she woke up four times, screaming at us."

She asked Katie if she remembered what had happened.

"It was a monster," Katie said.

Katie and her brother both seemed pretty happy. We played with them a lot, and Katie enjoyed the attention. They weren't thrilled about their parents freaking out, but there didn't seem to be anything abnormal about them.

Unlike the house, the kids were clean and seemed healthy. They also claimed Charlie had some experiences, but he was only one and a half, so there was no way to validate that. All children read off of their parents, though. That's a given anywhere.

During the walk-through we also met Pat, a family friend who was present for a lot of the phenomena. Teena met her through Raymond—they'd worked together—and at one point she said she worried they'd had an affair. Even so, Teena said she saw Pat as a blessing. They could always go to Pat's place if they had to flee. Pat, for her part, was there nonstop. Teena said she would come home from work to find Pat had been there all day with Raymond.

Nearly everything Pat said seemed geared to increase Teena's anxiety. For instance, when someone knocked at the front door Pat said, "Do not open it! It's the demon!"

Teena seemed to pick up on any cue from Pat. "Oh my God! Don't open the door, Ryan!" she'd said.

"You really don't want me to open the door, Teena?"

"Pat's never been wrong."

"So, you just sit here and ignore it when someone knocks?"

"It goes away if you ignore it."

"Well, that's what happens if you don't answer the door. The person will eventually leave."

When the knock came again, I said, "It's probably someone from production." And I swung the door open. Teena gasped. Sure enough, it was someone from production. I looked over at Pat and said, "See?"

That sort of thing continued all day. I wish I could say I was exaggerating, but I'm not. Pat had Teena believing so many ridiculous things, I was beside myself. Clearly Pat was trouble, even if she was ultimately trying to help.

I interviewed Teena and Raymond next. It was a small space, so Ray stood in the doorway.

"What caused it all to start, I don't know," Teena said. "I want to know. I really do."

I asked about Katie's monster complaints. "That's the night I woke up getting choked," Teena explained. "I had handprints on my neck." She explained that Raymond had seen the prints. Then they showed me the torn shirt he said he'd been attacked in.

"I was in the middle of the living room," Ray said. "I felt something really cold on my back, and it kept touching me on the neck. And I asked it, 'Who do you think you are?' That's when I got spun around. It ripped my shirt. All the shades went down all at the same time. And that's when it told me that it was B—."

We'd already cautioned Ray about saying the name, but he seemed intent on not listening.

Afterward, I spoke to Teena alone about their marital problems. She became very emotional, near tears. "When I really needed someone to talk to I couldn't go to him. He was withdrawn."

"What does he think when you tell him things like what happened with Katie last night?" I asked.

"He said he was ready to move. He didn't want to be in the house no more. Financially we can't do it. I know this entity is putting a strain on our relationship. We almost divorced."

My sense was that the activity was only part of the problem and I tried to explain that. "You take away the demonic, and there's still a lot of sadness, a lot of depression, and a lot of struggle. If the demons are here, they have a lot to feed off of. That's what it does, it sort of finds people who are . . ."

Teena finished the sentence, " . . . weakened to begin with."

She seemed to feel they'd brought things on themselves. It's hard to say what people bring upon themselves. While they may have contributed to the situation, I didn't think they started it.

Meanwhile, Ryan Heiser and another PRS member interviewed Ray, who was also convinced about the nature of the haunting. "This thing is demonic. I believe in God, you know, and if you believe in God, you've pretty much gotta believe in the devil," Ray said.

When they asked about the attacks, he again repeated the name. Since we'd already cautioned him, Heiser just said, "Ow."

Again, he was reminded. "Just for the record, it's not good to say the name you heard out loud."

Ray's response was strange to say the least. "It ought to be a fun night, then, because that's the third time I've said it."

It was a strange scene. His wife was crying in the other room. She'd reported being seriously abused by the entity and her children had experiences, but he wasn't listening when we asked him not to say the name.

As I said, the situation didn't lend itself to a lot of research. We tried to interview some neighbors, but Teena was worried about being judged, so we backed off to respect their privacy. Those we did speak to had no experiences in the park, and nothing negative to say about Teena and Ray. We did find out that the land had some Native American ties, but I didn't think that had anything to do with the phenomena. Every part of the United States has *some* Native American ties.

It was late by then, so we took a break for dinner, then came back. I took a walk with the team, trying to sort things out, going over how complicated the threads in this case were. There was the name, a wild variety of activity, Ray's reticence, and Pat's melodrama. It was hard to think where to begin, or how.

One of our producers ran up to us, saying, "Guys, Teena's calling for you. She's saying something happened in the house."

We went racing in. Several of the crosses hung in the house had been turned, some upside down, some sideways. Teena was visibly upset. "This isn't funny! We pissed it off," she said.

Was I suspicious they'd done this themselves? Sure. If I had to suspect someone, I'd suspect Raymond, but I had no proof. As much as we checked, there was no indication they'd tampered with any evidence.

In any case, Teena remained agitated. "I'm scared. This is

what happens every time it messes with the crosses. It's just shaking my belief." She also said that the demon was near Pat.

"He's here," Pat told us. She said things like, "The sense I'm getting? He knows you're here to get rid of him and he's fighting it. It's around me. It's trying to get to me. Get the Bible!"

So Teena found a Bible, got down on her hands and knees, and listened as Pat gave her instructions on exactly what to do. As Teena obeyed, reading from Psalm 7, she started crying. "Let the enemy pursue me and overtake me, and let him trample my life to the ground and lay my soul in the dust."

It didn't take a degree in psychology for me to believe that while Pat seemed to really feel there was a presence, she wasn't helping the situation. Teena was upset, yes, but Pat's melodramatic comments were apparently fueling the fire. I felt that in order to have a chance at helping Teena, I had to get Pat out of there.

"Something has to be done about this," Pat said. "It's going to attack me and attack them."

I always tried to be diplomatic with clients. Confrontation doesn't help. But here, I couldn't keep quiet any longer. I blew up and said, "No, Pat. I think you're part of the problem. You're making this family hysterical. Maybe the crosses *did* turn upside down by themselves. I don't know. But the last thing we need is for Teena to be in tears. You're not helping. I'd appreciate it if you left this house."

Put on the spot, she agreed to go. Before she drove off, there was a final interview with her in her car. "I don't know anything that would turn crosses like that. When he said, 'Turn around,' my eyes went right to that cross first thing. Upside down? It's been right side up since we put it there. It's in there."

Throughout, Raymond sat there, not showing any emotion at all.

At this point, I felt I needed help. Lorraine had other commitments, but I'd been in touch with Father Andrew Calder, a part-time pastor who was recommended to me by Chip. He claimed to have experience with the demonic and was involved in some social circles of the paranormal community. After his arrival, one of his first suggestions was that we move the clients to a safe location, and do a spiritual walk-through of the home.

After they'd left, we didn't rifle through their belongings by any means, but what was left out in the open held some surprises. Raymond's screen name was Tiny666. The numbers 666, as many readers will know, is famous as the "number of the beast" mentioned in the Book of the Revelation of St. John the Divine, in the New Testament.

The lights were turned off as we did the walk-through. Father Calder sensed a presence, and felt that in the dark it had gotten stronger. "Darkness is their realm," he explained. He also described what it felt like to sense the unseen. "When I'm dealing with a demonic entity, I will get pressure. I will get stinging sensations."

Chip had also been invited on this case; the father asked that he be brought in. As we moved through the trailer, Chip started acting very bizarrely. Because of what had happened last week in Elizabethtown, he obviously knew something demonic was up before he arrived. He seemed fine, but once inside, he got a bit crazy, talking forcefully, and faster and faster. In Katie's room, he felt hit in the gut. The presence, he said, was rattled because we were there.

Father Caldwell agreed. "We're all a threat to it."

"It knew we were coming," Chip said quickly, phrasing things in that quirky way of his. "I'm confirming that at this point in time. It knew we were coming. I am one massive goose bump."

During the walk-though, I was using a thermal camera, which basically shows the relative temperature of whatever it's pointed at, different colors indicating colder and warmer. It showed Chip's body temperature as unusually low. I didn't think this was paranormal, but it may have been an indication of his emotional state.

He went on, seeming more and more frantic. "It wants the child. There's something very negative in this house. And it wants the kid. Whatever is in here is very demanding, and this is the feeling I get, this big kind of energy. Whatever it is, is ramping up."

Suddenly, Father Calder said, "Okay, Chip, time to go."

He took him out of the house to calm down.

Chip did return for Dead Time later that night. In this case, since the presence certainly seemed demonic, it took place at 3:00 A.M. As Chip tried communicating, I sensed a weight in the house beyond the stifling clutter. If there was something demonic, it was definitely present.

There was little activity to speak of, though, beyond the brooding darkness, until we heard a sharp, constant, electronic beeping. After some effort at maneuvering the crowded space, I tracked down the source. It was an alarm clock, set to go off at 3:33, half of 666. It may well have been someone setting us up, or a coincidence, but it felt as if the entity was toying with us.

There was something unusual about the house that's hard to explain but that I've only experienced during demonic cases.

There's a disorientation, and shadows will flicker as if there's a candle in the room.

When it was over, we all left, Chip and Father Caldwell agreed that the presence was demonic. Part of the question for me was, was it B—, the name I encountered in Elizabethtown? It seemed a stretch. If the activity began after Charlie was born, it overlapped with what happened with Jodi and Nate on the other case. At the same time, things seemed linked.

Could demons be in two places at once? Perhaps, but Satan is often described as the Prince of Lies. As Lorraine said, demons try to deceive people about who they are, to pump themselves up in the eyes of their victims. I have no definite answers, and my own theories about these beings is open-ended. My sense, though, is that it was a network, two entities using the same calling card.

While Chip was getting strong messages that Katie, the girl, was its primary victim, I disagreed. It seemed to me that the force was more focused on Ray. There was the physical attack, his depression, his quiet, angry personality, Teena's claims that he'd changed when the activity started and last, the fact that it was Ray who repeatedly said the name. Taken together, it sounded like Raymond was experiencing oppression, an initial stage in possession.

Father Caldwell recommended that no matter what else we tried to do, the house had to be cleaned up first. How can you address a spiritual issue when the clients' lives are so literally and symbolically messy? It made a lot of sense. To get them on their feet, we had to get them to help themselves.

Beyond that, the spiritual situation required more than a

quick house cleansing. That meant that like the last case, we would have to return after arrangements were made. I was worried production would be concerned again, but maybe because we were already planning to return to "The Name," or maybe because of their own experiences, everyone agreed easily.

I rode with Teena to her church to explain. This is no exaggeration: McDonald's trash was piled above the minivan seats, all around me. I couldn't see the floor.

We sat down in the church. I told her what we'd learned about Ray's screen name. She said she was aware that devil worship had been part of his past, and part of the reason she felt the presence had been influencing him.

Then I laid into her, much more than I ever had with a client about what I felt should happen. I told her we'd be back, but only provided she did certain things. I said that her house and her life were a mess, and that we couldn't help her unless she did something about it. I actually gave her a list of tasks, including cleaning and counseling.

To my surprise she said, "You're right, Ryan. I do need to do these things."

It was a tough conversation, but afterward my producer complimented me, saying something like, "Ryan, if you're ever looking for another career, you'd make a really awesome motivational speaker."

I also talked to Raymond, telling him what we'd found out about him. "I hope you don't feel like I betrayed your trust, but I'm afraid this thing might be targeting you."

He had little response, as usual. He did say he felt the entity was more connected to Teena.

"No," I said. "Clearly this thing is more attached to you." I told him if he wanted it gone, he'd need to be more involved. His answer, pretty much, was stony silence.

Before we left, I sat in the car talking to Teena. She asked if there was anything from us she could have while we were gone. I was wearing a St. Benedict medal, so I handed it to her. She seemed so shocked and pleased that I was very moved.

"You need it more than I do," I said. "So keep it."

To be honest, as we drove away, I had, maybe not doubts, but certainly concerns about how things would work out. I worried that like "Paranormal Intervention" she would agree at first, and then go back to doing what I thought caused the problems in the first place.

I felt a very strong connection to Teena. She seemed so warm; I felt as if she were a friend I'd known for a very long while and now needed help. As I drove back to PA, I looked upward and prayed to God to please, let this case be a success.

We headed back to Elizabethtown to meet with Lorraine Warren and finish up "The Name." In the two weeks we were gone, Ray and Teena had minor experiences, but nothing extreme. The name did not come up again.

By the time we were ready to return, though, Father Calder wasn't returning my phone calls. Chip couldn't get hold of him either. Finally he texted me saying he was ill and couldn't make it. He later told me his illness might have been related to the demon.

In his place, I called Keith and Sandra Johnson, the laymen from "School House Haunting." Keith had come to UNIV-CON a few years running and gave a phenomenal workshop, which was always packed.

When it was time to return, I was apprehensive. Would she

make the changes we asked of her? Despite my concerns, in the short time we were gone it looked as if Teena had changed her life radically. When I walked in to her house, my jaw dropped. It was significantly cleaner. I wouldn't lick the countertop, but it was presentable. She also had a new full-time job, working as a secretary. She'd even reenrolled in college. All that in three weeks. I was stunned.

We had no church sanction in this case, so we originally only planned to do a house blessing, but as we worked, things changed.

We began in the master bedroom, making crosses with holy water on the doors and windows, telling the demon in no uncertain terms that it wasn't welcome.

Teena seemed to be quickly affected. "I feels like my legs are being tied. My legs are being tied."

So Keith prayed over her. "We ask for any unholy presence to release its bond on her."

When we reached Katie's bedroom, Teena felt the presence again. "It's with us."

"Any spirits, be expelled," Keith said. "Your right to remain in this room is removed."

During this, my team sat with Raymond. They said he was looking more and more angry, as if he were about to snap someone's neck. Soon he said he was feeling very off, telling Teena, "My head's on fire, honey."

Worried, she called us in. Once I saw Ray, it was easy to understand her concern. His skin was beet red. He was hot to the touch. Keith prayed over him and Ray reacted more and more.

Now it was clear to me that Raymond *was* the center of things.

Technically, as discussed last chapter, without church sanction, there could be no exorcism. There's been a lot of discussion about that in the church. In Mark 16:17, Jesus says, "And these signs shall follow them that believe; In my name shall they cast out devils . . ." This means to many that believers can call on him to cast out demons.

Others have done so, and with success. When someone tries to end a possession this way, without the official go-ahead of the church, be they priest or layperson, it's called a "deliverance."

It's difficult to keep the terms straight, and, in fact, in an episode from a later season, Father Bob, whom we work with regularly now, performs a deliverance that the episode text erroneously calls an exorcism. It was understandable. We work with different editors from time to time and if they see someone trying to get rid of a demon, they naturally figure it's an exorcism. It was a concern for Father Bob, who worried he might lose his priesthood if he were seen as claiming to perform exorcisms.

So, specifically, when Raymond became so reactive during the blessing, Keith began a deliverance for him. Chip, Keith, and I all put our hands on him and prayed.

"We rebuke any evil spirit . . ."

"I swear to go through with my promise to rid you from this house," I said.

As we worked, Raymond often stared at me without blinking. I had the powerful sensation that he was on the verge of grabbing me and trying to snap my neck. His anger and attention seemed focused on me, perhaps because I'd told him what we found out about his past.

I didn't believe he was possessed; things hadn't gone that far yet. I did believe a demonic presence was influencing him, that perhaps he was experiencing oppression, but not that he was totally under its control.

"Raymond, you need to let this thing go," I said. "Think of your daughter."

Suddenly, he began shouting, "Get out of here. Leave my home. Leave my body. Leave my family alone!"

The entire process took about ten or fifteen minutes, but there came a definite moment when it felt like it was over, that whatever had been tormenting him left. It wasn't gradual. According to Raymond, it suddenly felt like it was gone—bam! Raymond, and the house, became quiet. It seemed we'd succeeded.

Afterward, a more human breakthrough happened. With the deliverance complete, we took a break and I went outside. To get to our van, I had to pass by Raymond, who was having a cigarette. At this point, given how he was staring at me during the deliverance, I had no idea if he was still angry with me or not.

I quickly said, "Hey, Raymond," and kept walking.

This guy had never talked to me, never approached me, but now he said, "Ryan?"

I stopped and turned to him. "Yeah?"

I don't have a record of it, but this is how I remember the conversation.

He said, "This thing really was here, wasn't it?"

"You tell me."

He shrugged. "I don't know what to believe anymore."

He began a sort of confession. When I'd first said he was the focus, he was angry, but now, as he thought about it, he admitted to himself that I was right. He said he loved his family, that the one thing he wanted to do, even though he didn't have a job, even though he had his own problems, was to be able to protect them. He said something like, "But I couldn't even do that. I was so angry because I couldn't punch this thing. I felt so weak. So, I tried to make a pact with it. I said it could have me if it spared them. It took me, but continued to harass my family anyway."

It was a startling admission. I thanked him for opening up. "You have to understand that though your intentions were noble, these things don't make deals. It will pretend, but it won't follow through. You gave yourself, but that didn't give you any power over it."

"I realize that now."

"That's good, Raymond." As I walked away, snow began to fall.

I held a final interview with Teena at a local diner the next day. The activity had stopped completely that night. Teena seemed relieved, grateful, and full of hope. "I was just going day by day," she told me. "Now I'm looking forward to the future. You guys helped us to realize that the baby steps led to the giant steps. I thought I was beyond hope, and hope found me."

At that, we said our good-byes. Every few months or so, she'd call to update me. They did go through a few ups and downs, but for the most part, they were finally starting to lead a normal life.

As a coda to the case, on New Year's Eve 2007, almost a year later, I was in South Carolina, going to a party thrown by one of my high school friends. I'd just arrived with my brother, Jordan, and Serg when my phone rang. I recognized the CID as Teena's, so I picked up. It was Raymond. He'd never called before.

"Hey Raymond, is everything okay?"

"Yeah, everything's fine. I just wanted to call and talk."

"Oh." It was kind of awkward. "So, how are you guys doing?"

"We're fine." And there was a pause. "I just wanted to wish you a Happy New Year."

"Thank you very much. How's Teena and everything?"

After another pause, he said, "Ryan, you changed our lives. You showed us kindness that we'd never seen before and I wanted you to know that."

I felt very emotional. I didn't know what to say, other than "Thank you very much, Raymond."

It was the best New Year's I'd had in my entire life.

I began this case worrying this was the big one, that this thing had summoned me to Syracuse. At the same time, in the end, I never confronted or engaged the demon directly. In fact, I refused. Of course, if Keith and Sandra had gotten injured and someone needed to pick up that book and keep reading, I'd have done it in a heartbeat. But I was there to do as they asked, which was to sprinkle holy water and pray. Ultimately, I'm not an exorcist or a demonologist. I'm more like a sentry. I was there to bear witness, bring people together, to assist. In a way, I found my strength by finding my place.

It wouldn't be the last time I heard the name. During the last episode of season 1.5, "Asylum," a voice came through using the name again. That freaked me out for a while. It still comes up every now and then, but I don't react anymore. Chip will say, "It's claiming to be our old friend." Now I just roll my eyes.

In the end, I wondered if these two cases were simply a game of manipulation and intimidation. Both were ultimately mild as far as demonic cases go, but I think it may have been a test, as if the entities wanted the cases to seem more dangerous than they were, to see if they could convince me to back down through fear tactics.

Rather than destroy me, these encounters affirmed my faith in myself and as a Catholic. I also realized that the warning I was given two years ago was true: Now that I was known, I'd spend the rest of my life coming across these things. One day I might meet my match, but not today . . .

15

Living a Dream

If I die, I hope it's that way.

After "The Devil in Syracuse," we'd gone to Nevada for our twelfth episode, "Vegas." The original order from A&E for *Paranormal State* was for thirteen episodes. That meant, as far as I knew, that our next case could be the last for the show. It'd almost certainly be the season finale, so we all wanted it to be special.

When we first started planning the series, the producers asked if there was any particular paranormal site I'd always wanted to visit. Point Pleasant, West Virginia, immediately came to mind. I'm a huge fan of John Keel's 1975 book, *The Mothman Prophecies*, and the 2003 film starring Richard Gere, which takes place there. For years, I tried to raise money through PRS for a field trip, but never met with much enthusiasm.

Everyone was excited about wrapping things up after all the work we'd put in, so the producers gave me the opportunity to live out a fantasy and investigate the Mothman. It was a real charge, especially after the recent demonic experiences.

The creature aside, John Keel fascinated me. First and foremost a journalist, he began as a skeptic. His 1957 book, *Jadoo*, exposed mystic frauds in the Middle East and Asia. In the sixties, UFOs were the big unexplained phenomena, and he wanted to do a similar exposé. As he was documenting flying saucer cases in and around West Virginia, the original Mothman sightings occurred, giving him the opportunity to document firsthand an experience that ultimately changed his worldview.

The book was head and shoulders above the usual paranormal writing. No one had come close to that level of detail. There was philosophy, theory, and Keel's style was literary, engaging, and cinematic. He wasn't simply writing about events. He was also looking at how people structure and try to explain things they encounter but don't understand.

In my eyes, it is one of the most definitive books about the paranormal. His work is so inspiring that PRS now gives out an award for paranormal writing and literary excellence, known as the Keel Award.

To give you an idea, the book opens during a storm. A mysterious man in black arrives at a remote home and asks to use the phone. The figure seems "off," so the residents don't let him in. The next day they learn the same figure appeared at several other homes. Soon everyone is talking about the strange visitor. Was it an alien? No, it was John Keel. His car had broken down and his efforts to get help accidentally started the very type of story he'd come to study.

While people tend to focus on the creature itself, Mothman, there was a lot more going on at Point Pleasant. The book is more centered on what Keel felt was behind the activity: *ultra-terrestrials*, a term he coined. Despite popular belief, he felt that paranormal events might have nothing to do with aliens, ghosts, or demons. Instead he postulated an advanced species living on earth, visible to us only under certain circumstances, or through a chain of coincidences. His main concern was whether they were here to observe or harm us. You can see where that might be difficult to get across in a mainstream movie, but I thought they did a pretty good job.

John Keel passed away as I was working on this book, on July 3, 2009, but I was very pleased to have been able to speak with him on a few occasions. The first time I was just one of the millions of people wanting to talk to him about Mothman. "Now that it's all done . . ." I began.

"It's *not* done," he quickly corrected. "I'm still investigating."

He came across to me as a bit of a stern professor. If you were wrong, he'd be quick to call you on it, slam you a bit, and then teach you something new. At the time, he was following some events he felt were typical of ultraterrestrial phenomena, a huge flock of birds that suddenly dropped dead, that sort of thing. I don't believe he intended to publish a new book. He was in his late seventies, and sadly had it rough in terms of health. He'd agreed to come to UNIV-CON, but he had a stroke and couldn't make it.

Sometime afterward, I had an interesting conversation with Curt Sutherly, an author/investigator, who was somewhat mentored by Keel. We discussed some similarities between the concept of a demon and an ultraterrestrial. Both worked invisibly, often through coincidences. Both communicated in hidden ways, influencing lives.

That gave me a new perspective. Demonic activity is malevolent from a human point of view, but was it possible it *wasn't* a battle between good and evil, just another unknown form of nature? Animals devour one another, but in the end it completes a circle. Maybe what we perceive as demons are a form of ultraterrestrial that doesn't have our best interest at heart.

I'm not saying I buy that concept completely. How would the energy of Jesus Christ figure in? Why would an ultraterrestrial flee when you invoke his name?

As for our Mothman episode, everyone was willing to take more chances with this one, have some fun, and put some wit into it. It begins with a shot of the warm beaches at Cancun, and then slam cuts to the snowstorm back at Penn State, where your humble narrator and his intrepid team of paranormal investigators were huddled against the cold. Despite the snow, the time was spring break, so we'd again gathered while school was out.

The briefings were always an homage to *The X Files*, but here we went all out. It was snowing, so I showed up wearing what many called my Mulder-style trench coat and actually did a slide show for the team.

We found a great place to shoot, with a nice roaring fire and a huge projection screen. There I was, flipping through photos of Bigfoot, the Yeti, Nessie—all the *classics*, and talking about Mothman.

In the episode, my phrasing was a little off so it was interpreted that I was saying they were all debunked. I don't personally view *any* of those as debunked, even if certain evidence about them was. The 16mm Patterson film of Bigfoot was likely debunked when the guy who designed the suit and the guy who wore it came out and admitted it was faked. Likewise, the 1934 Loch Ness monster photo was debunked when one of the people involved admitted it was a hoax. Neither of which means Bigfoot or the Loch Ness monster have been debunked.

I remember watching a scientific investigation of Loch Ness that had nothing to do with the monster. As they took sonar readings, they got some strange images of a large living object about the size of a prehistoric plesiosaur.

Those stories are far from over.

During the slide-show/briefing I went through the Mothman basics. The first sightings, written about dozens of times, took place November 16, 1966. Two married couples, Roger and Linda Scarberry and Steve and Mary Mallette, were traveling late at night. As they passed an abandoned government factory, they saw two red lights by an old generator plant near the gate. Stopping to investigate, they realized the lights were actually the eyes of a large animal.

Roger Scarberry was quoted as saying it was "shaped like a man, but bigger, maybe six and a half or seven feet tall, with big wings folded against its back." Terrified, they drove away as the creature chased them at incredible speeds. They passed a dead dog on the side of the road, which was later identified by the dog tags. It was from another town. The rumor was that it'd been killed, and the body looked as if something with talons had grabbed and flown off with it.

Over the next year, the creature was seen by dozens of witnesses. The area also had a ton of other paranormal activity, which Keel felt was related: UFOs, men in black, poltergeists, Bigfoot, and black panther sightings. There were even animal and human mutilations. Things culminated December 15, 1967, when the Silver Bridge, a major route into town that crossed the Ohio River, collapsed during rush hour, killing forty-six people. Mothman and other activity tapered off, leading to theories that the creature either caused the collapse, or had appeared as a warning. Since then, Mothman's been sighted before tragedies such as Chernobyl and 9/11.

When we arrived for my first look at Point Pleasant, it reminded me of the town I was born in: Corry, Pennsylvania. Corry has always been a small town. There is a McDonald's, a Walmart, and that's about it. Most people commuted to a larger town for work. Point Pleasant was way smaller, and with a distinctly darker atmosphere. Of course, I was there because of Mothman, seeing things through that prism, but it was more than subjective.

I already talked about producer Alan LaGarde, who'd gotten his start in hard news. He'd gone undercover with street gangs and done some really wild news pieces. After scouting Point Pleasant, he came back and said, "This town is absolutely the most creepy place I've ever been to."

The Mothman Museum was our first stop. The impressive collection included the original handwritten police reports and witness depositions. I read for myself how all four eyewitness accounts matched up perfectly. The owner, Jeff Wamsley, said he received e-mails from all over the globe, nearly every day. Mothman was very much alive, at least in people's minds.

I was particularly excited to be able to interview two eyewitnesses, Linda Scarberry and Faye Dewitt. Linda was one of the original witnesses, while Faye and her brother claim they saw the creature a short while later, but didn't go public about it until years later.

Sadly, Linda was pretty much known around town as not being all there. She was cared for by her family, who didn't have a lot of money.

At the beginning of the interview, she says she saw Mothman "hundreds" of times: outside her apartment, outside her bedroom, in the yard. My sense was that the original sighting was so traumatic that afterward she thought she saw him everywhere.

I do believe she witnessed something that night four decades ago. After all, three other witnesses corroborated it. "It got its wings caught in the cables and couldn't get loose and when it finally got loose it took off for the powerhouse. We took off down Route 62 and it was waiting on us at a curve," Linda said.

She still seemed a little shocked about it, to the point where I was moved. That was after she's told this story how many times?

Faye Dewitt was very much the opposite of Linda. She definitely had her wits about her, and man, that woman talked. She was one of the few interview subjects I had to keep reeling back into the conversation. According to her, back in 1966 her brother thought the original sighting was a hoax. He was set on driving to the power generator with her to prove everyone wrong, but then he ran into the creature himself.

"All I can remember is turning off the main road," Faye said. "It was running alongside the car, looking in my side of the car window. All I caught were those red eyes."

Some claim Faye isn't a particularly trustworthy witness, that she wasn't there at all at the time of the early sightings and came on the scene much later, but I never found any evidence of that. As Jeff Wamsley said in the episode, there were just too many different people seeing basically the same thing for it to be a hoax.

There was some variation in the descriptions, though. Some witnesses said the eyes were in the creature's chest. Jeff also told us the sightings didn't instantly stop after the bridge collapse. It was more like they'd tapered off as the bridge tragedy seized the town's attention instead. At the time, his father collected newspapers and film footage about the collapse, all of which were on display at the museum.

In a town as small as Point Pleasant, the tragedy was extremely personal. Jeff remembered hearing a boom that rattled his house. Denny Bellamy, the gentleman in charge of the Visitor's Bureau, remembered that a girl in his class at school was on the bridge and her body was never found. Heather managed to interview a number of people who were there and still lived in town, including a woman who'd lost her first husband and son on the bridge.

The team regrouped to compare notes. Having done some research, Katrina related how witnesses arriving at the scene of the bridge collapse said the victims in the water sounded like cows. They were so cold they couldn't scream properly. The bridge itself was an eyebar chain suspension bridge. Built in 1928, it wasn't made to handle the weight of modern rush hour traffic. Investigators said the entire collapse was caused by a tiny defect a tenth of an inch deep in one eyebar. It's amazing how little it took to bring the whole thing down.

That night, we conducted Dead Time at the site of the collapse. Chip, who'd come along with us, sensed that at the time of the accident, the people involved knew they were going to die as soon as they went into the water.

"It's quick," he said. "I understand what's happening. I'm cold. I'm scared. Boom, it's over. If I die, I hope it's that way."

Strange phrasing, *if* I die—maybe he knows something the rest of us don't?

A weird bird cry filled the air. We also saw a red light in the distance, but never thought it was Mothman. It was certainly a sad, somber spot.

Chip also sensed a Native American component, but it was no secret that the story of the Shawnee chief, Cornstalk, was a big part of Point Pleasant's history. It was something everyone studied in school. He was buried in town, near the floodwall, and there's a monument to him there. Some of the townspeople were actually more open to believing in the legendary "Cornstalk Curse" than they were in Mothman.

Heather interviewed a resident, Robert Lander, who gave us some of the background. Back in colonial days, many of the Shawnee tribe fought against the settlers, but not Chief Cornstalk. For years he abided by a treaty with them. In 1777, during the American Revolution, the British urged the Shawnee to attack the colonists. When Chief Cornstalk heard about this, he, his son, Elinipsico, and other friendly Shawnee went to the fort at Point Pleasant to warn them. For their kindness, they were arrested. When a colonial soldier was killed elsewhere by the Shawnee, some settlers broke into the jail and, seeking revenge, killed Cornstalk, his son, and the others. Legend has it that as he died, Cornstalk placed a curse on the land.

Historically, Point Pleasant has had more than its share of misfortune. Some of that is because the river nearly overflows regularly. In 1913 and 1937, flooding nearly destroyed the city. But there were other tragedies. A barge explosion killed six townsmen in 1953. The Silver Bridge collapsed in 1967. Then, in 1978 a freight train derailed, spilling toxic chemicals that poisoned the town's water supply.

The Shawnee considered any spot where two rivers met sacred. Point Pleasant was at the intersection of the Ohio and Kanawha rivers, which is why so many natives fought to push the colonists out. This was also where they put their burial grounds. In West Virginia, Indian mounds were pretty common. Throughout the flat farmland there are dramatic hills, like bumps or pimples on the land, which turned out to be centuries-old burial mounds.

Shortly before WWII, the U.S. government built a secret explosives factory over an area that contained not one, but three vast burial grounds. This is where the original Mothman sightings occurred.

For the final part of our investigation, I took my team to this area. John Frick, a Mothman enthusiast, was our guide. He'd appeared on several shows dealing with Mothman and had extensive knowledge of the area and the subject. He was an invaluable person to have with us as we journeyed to this dark, overgrown area.

If the town felt foreboding, this was completely grim. We went at night, so it was hard to see clearly, but on the outskirts of the site, there was a warning sign saying the land was surrounded on all four sides by contaminated, polluted, poisoned aquifers. The sacred territory wasn't only invaded; it was completely defiled. Just being there made me nervous, especially knowing the burial site alone could contain thousands of angry spirits.

As part of the secret base, the government had built a series of concrete igloos. They sat beyond some dense growth, so we made our way slowly. As we walked, Chip felt as if something knew we were there. There were feathers on the ground. Heather and Katrina saw some geese, and we heard rustling in the brush. Geese can get pretty loud while defending their territory.

I tend to have a respect for the woods at night. It's not a fear, but rather a realization that I am a guest in the night realm. I want to respect the silence and order of things. These days I'll take walks in the forest in the dark, but I used to be very worried about disturbing something. It may be the Native American in me coming out, from my father's side. I have an innate sense that there are hidden things in the world that stay out of our way. The best place for them is where man hasn't conquered the terrain, the wilderness. So shouting in the woods seems disrespectful. My feeling is that you're on their turf; don't make a mockery of yourself.

At times I've had the same feeling indoors, like in the "Asylum" episode, discussed in a later chapter. That was not a place to go in and play foosball. It had a bad history. You just have to respect certain places because of the dark energy. That's how I felt here.

After a long walk, we came upon the igloos. The museum had a complete map of them, but scores had been demolished. According to John, this was supposedly where they stored the experimental explosives. If something went wrong, they didn't want the whole base destroyed, so they built these igloos. The buildings were mostly underground.

In response to John's explanation, Chip gave us a dramatic "I don't believe that."

The secret government base could have been working on much more than explosives. Some theorize the experiments there may have actually given birth to the Mothman. No one "officially" knows. I tried, but never got the government to say what they were used for.

Each igloo was kind of like a hobbit house, built into the sides of hills. Outside all I could see was the hill. Once I went in, there was a huge concrete space where a hundred people could fit comfortably. The ceiling was maybe thirty-five, forty feet up. In one igloo we saw a bunch of metal canisters, but they were all empty.

As we explored one, Katrina felt a stabbing pain. She became dizzy. Then the batteries on our EMF detectors started going out. Someone from town had told Chip the area tends to drain batteries. With some subjective experiences occurring, this seemed like a good spot to try to get in touch with any ultraterrestrials that might be present.

Chip opened himself and soon sensed a presence. He said it was very different from anything he'd encountered before.

"When I ask what it is, 'intelligence' is all I get as an answer, and that's not a word I've ever heard. I've heard 'spirit,' I've heard 'ghost,' now I hear 'intelligence,' " he said.

He also said it was communicating with us because we'd called to it. One of the big unanswered questions in the case is whether these intelligences had anything to do with the bridge collapse, so I asked.

"I can give you the answer to that, if you want to know," Chip said dramatically.

"Okay, tell us."

After a pause he said, "Absolutely not."

When I asked why they hadn't tried to stop the collapse, he said, "They can't." He felt they tried to get people's attention, but couldn't physically prevent the accident from happening.

I don't know if he was really in touch with anything, but it was one of a very few times he actually creeped me out. It felt to me as if something was there.

At that time, a very important personal moment took place, something that played out over the next few days. It didn't make it into the episode, but it so nicely sums up a lot of my feelings about being a paranormal investigator that I've saved it to discuss it in the book's epilogue.

For now, realizing we had no real way to prove or disprove something that occurred so long ago, I went back to my *X Files* roots and said, "I want to believe there was something here at Point Pleasant."

And that was the truth. I honestly have no opinion about exactly what went on. Some think Mothman may have been a big bird they had trouble with in the area at the time, a sand-hill crane, which has a wingspan of about seven feet. After seeing pictures of the bird, it doesn't seem to match the witness accounts.

Over forty years have passed since the bridge collapse and the original sightings. An older core group of townsfolk still embrace Mothman, partly because they either believe it or they were there at the time, and partly because it brings in the tourism that keeps the town alive. To the younger generation, though, Mothman's something they've only heard about, a legend. And more think that it's a joke.

For me, when I go to Point Pleasant—and I've been back since the filming of the investigation—it's like being a kid again. I've gone into haunted houses where five people have had experiences. Here's a place where people came from all over the world and had experiences.

There were things I wish we could have done. I would've loved to have had an interview with John Keel, but it wasn't possible. I would've loved to have the military go on record about the igloos, but we didn't have time to fully pursue that. One of my goals was to see if I could contribute something to the theories, but that was sort of the way some soccer players dream of being David Beckham.

I was in good company. Even John Keel, who wrote the most documented account people will ever see, didn't have a final explanation. The last line of the book is terrific. He quotes Charles Fort, an early twentieth-century writer who invented the paranormal genre the same way Poe invented the detective genre. Fort said, "If there is a universal mind, must it be sane?"

It's the author's way of saying that not only does he not get it, but also maybe we're not dealing with anything we *can* get. It blew me away.

FAMOUS CRYPTIDS

Cryptozoology is the search for and study of animals currently unknown to science, known as *cryptids*. Some may seem purely mythical, but it's important to realize that the mountain gorilla, for instance, was believed to be a legend until its existence was confirmed in 1902. More recently, in 1976, the previously unknown megamouth shark was discovered near Hawaii. In 2003, fossils of miniature humans were discovered on the isle of Flores in Indonesia and are believed to be a previously unknown species of man. A short list of some of the more famous cryptids follows.

The *Loch Ness monster*, or Nessie, is a creature some believe may be a prehistoric plesiosaur. It's been sighted in Loch Ness in the Scottish Highlands for hundreds of years. Despite hundreds of sightings, blurry videos, photographs, and sonar readings, no definitive proof regarding the creature has been found. Nessie belongs to a category of cryptid known as lake monsters, which includes Champy (in Lake Champlain, Vermont) and Ogopogo (in Okanagan Lake in British Columbia).

Bigfoot is a tall apelike creature that's been repeatedly sighted in the Pacific Northwest. Similar stories can be found on every continent except Antarctica. In 1951, when Eric Shipton photographed what he felt was a footprint of a Yeti, or the Abominable Snowman, in the Himalayas, the idea became popular again. Like Nessie, there are many photos and videos of such creatures, but no concrete proof.

Mokèlé-mbèmbé is a large cryptid reported by the native tribes in the Congo River Basin. Descriptions of the creature go back to the eighteenth century. Based on the accounts, some believe it to be a living brontosaurus. Many expeditions have attempted to find the creature with little luck, the most recent occurring in 2009.

The *Jersey Devil* is a winged, hoofed creature that walked on two legs and has the head of a horse. It is said to live in the Pine Barrens of southern New Jersey. Originally sighted in 1735, the most frequent sightings occurred in January of 1909 when it was seen by many people, and its tracks were found in the snow. Sightings continue to the present day and were the subject of a later episode of *Paranormal State*.

The *Thunderbird* is a large birdlike creature that some theorize may be a surviving species of pterosaur. In Arizona in 1890, two cowboys claimed to have killed such a creature, which was reported in a local paper at the time and believed to have been photographed. Sightings continue and in some cases attacks have been reported.

16

Paranormal Wait

When are these actually going to air?

As we were working, shooting, draining ourselves, and struggling to get things right, naturally I was also itching to find out when the show would premiere. By now I'd had enough experience to know what the production process was like, but the goal was to get out there, take part in showing the world what paranormal investigations were actually like, and fight the stigma that added to so many of my clients' problems.

Paranormal State was first scheduled to premiere in March 2007, but here it was February and that wasn't realistic anymore. I heard rumors about a May premiere, but the next date I heard, from Neil, an A&E executive, was January . . . of the next year.

It was like telling a kid Christmas was going to be delayed six months.

I managed to say, "Oh . . . why so late?"

He said it was just a scheduling issue. They really felt good about the show. Gary Auerbach, another executive producer added, "And they're already talking about more episodes."

Thirteen is considered the upper limit for any series that hasn't aired yet, so they'd already given us a big vote of confidence, but to me this was confusing news. We weren't going on until January, but we might shoot more episodes?"

In March, I was flown out to LA to do some voice-overs for my Director's Logs. I'd already recorded most of them, but then they'd decided the show should be more about the cases and less about our college lives, which was fine with me. While I was there, they showed me the opening titles, which I thought were pretty cool.

After that, after all that work, everything just stopped.

I spent the next months trying to figure out what to do with myself. It wasn't as if I could build anything new based on the show. It wasn't even out yet. I tried to kick back and relax as best I could. Summer 2007 rolled around. Still nothing. I worked on the next conference. I traveled a little. I even did a couple of new cases. Nowadays we get thousands, but at the time we didn't get many calls, so that didn't take up a lot of time.

Spiderman 3 was out at the movies, and I always like to go to New York City to see a new *Spiderman*. I dropped by the A&E offices to say hello, and met some of the people who were going to be in charge of our show, like our publicist, Barry. They were still considering more episodes, but there wasn't anything definite.

In August, I was back home in South Carolina when Elaine Frontain Bryant, an A&E executive, invited me in to go over their promotional plans. So I flew to New York.

From the beginning, things were different and impressive. It was a big meeting with twenty people. The digital department was there, as well as PR, the head of advertising.

"You know," they told me, "we're going to make this *the* event show in December."

They were talking about a huge promotional plan. *Paranormal State* ads would be on city buses. They'd make *Paranormal State* drinks for all the NYC bars. Then they said something that really made my jaw drop: *The X Files* was coming out with a boxed set that fall, and they'd gotten approval from the show's creator, Chris Carter, to advertise *Paranormal State* in the set with a promotional DVD.

Sadly, it didn't end up happening. For whatever reason, negotiations with Fox didn't pan out. There was plenty else to be excited about, though.

The decision had been made. Our first season would be *twenty* episodes, which meant we'd be back in production. They even gave me a new air date for the premiere: December 10, 2007. I also learned that the demo we'd shot, "Sixth Sense," had come out so well they wanted to expand it into a full episode.

A&E was also going to be sponsoring UNIV-CON that year, which was fantastic. They'd even agreed to screen an episode of *Paranormal State* there. After that, via satellite hookup, I spoke with about thirty A&E advertising departments across the country. I was shocked, excited, overwhelmed, astonished, and about a dozen other adjectives.

And of course, after all that wait, wait, wait, everything had to happen right away. We'd have to have six new episodes finished before the premiere, so I'd be available for promotion. But there was even a good side to that. Since we knew the show would debut in December and we only had to shoot six more cases, we didn't have to rush *too* much.

At the time, I was only renting part of that huge two-story house. Now I rented the downstairs level as well and turned it into an office. Previously, PRS had operated in a club room, a cubicle, and once in an investigator's basement for a while. In the old townhouse, the office space was next to the washer and dryer. This was the first time we had an official office with its own entrance. We also agreed on the need to have more people examining cases, so I was able to put Eilfie and Serg on salary to help out. It's not that they weren't paid for the show, but it wasn't huge money, and this was a way to compensate them more. We worked four days a week, finding cases, planning the conference.

Meanwhile, there was time to go back and think about our first thirteeen shoots and how to improve things. We all agreed our technology and evidence review needed to be beefed up. We also agreed on a rough structure, the briefing, the client meeting, the psychic walk-though, and so on. The crew would no longer relocate to State College. Since the show would focus on the cases now, they could remain in NYC and travel directly to the investigations.

Another issue we reviewed was the breakneck schedule. Now we planned to prepare a case or two, shoot two back-to-back, take a break to prepare the next two, and so on. It sounded like it would be more like the investigatory process I'd established and enjoyed before the show started.

With the improvements, the promotional efforts, and the upcoming premiere date, I went back into production for season 1.5 in September 2007, all jazzed up and raring to go.

PARANORMAL BILLBOARDS

Among the exciting things A&E used to promote *Paranormal State* was a billboard using an innovative Digital Audio Technology (DAT) that could direct sound at people's heads, making it seem as if someone who wasn't there was whispering in their ear.

The new technology, first used in England, transmitted low frequency sound waves that made the human skull act as a sort of speaker. People in range of the transmitter would hear an unnerving woman's whispering voice saying, "It's not your imagination."

This amazing promotional device was installed in SoHo in New York City and quickly caught the attention of national and international press, including the *New York Times*, National Public Radio and newspapers as far off as Asia.

On Sunset Boulevard in LA another great billboard, this one 3-D, was installed. It featured a slowly emerging screaming face reminiscent of Munch's *The Scream*.

17

We Find Something

If you want to go in you're welcome to,
but I think I'll stay on the porch.

Our first shoot for season 1.5, which would become "Pet Cemetery," was an amazing case where a lot of crazy stuff happened. It was so intense and in-the-moment there were times I felt like I was living in a Stephen King novel.

The client fell into our laps. We were looking at a different haunting in Maine. A couple said they'd found blood in their home, where apparently some dark things had happened, including a murder. The producers scouted it and at first I was interested, but the stories didn't add up. The blood turned out to be paint. The woman was also on several medications. In the end we decided against it. What I think is interesting, and that the audience doesn't get to see, are all the cases we turn away or look into but don't work out. Sometimes I think it'd be fun to show that process.

But while in Maine, the producers also met Sybil Howe, a divorced nurse who'd been driven out of her house by paranormal activity. Her dog seemed to sense a presence, too. Two other dogs had been run over near the house. It sounded like a creepy location—a remote house—but I wasn't sold. The story seemed to be mostly about dead dogs, which was sad, but not intriguing. When I learned that Sybil had also been in touch with Lorraine Warren, I took a closer look and learned there were rumors of strange rituals taking place on the property. That caught my interest. After speaking to Sybil, I was hooked.

She described a latch on her door popping open for no reason. While showering, she felt as if something was watching her, and then she heard what sounded like a hand slamming into the wall next to the shower.

She seemed legit. She didn't just say, "Oh, my dog is growling at something invisible." The pieces of each experience were there. "I'd wake up, feel a presence, see my dog, Lucy, staring at something. Then she'd start growling." So we went for it.

The episode was shot during school, and, unlike our previous efforts, during the week. We found the Parsons Memorial Library near Sybil's, and shot the briefings for this case and the next there. It was senior year for Heather and Katrina, a busy time, so Heather wasn't there for this episode. In the next episode, Heather would be there, but not Katrina. With a number of shows under our belt, we felt more confident. It wasn't as big a deal as when Serg wanted to study while we were trying to shoot "Freshman Fear." Serg and Josh had both graduated by this point.

As I explained at the briefing, animals are very sensitive to their surroundings—able to sense earthquakes and tornadoes before they happen. They're also traditionally thought of as able to detect spirits. This seemed extreme, though. Lucy, Sybil's black Labrador, even refused to go up to the second floor.

At this point Sybil wouldn't enter the house at all, so she and Lucy met us in town. She was a little more open to the paranormal than the average person. She had brought in a psychic before we'd been there. Here, though, the psychic wound up picking up things our own experiences later confirmed.

It's not mentioned in the episode, but Sybil also had experiences before living in the house. Apparently she'd known someone who'd gotten into some dark, questionable practices and talked about using blood and animal parts as offerings, something in which Sybil hadn't been involved. This person was gone, but as the case developed, I thought there might be a connection between that relationship and this activity. After "The Devil in Syracuse," the possibility of demonic involvement no longer rattled me or my team quite the same way.

At the house, things started the first day she moved in. At night, she heard footsteps overhead. Over time, she said there were bells ringing, lights going on and off, and a gross fecal odor following her around. Meanwhile, she said that Lucy was constantly begging Sybil not to leave her alone. The dog was particularly uneasy if Sybil, or anyone else, went up to the second floor. At one point Lucy developed a limp, as if something in the house had hurt her.

One night, Sybil said she found herself mysteriously locked in the bathroom. She was able to get out, but that was enough for her. When she bought this place, she hadn't sold her first house yet, so she moved back to her old home. Now she didn't want to sell the house because she felt it unfair to pass the problem on to someone else.

When we arrived, she hadn't been at the property for a while. I tell you that place was creepy. It was in the middle of nowhere. The closest neighbor was a quarter mile or more away. If you screamed loud enough *maybe* someone would hear you.

"If you want to go in you're welcome to, but I think I'll stay on the porch," Sybil said.

So, in I went. I'm not the type who typically senses things. In "Beer, Wine & Spirits," for instance, I didn't feel the same creepiness others did. Here, the moment I walked in, the whole place felt dark. There was definitely heaviness in the air.

Among the activity, Sybil mentioned a ringing bell. As I first toured the house alone, amazingly, I heard it. It sounded like a toy or something musical.

I was thinking, "Wow."

In trying to pinpoint it, though, I eventually figured out it was the refrigerator. Once I unplugged the fridge, the sound stopped. That turned out to be one of the few mysteries here that was actually solved.

From the state of things, it was obvious Sybil had left in a hurry. There were half-unpacked boxes and plastic bins all over, so she hadn't even completely moved in. Remodeling had begun on the second floor, where she planned to put her bedroom, but it was never finished. I searched for evidence of an animal infestation that could explain the strange sounds and smells—and caused the dog's reaction—but I didn't see anything.

Next I tried to coax Lucy in. She wouldn't go past the threshold of the front door. The moment I started up the stairs to the second floor, Lucy barked and kept barking. You can see this in the episode; the sequence is completely in real time. I hit the stairs and the dog becomes upset. Lucy would not go in.

Dark as the property and the house felt to me, the feeling definitely intensified on the second floor. It was different, as if at any moment something would jump out at me.

Something else that didn't make it into the episode was the fact that we'd brought Xander, my own dog, with us. Given Lucy's reactions, I wanted to bring him into the house to see what he did. Once we took our first look at the place, everyone tried to talk me out of it, including the producers. At the time we didn't even know *how many* dogs had died here.

It may seem callous that I wanted to take my pet in, but I knew in my heart Xander wouldn't be hurt. I'd stay with him, and I wouldn't let him run around unattended. Serg, who co-owns Xander, was open to trying it, but he felt everyone else had a good point. Why take the chance? So we decided against it.

That created the issue of what to do with Xander. I couldn't just keep him locked in a car, so I had to find a kennel, which led to an interesting turn. The kennel we found was run by a dog whisperer. This isn't a psychic. It's someone who's studied dog psychology well enough to communicate with canines in ways they understand. This connection provided an opportunity for the case, which I discuss toward the end of the chapter.

Meanwhile, Eilfie did some great work researching the property's history. She managed to come up with a list of all the previous owners going back to 1893. There were at least a dozen. I don't necessarily attribute the large number of owners to the paranormal. In cases where there really does seem to be something going on, it's particularly important to explain whatever aspects are explainable, to leave a clearer picture of what, exactly, is unknown.

A more "natural" explanation for the number of owners is the home's remote location and size. It was a starter home, inexpensive and small enough for a single person, or, at most, a couple with one child. There were also those who'd buy the house to stay in over weekends. Could other reasons have caused people to move out? Sure. But the turnover wasn't surprising.

The most recent owners, Sybil told us previously, were her son and daughter-in-law, Melanie, and their daughter, Coley. They'd owned the two dogs we knew of that had died.

Katrina interviewed Melanie. She hadn't really noticed anything off at the house until their first dog, Zeus, got out and was hit by a car. About a month later they'd bought a second dog, Bailey. In short order Bailey also got out and was hit -and killed.

This was genuinely odd. The house was in the middle of nowhere. We spent a lot of time there, and a car came by maybe only once every half hour. There was no blind spot, so when a car did drive by, you'd be able to see it coming a good distance away.

After the death of the second dog, their toddler, Coley, developed an invisible friend she'd named Deppy Zoe. Invisible playmates at that age are common, more likely the result of an active imagination than a child seeing spirits, but naturally Katrina asked Coley about Deppy Zoe.

"Did she say anything to you today?"

It was like the kid had multiple personalities. In a squeaky voice, Coley said, "I don't want to die in the road." Then, in a deep voice, she said some things we couldn't make out. Finally, in a third singsong voice, she added, "I want to die."

The look on Katrina's face is priceless. It was such a strange moment the producers thought about investigating that angle, centering the episode on a witch named Deppy Zoe. It made sense that Coley would be a little weirded out after hearing her mom discuss their lost dogs. This little girl had lost two pets in a violent way in a short time. That'd be tough for an adult, let alone a toddler, to process.

Melanie told Katrina that after the dogs died, she woke up in the house once and felt a presence. But she'd had no experiences beyond that. Sybil's son didn't want to talk to us. He hadn't had any experiences and wanted to let it be.

With the list Eilfie put together, we were able to make calls to several previous owners. Two got back to us. The first was Gail Kass, who lived there from 1984 to 1986 with her husband, Ryan. They'd also had experiences. At night, they heard choral music in the woods, people singing, but no songs they recognized. Gail felt that the strangest thing that happened was that *her* dog died while they were away on vacation. Apparently, she received a call from her house sitter, who didn't know how it happened. She said that suddenly the dog went crazy. The dog just ran out and bam! Gail said she felt it was the weirdest thing, confirming what we'd seen for ourselves, that people rarely drove on the road.

Next I spoke to Erik and Rhonda, who lived there from 1986 to 1988. They said they'd never heard any rumors or experienced anything strange on the property, at least nothing they considered strange, except for the fact that their dog had an aversion to the second floor, just like Lucy.

"She would sit at the base of the stairs while we were up there, and whine the whole time," Rhonda said.

That was already a wild coincidence, if it was just a coincidence. Not knowing the history of the house, they didn't mention it until I asked, but that dog had *also* been hit by a car and died. By the end of the day, I learned there'd been a total of *four* dogs living at the property that had been hit by cars on that normally desolate road.

And things were about to get even stranger.

Chip Coffey, who was with us regularly now, was there for our psychic walk-through. Now that we'd had a chance to review our procedures, we were even more cautious about making sure our psychics didn't know anything about the case beforehand. When he wasn't shooting, the producers kept Chip locked in a van. And this is one episode where Chip really proves himself.

Though she hadn't fully unpacked, Sybil had already decorated with a lot of small porcelain knickknacks in the house—angels, clowns, and so on. They were all different types, and all over the place. Chip walked into the house and headed to the cupboard area. There, not in the open and not a huge piece, was a small porcelain necklace with a two-inch picture of Lucy.

Chip grabbed it. "There's something about this dog . . ."

That shocked me. It was a huge leap.

He also felt drawn upstairs, where he asked about a female with an "M" name, Margaret. It struck him so powerfully that he made sure I wrote it down. Margaret. He picked up on more, a live dog and a dead dog, and then wondered if there was anything ritualistic going on.

"There's something buried on the property," he said, and started pointing outside.

He was hitting so well that I decided to see if he could pinpoint the area. We went outside and I followed him through the woods near the property. Chip didn't find anything, but on our way back, he stopped short.

"Margaret! Margaret!" he yelled.

He pointed to a gravestone with the name "Margaret" carved on it. It was right off the backyard, barely into the woods. There was no cemetery, nothing else, just one tombstone. I'd seen the stone itself before and hadn't thought anything of it. It looked like a rock. You'd have to be within a few feet to notice the writing. There was no last name, just Margaret.

With no Margaret listed among the owners, Eilfie went back to the library for more research. Meanwhile Chip met with Sybil and Lucy to ask about the ritualistic aspect he'd sensed. Apparently neighbors had told Sybil that in the sixties an older woman lived in the house. She was supposedly a very mean person, and hung out with a strange man who used to kill dogs.

That provided the rudiments of a theory. If the area had been the site of ritual killings, because of her friend's dabbling in the occult, it's possible Sybil's presence escalated the activity.

Sybil had already been in touch with Lorraine, so the case provided a nice opportunity to work with her again. Like Chip, Lorraine was dead-on in what she sensed in the house. She felt the presence of an older woman, then headed straight up to the second floor, and sensed something she described as horrible.

"I feel like I'm being choked. I feel that hurt in my throat. Who would want to live in this house? I couldn't live in here. I wouldn't even want one of my animals in here," she said. Under the circumstances, it was quite surprising to hear her mention animals.

As I mentioned, Sybil had originally spoken with another psychic who'd sensed similar things. According to Sybil, as they stood next to the house, the psychic pointed up at the window to the tiny room where most of our experiences took place and felt something there. She also saw a man who seemed malevolent. So here we had three psychics who had no contact with each other that I knew of getting basically the same information. It was *incredibly* unusual.

Meanwhile, for the second time, Eilfie's research paid off. She'd managed to track down a neighbor, Fern, who'd grown up in the area. Fern was able to confirm some of the rumors about the property. When she was ten years old, an older woman *had* lived there.

"She had a male friend who used to ride on a bicycle, and he killed our dog," Fern said.

That was the *fifth* dead dog we'd heard about connected with the property. Apparently he had a stick with a nail on the end that he'd use for killing dogs. Fern also knew the first name of the woman, Margaret. At this point, I have to admit, I was pretty damn impressed with Chip and Lorraine.

We never did get Margaret's last name. She may have rented the house, or it could have been in her husband's name, and she inherited it when he died. This was a very, very small town, and try as we might, we couldn't find more information about these people—no family, no descendants, nothing.

We were able to determine that the stone wasn't a grave site. I'm not clear on the details, but someone close to Sybil had a wife, who, by a surprisingly eerie coincidence, was also named

Margaret. When she died, they had the tombstone made, ended up not using it, and left it there.

With all this data feeding the already heavy atmosphere, we went into Dead Time. Half of the team stayed by the tombstone while Chip and I were stationed on the second floor of the house. Early on, Chip sensed a spirit at the bottom of the steps, but couldn't confirm who it might be. When he asked whatever might be present to communicate, we heard a tap and a barking dog. I did hear dogs in the neighborhood once in a while, so that was likely yet another coincidence, but then a motion detector went off on the second floor. We had a camera synced with it this time, but the photos didn't catch anything.

We knew something was going on, but coulnd't figure out what. To try to get more information, Chip offered to try channeling. Unlike a possession, where the host is unwilling, when channeling, a psychic invites the spirit to use their body to communicate. We hadn't done anything like that previously on the show, and I'm always dubious about claims of mystic abilities. It seems possible, but especially with channeling, you have to trust the medium. I did trust Chip, so I opted to give it a shot.

After about ten minutes of attempting to channel, Chip's demeanor changed. He looked very frightened and actually started weeping. It seemed to me as if he was genuinely coming under the influence of another personality. Whether that personality was imaginary or not, I don't know.

When I asked if it was human or a demon, Chip couldn't speak. He was only able to shake his head, "No."

Aside from apparently being mute, while in the trance Chip didn't know how to use his hands. He kept them balled up like paws. He later said that sometimes when human spirits enter a medium, they don't quite remember how to use a human body. It's possible, though, that he was channeling the spirit of one of the dead dogs. In the end, it was extremely interesting, but didn't provide any additional information.

In all our cases, I try to put together a complete picture of what's going on. Here, again and again, it felt as if we were on the edge of something, but we couldn't quite get to what we needed to know.

Frustrated, while Chip was in the trance, I asked the spirit to pull all its energy together and give us some definite sign or clue about what was going on. As if in response, there was a *loud* bang to my right.

It wasn't a rustling, a scratching, or a thump. It was a banging, so loud it made us all jump.

I was *sure* the recorders had captured it, but in a big disappointment, on playback, the sound was barely audible. Whatever it was, it was loud enough to take Chip out of his trance.

What the episode also didn't show was that I investigated the sound. It was so loud, so intense, that I ran over to the right side of the room with a flashlight to see what had moved. Even though I was in the room with Chip and a camera guy, I suddenly felt a prickling feeling up my spine. I felt like something was eyeing me, like a predator watching its prey.

In the episode, the time crunching makes it seems as if right after leaving his trance Chip led us to a small pile of rocks, but the full story is much more interesting.

When we walked through the woods earlier, I'd spotted not one, but several piles of rocks. They were in various places, and each pile looked as if it were marking something. Eilfie thought they might be trail markers or fire pits that had been filled in, but they didn't look like either. Most were stacked about four feet high.

One dog had been buried on the property, but we knew the location, and the stone piles didn't match. Two of the other dogs died at the vet and weren't buried on or near the property. I didn't know what to make of the stone piles, but it looked like something was going on. Early on I had Josh and Serg start digging. By this time, they'd dug up two pits, but found nothing. The third they started on was different from the others. It was smaller, but more distinctly piled.

After they'd been at it awhile, they called and said, "Ryan, I think we might have found something."

"You found something? Are you sure?"

I was floored. That was big news. We dug for things at least four times each in our second and third seasons and never found a thing. I've had people with sophisticated ground-scanning equipment *tell* us we'd find something in a certain spot, but we came up with nothing. Here, we go to Maine in the woods with a couple of shovels and find something.

I went over to them immediately and looked into the bottom of the hole. In it lay a blue plastic tarp, half covered in dirt, bundled up, and tied with rope. Some thick tree roots had grown over it, and to get to it, Josh and Serg had to cut them away.

I decided to pull it out and have a closer look. We had masks on as a precaution, and as we started moving it, the tarp shifted and an awful smell came out. Even with our masks on we had to back away. At that point we knew we had a dead body.

We were really freaked. What on earth was it? Another dead dog? A dead baby?

My heart was racing as we dragged the tarp up and out of the hole.

"Oh, God," I said.

"Oh God, doesn't sound like a good thing," Chip said.

Once we opened it up and saw the corpse inisde, it was obvious it was a dog. It looked like a medium-sized breed, black or dark brown. As far as I could tell it didn't have a head; it was decapitated. The body was also very moist, fresh. It's possible the plastic tarp kept it preserved, but the thick roots growing over it meant it'd been buried a long time. Of the dead dogs we knew about, three were accounted for, and the others had died nearly twenty years ago. That's a long time for a body to still look fresh. I wanted to get a vet to examine it, but we couldn't find anybody available.

After regrouping back at the house, Lorraine told me that the "freshness" of the body, the lack of decomposition, was characteristic of ritual slayings. She and her late husband, Ed Warren, having done many occult cases, theorized that in these sacrifices the supernatural component slows down the decomposition, as if to defy, or mock, the natural order.

Was this another animal victim of Margaret and her dog-killing boyfriend? There was no way to know. The mystery of this place just kept getting deeper.

That night, there was one major experience that didn't make it into the episode, basically because no one was awake for it except me. As usual, the team slept at the house that night. After the film crew took the lights and left, the desolation and the dark atmosphere really sank in. I remember thinking that staying might end up being something I'd regret.

Unlived in for so long, the house had no food, so we decided to get some snacks. To give you a sense of how isolated the house was, we had to drive thirty minutes just to reach a gas station. When we came back we stayed together on the second floor. We put two mattresses together with three blankets so we were literally sharing the sleeping space. We played cards and talked. Around 1:00 or 1:30 I crashed on the bed and passed out. The others had on a radio and listened to music as I fell asleep.

I don't remember if I was dreaming anything, but a sound, like an audience's laughter, but loud, woke me. With my eyes still closed, I was sure it was the team, still playing cards, or the sound of their radio, but when I opened my eyes, it was dark. The radio was off and everyone was asleep.

I looked at the clock on my cell phone: 3:00 A.M. on the dot. All of a sudden, I heard shuffling downstairs. I had "that" feeling, as if I were being watched. It was a particularly strong, uncomfortable, intimidating feeling.

I considered waking everyone, but took this as a challenge. After "The Name," I decided I wouldn't let my fear get the best of me. I could always shout if something happened. So I got up to investigate.

As I leaned over the stairs I could see down into the first floor kitchen. There was a light we'd left on below. Near that I saw a moving shadow.

That really freaked me out, but I walked down. As I made my way down the steps, I was thinking it could be an animal, a ghost, or possibly an intruder. Looking back, it could have been both. I didn't see anything, and didn't know exactly where the shuffling had come from, so I checked around. The doors were all locked, the windows all closed. All the while, my instincts were on fire, telling me something was watching.

The sound came again. It was from behind me, in the kitchen. It sounded like one of Sybil's boxes was being dragged across the floor. When I went there to check it out, I heard it again, only now it was coming from the living room. It was a game I'd been stuck in before, as if something was teasing me, leading me back and forth just to scare me. And it was working. The feeling of being watched kept growing until it became overpowering. I'd experienced presences, but this was one of the strongest.

My fear *was* about to get the best of me. I was ready to run. I was ready to pack up and leave. But I didn't want to give in, and instead became defiant.

"You're not scaring me," I said to the dark.

I recited the St. Michael prayer. Saying it again, I walked around the room.

"You will stay away from me," I said under my breath. "You're not going to come near me. You're not going to drive me out of this house. You tried and you failed. Do not intimidate me or I *will* get rid of you."

The more I talked, the more pissed off I got. In a way this was the fruition of my efforts during our last demonic case. I'd made a decision, and now I wasn't going to quit. I wasn't going to give in.

Finally, the feeling lifted. I had the sense that whatever it was had backed off. I went upstairs and back to sleep. When I woke up, it was morning.

No one else had an experience that night. Looking back, I wonder if I should've woken my team, but my gut tells me that the experience wouldn't have happened if I had. There are some things you just have to face alone at night.

I wasn't thinking this haunting was demonic, per se, but I did believe at the time that this sort of presence was evil, so that's how I reacted. In the years since, I've come to think I could be wrong about that. It's possible that when you're around any spirit or sensing anything that you can't see, the mind automatically interprets that as a threat. These days I try to take a more curious attitude.

Having found one body, the next day I had everyone spread out and dig at the other stone piles. We got a little trigger happy and started with the bigger stone piles, figuring maybe there's something bigger buried there, but we didn't find anything. There were many piles we never got to, but we were running out of time and had to move on.

Back when we shot "The Devil in Syracuse" and "The Name," I'd dropped by a Catholic store and bought a book with prayers for all occasions. It came in handy here. As part of the closing for the case, I read a prayer for animals from it:

God, loving creator of all life,
Help us to treat with compassion the living creatures en-
trusted to our care
May they never be subjected to cruelty or neglect
So that through them we come to a greater appreciation
Of your glory and creation. Amen.

With Lorraine's help we buried blessed medals on the four corners of the property. Afterward, we went into the house. Sybil felt it was cleaner, lighter. She was laughing. She was back in the house. Lucy was with her, and now roaming about much more freely. Over the closing credits, there's footage of the dog whisperer walking Lucy around on the second floor.

Sybil ended up keeping the property. For a while, she promoted it as a house that appeared on *Paranormal State*, renting it to curious ghost seekers. At the time of this writing she's been in touch recently and said she was living in the house and doing fine.

Also, as I mentioned, meeting a dog whisperer created an interesting opportunity. I invited the dog whisperer to the house to meet Lucy. She worked with her awhile, started praising her, conditioning her, and so on. Much in the same way we try to empower the clients to confront whatever's haunting them, the dog whisperer worked to empower Lucy.

Soon she was able to bring Lucy into the house. The dog was clearly nervous about it (and she hadn't been the only dog with that issue), but in she went. Even then, Lucy remained very hesitant about the second floor, but with the dog whisperer, in time, she even went there.

The whisperer believed that at least part of the reason for Lucy's refusal to enter could have been the dog's extreme sensitivity to her owner's emotional state. This is a common characteristic in dogs, and Lucy could have been sensing and reacting to Sybil's fear.

It was fascinating, but I don't think that proved anything one way or the other about the house. It does call attention to the fact that even with dogs there's an emotional aspect to activity.

After leaving Maine and returning to State College, both Chip and I had two very bizarre experiences. Not even a week after being back, my dog, Xander, who has never jumped into our inground pool unaccompanied (he's a little chicken), was suddenly found out in the backyard, caught in the pool cover. He had been trying to get out, but to no avail. By the time we realized he was no longer in the house and found him out back, he was exhausted. I'm not saying this is necessarily paranormal, but it is a bizarre coincidence. Had I not found him so soon, I shudder to think what would've happened.

Chip, on the other hand, claimed he was on the phone when suddenly all of his dogs went crazy. They started to fight. In the process of trying to break it up, he was scratched and bitten. "That has NEVER happened in all my years of having them," he said with bewilderment. Later that night, he awoke to a loud pounding on his walls, as if someone was beating their hand against the wall. He looked at the clock. It was 3:00 A.M. Both of our experiences took place on the same day.

With all the wild experiences and the history behind that place, this is one case I look back on and feel that we definitely missed something. If we ever went back, I'd love to dig up more of the rock piles, do some more historical research, and try to find out more about Margaret and her strange friend who used to kill dogs with a stick.

Sometimes, though, you have to live with not knowing.

TRANCE CHANNELING

Channeling is a form of mediumship that gained popularity in the second half of the twentieth century. With it, psychics claim to become the vessels for spirits, angels, alien entities, and transcendent beings from other dimensions, who speak through them offering everything from advice to apocalyptic warnings.

Prior to the rise of the concept, Edgar Cayce (1877–1945), while trying to cure his chronic laryngitis through hypnosis, would go into trances during which he referred to himself in the plural, as "we." His laryngitis disappeared and he soon began channeling health cures and a history of the lost continent of Atlantis. Though a devout Christian, he's considered by some to be one of the founders of the New Age movement.

J. Z. Knight, another famous channeler, claims to leave her body while the spirit of Ramtha, a 36,000-year-old entity, speaks through her. Ramtha said he was originally a warrior from another lost continent, Lemuria, which once did battle with Atlantis. Through Knight, Ramtha teaches enlightenment and has written a series of books.

ANIMAL SACRIFICE

Animal sacrifice is one of the oldest methods of attempting to appease gods or spirit forces. It has appeared in practically every culture, in the Old Testament, and it still exists.

In Santeria, for instance, today, the blood of the sacrificed animal is thought to contain life energy. Some villages in Greece currently sacrifice animals to Orthodox saints in a practice known as *kourbània*. It is thought to be a holdover from pre-Christian beliefs. It is also used in various black magic rituals.

Human sacrifice has also taken place throughout history. Likewise, it still occurs in remote parts of India and sub-Saharan Africa. It is not condoned in any country and is treated as murder.

18

I Open a Portal

It doesn't have a human face.

Directly after "Pet Cemetery" we went to our next case. With our new schedule, we were doubling up on cases, shooting two back-to-back, taking a break, then shooting the next two. Though we only had six more episodes to do, between UNIV-CON, the series premiere, and promotion for both, a lot was coming up.

This time we found our client through our previous client. While in Maine, we asked Sybil if she knew anyone else who'd been experiencing activity. She told us about a woman she worked with as a nurse, Georgia Poole. Georgia was single and had lived in the town of Chapley for about ten years in the same house with her daughter, Katie. There'd been activity from the beginning, but more recently, Katie claimed she'd been attacked by a thing she described as half human, half animal. Georgia was concerned for her daughter and we'd never dealt with this sort of creature on the show before, so it was a perfect fit.

The briefing was again held in the Parsons Memorial Library. This time Heather made it, but Katrina had to go back to Penn State to get some of her schoolwork done. As I explain in the episode, which would come to be called "Shape Shifter," Georgia and her daughter often heard strange noises, unexplained growls. More interestingly, one night Katie said she heard the fluttering of wings, and then felt something on top of her pinning her down, a squat animal-thing.

Georgia had seen something herself once, but unlike what Katie experienced, she saw a tall, deformed shadow figure. They were both petrified, so our main concern was trying to get rid of whatever was there so they could get on with their lives.

Katie was now a college freshman, but she took off from school for the shoot. That made Georgia worry that she'd put her daughter in danger by bringing her back. From the moment we arrived Georgia struck me as very on edge. While it's natural for people to be a little tense when we show up with the cameras and the crew, this seemed to go beyond that. It was clear it was the house and her fears for her daughter's safety. Georgia had been feeling the presence more and more, and feared that this thing, whatever it was, was getting bigger and bigger. Worse, at 7:30 that morning Katie had experienced another attack.

Katie, a very athletic, gorgeous girl, wasn't quite as nervous as her mom. She told me about her own experiences, saying that for years, she'd sometimes hear someone call her name. As she slept, she heard a sound like an animal scratching near her head. The attack that morning was more extreme.

"I heard a huge wind," she said. "Something jumped on the

foot of my bed, and slowly crawled on top of my feet, along my body, until it was staring at me. I could feel it breathing hot, hot, hot, *awful* air right on my neck . . ."

The creature growled. Katie described the noise it made as being somewhere between a cat's hiss and a rattlesnake. It wasn't huge, maybe four feet tall, about the size of Gollum from *The Lord of the Rings*. Katie had seen it previously, but generally out of the corner of her eye.

It sounded as if it might be sleep paralysis. A lot of the signs were present. I asked Katie if she tended to see this thing when she was stressed or tired, but couldn't find any correlation.

I also asked about any personal trauma they may have experienced. I never had the sense they were keeping secrets. To make sure, though, I also spoke to them privately. I was comfortable there wasn't anything else major going on, beyond the fact that Georgia, of course, was concerned for her daughter.

As Georgia put it, "She's my baby."

Georgia was single and seemed very connected to her daughter. Katie's recent move to college was big for both of them, and I do think that may have had a lot to do with aggravating the haunting. And there was one important thing that didn't fit in with sleep paralysis. Katie's childhood friend Chris had stayed over, and also saw the creature.

Speaking in a low, frightened voice, Chris managed to give me the fullest description: "It doesn't have a human face. It's got really thin lips that are red in color, like there's a red strip. Its nose isn't a full nose. It's like a strip of red. It's like the nose stopped growing. It had whitish skin and the teeth are narrow and pointy. It's the scariest thing you'll ever see."

Unless it was hysteria, or Chris was imaginative, it sounded legitimate.

I also considered the possibility the activity was related to some surrounding cemeteries. The house was in an area with a lot of old graveyards that aren't fenced off or cared for.

While staying at the hotel between shoots, I'd go for a run down a road between two woods and think about the case. Right on the side of the road, I'd see a cemetery. It started out as a couple of tombstones, and then there were maybe twenty, very old, possibly from colonial times.

At the same time, this sort of creature attack isn't characteristic of a haunting. If something's assaulting the client this way, it's generally not a human spirit. Yet, given the descriptions, I didn't consider it demonic. If anything, it seemed outside the family's, or my own, cultural experience.

The possibility that this was some form of nature spirit was something the clients had already considered. They'd worked with a Native American spiritual leader, Brent Allaire, who'd tried a house cleansing that apparently didn't work.

Research is always important, but learning anything about the history of this property was particularly difficult. Chapley wasn't a sprawling city with historical societies or many neighbors to interview. It was a chunk of land in the middle of nowhere. There wasn't even any official town where the documents were kept. We had to go to the next town over, about twenty minutes away, for any information.

There, though, Eilfie managed to find a deed for the land dated 1660. It stated that a John Henderson and John Scadlocke bought the property from a Native American named Segeweha.

That name is common to a tribe called the Almouchiquois that once lived in the area. They paid for the land with very little money and some supplies. Back then there was plenty of land, so many Native Americans figured they'd just move to the next spot, until one day they had nowhere else to go.

Given this background, the Native American spirit theory began to make more sense. Still, there was no specific indigenous myth we knew of that matched the experiences Georgia and Katie described. There was the wendigo and the trickster, and we discussed both, but neither fit.

Hoping to learn more, I asked Brent, a member of the local Penobscot tribe, to return. Like the Almouchiquois, the Penobscot were related to the larger Algonquin tribe, sharing language and culture. I don't think Brent had a title, per se, but he and his people were very open to spirits.

After arriving, he described his belief that something had been done on Georgia's property a long time ago that angered the spirits. As he put it, "The ground is unhappy."

He felt he'd already pinpointed the source of the problem as a pile of stones in the backyard about a hundred feet from the house. When we examined them, they seemed to me just a pile of rocks, not huge or in a special pattern. We'd just dug up a lot of rocks in "Pet Cemetery," with interesting results, so I asked Brent what would happen if I disturbed them.

"It would be extremely dangerous," he said. "You've got good and bad down there and you've got to know which one you're dealing with. They will try to kill you."

It was a pretty strong warning. Since Brent's first effort hadn't ended the activity, he planned to return the next day with a tribal elder. Though I didn't know the details, I understood that together they would perform a more complete cleansing.

Meanwhile, Chip arrived for the psychic walk-through. I believe this is one of the first episodes where I "officially" ask if he knows anything about the case. That's now a standard part of the show, like a little oath. If memory serves, it came up because we'd all been thinking more about our investigatory process. There are times when Chip has been so accurate that I worry he'd overheard something or read a local article. So I started giving him this one chance to come clean.

"You keep me very much in the dark, Ryan," he said.

Here again, Chip's pretty on the mark. He senses that Katie is "a or *the* target," that the troubling spirit comes into the house from outside, and, disturbingly, that the entity is pleased by Katie's fear. When we take him outside, Chip hits again, sensing something Native American involved. I asked him what it looked like.

"Half animal, half human."

After the walk-through, we prepared for Dead Time. Chip and I remained in the house with Georgia and Katie, while Josh and Eilfie worked in the woods. Often, we get nothing, but this session was particularly interesting. Georgia heard a faint growl. Chip sensed the source and we followed it downstairs. There, he felt it'd ducked behind a door. At times I felt teasingly close to some kind of breakthrough. Whatever we were tracking inside moved around a lot.

The most fascinating thing happened outside, though. After hearing a slight rustle, Josh asked any entities that might be listening to make another noise indicating their presence. A series of weird, plaintive cries erupted from the woods.

Inside, we didn't hear them at all. Outside, the sound came

and went, but overall lasted a good twenty minutes. We hadn't heard many other noises, maybe a dog barking once in a while, faintly, and this was clearly no dog. Josh and Eilfie wanted to try to get closer, but they didn't know what direction to head in. It sounded far off, like a quarter or half mile.

This time, the sound was captured.

The next day I led an evidence review centered on that recording. One of the things that seldom makes it into the final episodes, for obvious time reasons, is our lengthy conversations about what evidence we do have, and what explanations there might be for it. But man, this sound was weird, like a whole pack of some sort of animal. It was nothing recognizable to any of us. Georgia and Katie had never heard anything like it either.

We searched the Internet for coyote and other animal sounds to compare, but nothing came close. It sounded sort of like hyenas, but there aren't any living naturally in North America, let alone Maine. With the nearest neighbor at least a mile away, there wasn't anyone else to ask about the cries.

Stumped by the recording, but more and more curious, I decided to take a look under those rocks in the yard. Some viewers felt I wasn't respecting the beliefs of the Native Americans. This couldn't be further from the truth. On a regular basis, however, religious tradition and the investigation process are at odds. For the sake of the clients, I needed answers. I explained my reasoning to Georgia. The Elders *assumed* there was a portal, but we wanted to be sure. If it was a significant source of paranormal energy, there could be markings or even a cursed object planted there. Knowing more would better help us understand how it was affecting the clients.

In the end, someone simply saying, "the problem is coming

from over there by those rocks. But don't open it or investigate it" isn't a strong enough argument to stop the investigation process, whether the person is Catholic, Native American or Buddhist. If someone says there's a portal to hell under some rocks, you bet your ass I'm going to move them.

Together with Eilfie, we removed the rocks to see if there were any occult or religious markings. Underneath, the only thing we found was a rotten tree trunk, a stump. At the time it felt like a dead end, certainly not the wound in the earth Brent described.

Brent and the tribal elder would be arriving later that morning. I wasn't sure what to expect from the elder. I pictured the stereotype—some wizened man in robes with a gnarled wooden cane. Not knowing the specific tribe's culture, I was also concerned we might accidentally offend him and wanted to make sure we were respectful. Eilfie knew enough about Native American tradition to tell us that when an elder visits, you're supposed to offer a gift. She felt the safest thing was tobacco, so we bought some and Eilfie took the time to make pouches for it. As we're reviewing the animal cries, you can see her sewing the pouches in the background.

The elder, Ron Strongheart, didn't match my preconceived image at all. If anything, he looked a bit Italian. We gave him our gift and he accepted it. He didn't seem surprised we'd offered it, so it felt like the right thing to do.

At first, I was pleased not to have offended him, but that didn't last. Maybe I should have expected it, but he and Brent were both upset that I'd disturbed the rocks.

"I wish you didn't move the rocks until I sealed it," Brent said.

The hole and the tree stump didn't feel evil to me, but Brent and Ron were convinced they were. Looking back, I think our moving the rocks was a positive thing. Once we told Brent and Ron what we had discovered, they felt it was proof that it was indeed a portal. According to them, the tree root was a connection to the underworld. They said again that someone or something had wounded the land, perhaps cutting down a sacred tree without the proper atonement. Maybe the stump I saw was what was left of that sacred tree? In either case, they felt this caused a portal to open to the spirit world, allowing evil to pass over.

"That hole in the ground is where the vortex is," Brent said.

As they explained further, I understood that they felt there were two issues, separate but related: the vortex and the creature. Brent believed that when he first cleansed the house, he'd trapped the evil spirit in the hole. The trap wasn't strong enough, though, so at times it was able to get out. He originally figured if he and Ron closed the vortex, they'd be done. Now that I'd moved the rock, he was concerned that I may have opened it completely again.

I wasn't sure what I believed at that point. When I asked about the animal sounds, interestingly, they didn't want to hear the recording, Brent saying that a spirit could take any shape or form, as if the specifics didn't matter.

As a result, they wound up not only cleansing the land but also going back into the house and doing a second cleansing.

Importantly, what's shown on the episode is not their complete ceremony. They felt that would take away from the tradition's privacy. Many cultures share those feelings. Eilfie, for instance, was very reluctant to allow the pagan banishment ritual she performed in "Dark Man" filmed. And it's next to impossible to find a Catholic priest willing to allow an exorcism to be filmed.

They did explain the "smudging" process for us on-camera, showing us the eagle feather and abalone shell they'd be using, and reciting some of their prayers. The word "smudging," by the way, has been adopted into English from these original Native American rituals. It involves binding certain herbs and grass into smudge sticks. The sticks are lit, and the smoke is used as part of the cleansing.

"As the smoke rises, it will be sealed," Ron explained.

In some ways, Ron and Brent came across as psychics, but there was an important difference. They didn't walk in and start saying things based on what they sensed at the moment, the way Chip would. They felt their insight came from meditation and prayer, through rituals they'd performed on the reservation before they arrived. While the role is embedded in a cultural hierarchy and process, they also believe everyone has an intuitive spiritual ability.

Their understanding seemed to match a lot of what was going on here, and my take is that they were close to the truth. The Native American element seemed genuine, and it involved something that was, at best, unfriendly. But, having failed to remove the entity once, would they now succeed?

After the ceremony, Chip walked through the house again to see if there was any difference. Unfortunately, he soon tensed up and shook his head. Whatever it was, he felt it wasn't gone. He felt part of it had been taken care of, but not the whole thing.

We didn't share this with Georgia, but she went back in as well. We all had dinner, but afterward she came up to me, upset.

She said that in the basement, she'd just felt something around her throat. After putting a lot of hope in the ceremony and our work, she appeared frustrated and frightened. More than that, it looked as if she was starting to become hysterical.

In the episode I'm seen cautioning Chip that the family's on the edge. I was basically telling him not to be too superdramatic, not to scare them more than they were already.

At this point, I decided to try a second Dead Time, not so much to contact the entity but to empower the clients, to make them understand that whatever was going on, conquering their fear and reclaiming their home was up to them.

I don't know if it's the state of Maine or that particular area, but we again had a very active session. Chip sensed a presence once more. A slight animal moan came from upstairs, so we followed it there. A motion detector in one of the bedrooms went off. Again, the entity seemed to be moving around a lot. Finally, Chip felt he'd narrowed it down to a spot outside one bedroom. There, Katie said she sensed it watching her.

And I actually saw something.

Just for a second, I glimpsed a shadowy figure moving, kind of walking. It wasn't short, as Katie described. It was adult-sized, more like what Georgia had seen, a shadow that blended in with one of the doors.

Whatever it was, I felt the thing was as present as it was going to get. Chip invited Georgia and Katie to confront it, to demand it to leave their home.

Georgia began very softy, almost whispering. "By the lord Jesus Christ . . ."

The more she spoke, the louder and angrier she became.

"You have no power here! You have no right here! Get out of my house now!" she shouted.

As she rallied her rage, you can actually see, on camera, the change that came over her. It reminded me of Helen in "Dark Man" or my own experience alone in the house during "Pet Cemetery." Georgia believed the thing she was confronting had been hurting her daughter; now she was fighting back. I can only imagine how liberating it must have felt.

Katie was there with it, too. When Georgia found strength, Katie took that signal and found strength within herself.

FDR said we have nothing to fear but fear itself. I don't know if that's true, but to my experience it's always more than half the battle. The next day, that difference in them remained. A lot of the agitation I sensed in Georgia when we arrived had melted. They both seemed relaxed and happy, more comfortable in their own home. Katie was pleased she'd come home, so they could fight it as a family.

I buried blessed medals on the four corners of the property and gave one to Georgia as well. After that, the activity really, finally, seemed to stop. I think it was a cumulative effort, started by Brent and Ron, but culminating with Georgia and Katie reclaiming their home.

I do feel we never got to the heart of the story. I hadn't previously worked with cases where someone claimed a half-human creature was sitting on her chest. It was something we had to learn about on the fly. We did manage to help the clients find the power to face whatever it was that the vortex, or circumstance, allowed inside their home, so that much was a success.

Often, the people who contact us for help seem to think they need some magical, complex piece of investigation and religious ceremony to remove the spiritual. In truth, the number one cause for spirit removal is through client empowerment.

Almost always, whether it's through parents who feel powerless that their child is experiencing phenomena (as in "Sixth Sense"), a bar owner who feels like the activity is negative and trying to destroy his business (as in "Beer, Wine & Spirits") or in this case, a woman and her daughter who felt that a spirit creature from the woods was taunting them, getting rid of their fear and teaching them to get back on their feet is the most powerful weapon.

We live in a very technologically oriented society, many of us increasingly detached from religion, spirituality, and nature. When faced with whatever supernatural force is out there, we've lost an older sense of how to cope with it. We've forgotten that the supernatural is part of a normal life's journey. So we work to reconnect our clients with the spiritual, to help them remember that there is something more out there than money, jobs, and TV. You can try to spend your whole life trying to ignore the other side, but when it comes knocking, it is one guest you cannot refuse.

NATIVE AMERICAN MYTHS

In trying to determine the nature of the spirit that attacked Katie, I considered a number of possibilities relevant to the beliefs of the Almouchiquois/Algonquin tribe that had once lived on the land.

The *wendigo* was part of the Algonquin belief system. It was a malevolent cannibalistic spirit that humans could either transform themselves into or become possessed by. Humans committing the crime of cannibalism were more subject to takeover by this spirit. The wendigo were giants—thin and famished, but also gluttonous—constantly eating human flesh. There was no indication of a wendigo spirit in this case.

Trickster is a more general term for a figure that appears in many myths: a clever, clownish spirit that likes to play tricks on both human and god. Coyote is a popular trickster from Native American myths. The Algonquin shared traditional beliefs with the Anishinaabe, which had a number of trickster figures, including

Nanabozho and Wemicus. Tricksters are not malevolent figures and therefore can be easily ruled out.

But also among the Anishinaabe was a belief in dwarf creatures called *memegwesi*. Hairy-faced, riverbank-dwelling dwarfs, they often travel in small groups, appearing only to children and those of "pure mind." Their short stature makes an intriguing connection, but the memegwesi are not half animal.

Eilfie Music on "Shape Shifter"

During this case, Josh and I encountered some really strange audio phenomena. At Dead Time, we were facing the woods, sitting around a candle as Ryan and the clients worked inside. As we asked the standard "Who is here?" and "Where do you come from?" questions, we heard a sound that started off as howling, then became more like laughter.

The sounds would always occur after we'd asked a question. The noise would get louder and softer, moving around the edge of the woods. It was the strangest thing we had ever heard. The laughter was the craziest, since it sounded like a bunch of people laughing at us. Luckily we were able to get it on audio.

Some people have suggested to me that it was possible there were coyotes roaming around, but this was one of the very few times that something this inexplicable happened for me during Dead Time.

19

Out of the Shadows and Into the Limelight

What the hell is this?

Between "Shape Shifter" and the next case, "Requiem," UNIV-CON took place. That was a very special experience for the team and me, since it was there we premiered *Paranormal State*. Of course it was a huge honor. To premiere my own show at UNIV-CON had been a dream of mine since we first came into the media spotlight during the Cindy Song case.

There was an audience of about seven hundred paranormal enthusiasts and Penn State students. Both sides of my family came up; my mom, my stepdad, my siblings, my grandmother, my dad, and my paternal grandparents were all there. I had maybe sixteen relatives there.

Before that, my impression was that my dad's side of the family felt my paranormal investigations were basically stupid. They came from a very small town and led a pretty insular blue-collar lifestyle. I was the first Buell to go to college. So I think they didn't understand it. You're investigating ghosts? What the heck can you do with something like that? Now, all of a sudden, I was doing a TV show, which, I'm pleased to think, helped changed their perspective.

My mom's side had been a little more open-minded and supportive. She's told me she was sorry for not believing me during my childhood experiences, and for not knowing what to do. I don't hold anything against her for that. I talk to her almost every other day. I go home whenever I can and miss them when I'm not there.

After all, my parents are human beings. My mom and dad were just out of high school when I was born, dealing with a lot as they were raising me. If I had led a similar life, right now I'd have a nine-year-old son. Adding to that, I imagine myself trying to get a career off the ground while my spouse is in a war, working and taking care of the kids and having no time for myself. If my son started complaining about seeing a grinning, floating monster in his room, I wouldn't necessarily know how to deal with it, either.

By now, I'd seen cuts of the first thirteen episodes. This would be the first time, however, anyone outside our circle would see the show. The place was packed. It was crazy. All the A&E people were there, along with the entire crew. Before I went up onstage, they coached me on what they thought I should say: It wasn't a finished version, the premiere will be December tenth, and so on. Unlike the "Dark Man" shoot, their input here didn't rattle me. I was already as nervous as I could get.

Chip introduced me and I stepped up, trying hard to contain myself. Until then I hadn't done much in the way of public speaking. I'd do workshops at the conference with smaller groups, but I never addressed a big crowd like this. I went up, introduced the show as best I could, and then sat down in the front row with Heather, Katrina, Eilfie, Serg, and Josh. We were all there, all jumpy as hell.

Finally, the lights dimmed and the show went on. I was still panicky, but as soon as it played, I sat back and started watching. The episode was "The Name"—definitely one of the signature shows from season one. I felt it was one of the strongest episodes from a TV show that was completely different from what people were expecting.

When it was over, it received a standing ovation. Katrina looked at me. "You must be so proud. I'm very proud of you. Get up there."

So I went up again, along with the team, and we all did a quick Q&A. Part of the reaction we got was "What the hell is this?" Some people said it was cool to see the spirituality in this format, but others were, well, "Where's the evidence? Where's the investigation?"

One guy asked if this was really based on the PRS team "because you are all, coincidentally, very attractive."

I think people were expecting something more like *Ghost Hunters*, which at the time was the only major ghost reality show out there. It enjoyed three years of being the only outlet for those interested in the paranormal, but that was about to change. We were going for something different. I explained that finding evidence was only part of what we were about, that the story we wanted to tell also included the client. Still, I could see where someone watching "The Name" might think the whole series was about demons. It was one of our best, but looking back, I wonder if we should have shown something simpler first, more direct, like "Beer, Wine & Spirits" or "Pet Cemetery." Viewers may have had an easier time appreciating "The Name" if they'd known more about where we were coming from.

At the same time, moving forward, I took the comments to heart. For the last four episodes we became more focused on delivering certain things. We tried harder to bring more evidence in, and to experiment more, by using Frank's Box (see sidebar on page 353) in our final episode, "Asylum," for instance. There's always room for improvement, and now that we had a small sense of what audience reaction might be like, we could look at things from a new perspective.

20

Sickness and Suicide

I went out to get it and his skull was still in it.

We went into our next case, which would eventually be called "Requiem," after the feedback from UNIV-CON. The case itself came to us sometime in September 2007, when we received an e-mail from a college student named Kristy Warren. Her family had moved into their house in Morris, Pennsylvania, about eight years ago. That was the summer before Kristy entered third grade, making her about seven years old at the time, not far from the age I was when I had my first experiences.

She said her experiences centered on her bed, where she'd feel as if someone were there, pushing up and down on the mattress. The problems continued through the years, and more recently she'd said she'd felt icy sensations on her feet, and, most upsetting, a hand across her throat. I knew from her e-mails that a previous owner, after discovering he'd had Alzheimer's, had committed suicide on the property. There were also rumors that years ago a boy had died in the house.

As a possible multiple haunting, with one of the spirits conceivably experiencing a mental disease, the case sounded interesting and different. After the mess with "Freshman Fear," though, I was very hesitant about inquiries from younger people.

Kristy herself won everyone over. Her e-mail was thoughtful and well-written and when we spoke, she came across as intelligent and together. The more I found out, the stronger that impression became. She was well respected at her college and her professors thought highly of her. She also didn't have a huge interest in the paranormal. She wasn't out investigating haunted houses or reading a lot on the subject, meaning she was less likely to have a bias about what was happening to her. We were also the first investigators she'd contacted and it was clear how honestly upset she was. Once I realized she was serious about the commitment, and unlikely to be making things up, I decided this was worth getting involved in.

The briefing was shot at Pizza Hut—where we've gone a few times over the years. As we enjoyed our stuffed pepperoni and Serg dipped into his ranch sauce, I delivered the basics. Aside from the shaking bed, Kristy reported having experiences in a barn on the property. Our goal would be, as it often is, to try to find the source of the haunting and, if it was paranormal, to see if we could get it to leave.

The first day we made the drive and arrived at a nice neighborhood. Until now, many of our cases involved working-class people, but the Warrens were a comfortable upper-middle-class family. Paranormal activity cuts across all socioeconomic boundaries and I was happy to have a chance to show that here.

Much as she'd been in her e-mail and on the phone, Kristy came across as an intelligent, concerned person who was having upsetting experiences. As I interviewed her, she described feeling a "black hand" that touched her throat. Interestingly, she said it didn't choke her, or do anything aggressive, but simply slid across her neck.

With the activity having gone on for so much of her life, over the years her parents had taken her to doctors, to see if she was having panic attacks, but that was ruled out. She also went to a therapist, to see if she was having trouble adjusting to the house, but that didn't seem to be the issue either. Kristy didn't strike me as an anxious person. The tension she expressed seemed centered on finding a resolution. Having tried so hard and so long to find answers, she hoped we could uncover some.

Her parents, Susan and Glen, hadn't had the same sorts of major experiences themselves, but they told us they'd seen and heard enough to make me think a true haunting was plausible. In this case, I felt that their personal beliefs about the paranormal were irrelevant to them. Kristy had recently moved out to live at college, and their feeling seemed to be "Let's see what's wrong, because we care about Kristy and want her to be able to come home and feel comfortable."

As part of the house tour, they took me out to the barn, where the previous owner had shot himself. Though the house was supposedly haunted, too, the barn had a very different feeling. I didn't sense anything strongly, like I did in "Pet Cemetery," but it felt uneven, as if something wasn't quite right.

Kristy's bedroom was the source of most of the activity, but she didn't like even being in the barn. She said that whenever she had to go there, she wouldn't stay long. It was there too that her mother, Susan, once had a minor experience. While sorting some cans, she said she heard a noise. She turned and saw a black blur, followed by what sounded like a gasp, or some sort of labored breathing.

As for the history of the property, Glen and Susan had learned about the suicide shortly after moving in but kept it from Kristy, who was very young at the time. The former owner, Jim Barnes Jr., had been diagnosed with Alzheimer's and, having seen his father go through the stages of the disease, killed himself. After he died, his wife sold the property and ended up moving out of state.

As Kristy got older her parents did tell her the story. When she heard about it, she told us she connected it to the experiences she was having and worried that Jim Barnes's spirit was lingering. She was afraid he felt there were "people in his house that shouldn't be."

As she talked with me about this, she became very emotional. She said she hated the idea someone might feel as if they didn't belong in their own home. She felt that way herself at times, and wondered if she'd been picking up on his energy.

What she said hit on a big issue in our investigations. Feeling like a stranger in your own home is the major reason many of my clients feel victimized. I reassured her, explaining I didn't think *she'd* done anything wrong. If Jim Barnes's spirit was bothering her, he was the one intruding.

Had Kristy had any experiences away from home I'd have been more concerned about what sort of haunting this was, but the phenomena presented as localized. Her recent move to college did seem linked to an increase in the activity but it was still something she experienced only when she returned home.

I felt there were a number of possible explanations. The spirit may have sensed the change in the household, or could have been using the excess energy that the change generated. I suspect that anyone who's moved away from home and then returned has that odd feeling: This is my room, but it's not. I'm living somewhere else now. It's the sort of emotional shift I believe hauntings thrive on. It's also possible Kristy was correct, that her feelings about being a stranger were reflected by a spirit that felt invaded itself.

With the barn, and a large house to deal with, setting up for Dead Time was a challenge technically. We'd improved our technique and were pushing ourselves more for these episodes in several ways.

For instance, before the show ever began, we'd have weeks to analyze any evidence we gathered. Now, to get the analysis in the episode, we had to do it on the fly, so we now developed an entirely new system for capturing and reviewing data. The system Serg designed could measure EMF and temperature fluctuations through different nodes that were wired back to a central hub. Also, instead of the six monitors we had in season one, we now had twelve, not to mention better cameras, audio recorders, and night-vision equipment.

But this was the first case in which we had to cover such a large area of ground. We had to run cables not just inside the house, but also outside to the barn, and we were working with technology that was still pretty new to us.

Despite our new effort to focus on evidence, Dead Time that

first night was probably the deadest of the season. All our efforts to contact Jim Barnes were uneventful. It made me question whether or not the activity was paranormal.

It's not to say I felt we were being tricked. Here, given the deaths on the property, the Warrens had good reason to believe something was going on. If anything, since we hadn't experienced any activity, I considered it possible they were misinterpreting or subconsciously overhyping their experiences. We ended Dead Time with nothing to show for it.

Forty minutes later, a very exhausted Chip arrived for the psychic walk-through. He'd been doing a series of college lectures and this case occurred right between two appearances for him. In the edited episode, he lies down in Kristy's bed and feels as if something is above him. He also picks up on "a child who died" and something that "looks in through the window." In the barn he detects a nastier presence, but it dodges him.

"It doesn't want to have anything to do with you. It wants you to keep the fuck away from this place," Chip said. "He's being invaded. You're walking on what he considers his property. Leave it alone. Get out."

I pressed him on how this person died, but apparently the spirit didn't want to say. "Fuck with me and I'll fuck with you. He doesn't care who's here. He just wants to be left alone. He doesn't do anything that's that bad."

When I pressed him further, Chip said, "You said something about hand to the throat? That wasn't him. I really think that's the kid."

To be fair, while Chip hit on some things, this was also the first time, in my experience, he was completely off on some big issues. The episode doesn't show how he felt the barn entity was a presence from thousands of years ago. More important, to my mind, he never picked up on Jim Barnes's suicide.

I don't necessarily bring this up to discredit Chip in any way. He'd already blown me away on more than one occasion. And there are those viewers who rightly ask, "Why is Chip *always* right? No one is right *all* the time." It makes some think we're feeding him information. The truth is, on occasion he is very off. I notice that he tends to be inaccurate, especially when he's tired. Is that a direct correlation? I don't know. To me, those mistakes are part of what makes him legitimate.

Meanwhile, for day two, I decided we should focus on the historical aspect, to see what we could uncover about the deaths. Katrina and I interviewed two neighbors, Raymond and Peggy Butters, who knew Jim Barnes Jr. They remembered him as a good friend, always ready to help. While nothing they said matched the angry cursing figure Chip sensed, it's possible the rage was related to the Alzheimer's diagnosis, and the fear that must have brought with it.

The Butters remembered Jim as a very respectable man, someone who was about honor. Raymond became quite emotional as he talked about it. Neither knew about the Alzheimer's diagnosis at the time of his death. They had a police scanner in their home and heard the call come through. Raymond felt that Jim had killed himself so he wouldn't be a burden to his wife. They were both impressed with her strength in moving on after the tragedy.

I asked about the other possible spirit, the child who'd supposedly died in the house. Peggy not only confirmed the rumor, she told us the child was named Walter. She even put us in touch with his sister, Alma Jean Mosier, who was living nearby.

With that productive interview complete, for our next step, Katrina interviewed Alma Jean. The fourth of nine children, she told us that her family had lived in the house nearly six decades, from 1921 to 1984. Walter was an older brother. He'd suffered from croup and died at the age of eleven.

Croup can be a very serious, sometimes fatal respiratory disease involving blockage of the larynx. Interestingly, Kristy's mother, Susan, described what she heard in the barn as labored breathing. I'd been thinking of that as Jim's territory, but who's to say Walter's spirit hadn't followed her out there that day?

Alma Jean showed us an old black-and-white photo of her brother. That image of Walter is very evocative, and, frankly, unsettling. His face seemed malformed, parts of his skull swollen. It's seems he suffered from ailments aside from croup, but it was so long ago, his doctors were likely only guessing at what was wrong. In one of a few coincidences that occurred during this case, Alma told us that Walter passed away at 3:00 A.M., Dead Time.

Spirits often remember houses not as they are, but as they were at the time they'd lived in it, so I invited Alma back to describe what it looked like when she was growing up. She pointed out an area now near the kitchen and said that was where an old potbellied stove once sat, near the bed Walter slept in the night he died.

Having a stronger bead on Walter, we also wanted to continue researching our other spirit, Jim Barnes Jr. I called his widow, Ruth Anne, and she kindly agreed to talk to me about that sad day. She told me they'd moved into the house in 1987, after Jim had retired from the army. About five years later, he was diagnosed. Naturally, they were both depressed by the news, but Jim's death occurred too suddenly for them to seek any counseling.

"He didn't wait around for that," Ruth Anne explained.

She said there wasn't any sign he was planning to take his own life. That morning, he'd made breakfast for her before she left for work. When she came home from her shift that day, she was surprised to see Jim's beret in the driveway.

"I went out to get it and his skull was still in it," she said.

In the barn, she found his corpse, still warm. Apparently the shotgun blast had carried his beret all the way out to the driveway.

There was no way to know if his death was planned or spur-of-the-moment. She felt there wasn't anything to suggest he was suicidal for a long period of time.

Two big revelations came out during that interview. There was no crime-scene cleanup facility in the area, so while the authorities took the body away there was brain matter left lying around, as well as the hat with a piece of Jim's skull. As part of her own cleanup, Ruth Anne buried it. It was still there, as far as anyone knew, on the right side of the driveway, near the path to the barn.

The Warrens knew about the death of Jim Barnes Jr., but they had no idea that part of his body was buried on the property. That was a situation we hadn't dealt with since the urn in "Cemetery."

In a second surprise, Ruth Anne told us that the day we interviewed her was the anniversary of Jim's suicide. He had died fifteen years before to the day.

A coincidence? We didn't plan it, but as Chip later said, "Maybe it planned you." It certainly was something I should've noticed sooner. Once we started compiling articles about Jim, the death date was right there in my face. That sort of thing reminds me how much more I, and everyone else on the team, can do to pay attention. The small details we tend to miss are sometimes the most important.

Since Jim Barnes had Alzheimer's, it raised the question of whether his spirit might believe and act as if it had the disease as well. To explore the issue, I interviewed a neuroscientist specializing in the subject and asked about the psychological and emotional makeup of someone who has Alzheimer's. I wondered if it was possible a spirit might somehow still have the disease, or at least behave as if it did. The neuroscientist felt that once you accept the possibility there are spirits—then, yes, it was possible.

Some theorize that spirits, especially those that die suddenly, continue to assume things are as they were when they were alive. So, Jim's concern about his disease may have been part of what was keeping him there.

Since this seemed to be a multiple haunting, I also want to point out that there's evidence and testimony from many cases suggesting it's possible for spirits to be aware of one another, even if they're from different eras. During psychic or EVP sessions, sometimes one spirit names the others. On the flip side, it seems that in some cases one spirit has no idea the others exist. I think that's fascinating.

That night, when we went into a second Dead Time, I was determined to try to make contact with both spirits. As I spoke,

I tried to tell Jim, if he were present, that Alzheimer's wasn't something he had to worry about anymore.

Despite the quiet first night, our second session was much more active. Chip sensed Walter edging up to us, in the hall. I try to coax him in, but Chip said he was keeping his distance. Whenever Chip tried to approach, he sensed Walter move away. Serg reports that the door to our headquarters suddenly opened by itself, but on later inspection we were confident it was due to the wind.

Another interesting thing was the fact that Chip had been traveling with a friend, Patti Star, a ghost hunter. They'd been together on a college speaking tour, so she came along with him to the case. Patti claimed to have psychic intuition but didn't consider herself a full-blown psychic.

During our second Dead Time, a thunderstorm rolled in. Patti was in a truck out in the back when she opened her eyes and saw a tree shaking from the wind. She said she saw a man standing there, holding on to the trunk, and later she pretty accurately described what Jim looked like.

She said he was swaying, rocking, and in her mind she heard him saying, "I did a bad thing. I did a bad thing."

It's possible Patti was exposed to some details of the case, but here was something to suggest that Jim's spirit was remorseful over his suicide. When I heard about this, I wanted to ask Patti back for an interview, but she and Chip left pretty early the next morning.

The most exciting event during that Dead Time occurred when Chip announced that Jim Barnes Jr. would show himself in the barn. "Just watch, that's what he says, just watch."

Then . . . bam, bam, bam, bam—four cameras malfunctioned, one after the other. First it was Kristy's bedroom, then the kitchen area where Walter died, a second camera in Kristy's bedroom, then the barn. These were all areas directly related to the activity.

The cameras didn't simply go black. Each image dimmed, as if the camera were losing power. Everything got darker until the screen was suddenly tinted a bloody red. Then, it blacked out for half a second. Three to five seconds later the cameras all returned to normal.

There was no easy explanation. All our cameras pulled power from the same source, a cord that ran to the tech HQ computer. If the electricity had stopped or been interrupted, *all* the cameras should've been affected, but it was only four. It was something that'd never happened before, and to this day we have no idea what caused it.

Having done all we could, by about 4:00 A.M. we brought the family back to the property, to share what we'd learned about Walter and Jim. Chip explained his sense that Walter was simply mischievous, that his actions were more playful than harmful. He told Kristy that it didn't seem to him as though there was anything in the house out to get her.

As for Jim Barnes, I considered exhuming the piece of skull and burying it with the rest of his remains, but it would have been too complicated. Not only did we not know exactly where it was, but the Warrens had expanded the width of the drive-way, so the asphalt would have to be ripped up to get to it. With our limited time it seemed futile to even try.

But I did want to honor Jim's remains in some way, and possibly release him. So, I asked to have a memorial guard perform a military service for him on the property. I believe that service, coupled with our efforts to tell Jim he no longer had to worry about his disease helped set him at rest. Afterward, the activity in the barn stopped.

As for Walter, I didn't have a priest formally come in, but I gathered everyone for a small prayer where we asked him to move on. I also laid some blessed medallions around.

A few weeks later, Kristy contacted me through Facebook to report she felt much better. A lot of her concern was that the spirit was angry, and Chip's description of Walter set her mind at rest. The last I heard, Kristy still feels Walter around sometimes, but she is no longer afraid.

SYNCHRONICITY

Synchronicity is defined as two or more events that don't seem to have any physical connection, but occur in a manner that seems meaningful. You think of a friend, the phone rings, and it's them. Throughout the series, we've encountered a shocking number of synchronicities, such as in this episode, where we happen to arrive on the anniversary of a suicide. I think it's happened at least half a dozen times in the first season alone.

I don't have an explanation, just some vague thoughts. We relive anniversaries all the time. There's an energy and concentration around dates that are important to us. People tend to die near their birthdays, for instance. A 1992 study of nearly three million people showed that women are more likely to die in the week following their birthdays than in any other week of the year, while male deaths peak shortly before their birthdays. So, it'd make sense for a spirit to become more active near such a date.

If the case has already been given to me, if PRS is aware of it, the increased activity would draw our attention to it. Of course, I'd want to investigate while the spirit was active.

In that sense, it might be like the butterfly effect, the theory that the flapping of a butterfly's wings can cause a tornado a thousand miles away. But it's always surprising and often mysterious the way things wind up being interconnected.

21

I Don't Believe

If a priest was standing here and it did that,
he'd take it as a sign. I'm sure.

As with some of our other cases, Peg Knickerbocker got in touch with us through the publicity and articles we'd circulated back around Halloween. She and her husband, Myrle, owned a 131-year-old building in Linesville, Pennsylvania, and ever since they'd bought the place they'd been experiencing activity.

I knew from the start that Peg welcomed psychics and paranormal investigators to her hotel. The spirits were part of the draw for customers. Since it was evident that Peg was okay with publicity, I did worry about the legitimacy of the haunting, that it might be a stunt. In general, though, PRS doesn't mind doing a case just because a client wants publicity. We do want to be sure that (1) the client genuinely believes in the phenomena and, (2) that there's some sort of scientific or ethical merit to doing the case.

We always have an eye to our overarching goals of furthering the understanding of paranormal phenomena and helping clients, but sometimes an investigation can be more of a fun exercise for the group, like "Mothman." If, in the process, we can document evidence or improve our technique, then I feel there's merit in it. Here, the Knickerbocker Hotel seemed like a cool, creepy location. I explored further, wanting to know how active the haunting was and so on.

Through our preinvestigation and research, I became more dubious about the claims. Aside from all the psychics and investigators who had visited, I also saw a very hokey brochure advertising the spirits in a way that fed my doubts. I didn't think the client was lying, but rather that, wrapped up in the atmosphere and her own beliefs, she might be misinterpreting natural events.

When Peg spoke over the phone, even in initially talking to the producers, she seemed very careful about what she said, and kind of passive. I knew, for instance, that there'd been some deaths and injuries involving people close to Peg who'd been at the hotel, but she didn't want to talk about that directly. She did report that there was a particular bedroom where she wouldn't stay because she'd wake up feeling choked. Apparently more than one person had seen apparitions and they had mediums over regularly to perform séances.

I try to start out open-minded, but sometimes I get warning signs that I don't want to ignore either. As I started theorizing with the others about possible natural explanations, I began to worry that the case could be a disaster—a situation where the client was so set on believing in the ghosts, that there'd be no reasoning with her.

When we headed to Linesville, and held our briefing on the first floor of a local historical building, I was already taking a slightly more skeptical approach than usual.

"I definitely do want to pursue debunking some of this stuff," I said. "As well as trying to give the clients the benefit of the doubt that maybe what they're experiencing is real."

To me, if we're thinking it *isn't* paranormal, that's a legitimate part of the process, too.

The Knickerbocker Hotel is a three-story building on the corner of a busy street. The current business was established by Peg and Myrle in 2005. During our tour, she told us it was built in 1882 by Milo Arnold, and originally called the Arnold House.

Though it was called a hotel, it was set up more as an event space for reunions, meetings, paranormal groups that would come to investigate, and that sort of thing. The rooms are mostly decorative. Peg said she wanted it to be a place where people could come and have their picture taken on the stairwell.

"But who's going to have their picture taken on the stairwell if someone is going to try to push you down it?" she asked. According to Peg, many people had felt something come from behind them while they were on the stairs and try to push them down. "That's happened to my husband, my son-in-law, my daughter-in-law . . ."

She also showed us the "choking room" where she'd woken up and felt unable to breathe.

As I sat down to interview her, I kept in mind that she was, in a way, an entertainer, as a hostess for the hotel. I had the sense she felt as if she had to be engaging and entertaining for the camera.

It was clear she loved the place, and they'd put a lot into preserving it. It didn't seem as important for their income as much as it was a labor of love. They may have lived there at some point, but at the time of our investigation they were living nearby.

Peg told me there'd only been two séances at the hotel. The number seemed small, so I was concerned she might be misleading us. In the end I don't think that was the case. Others interviewed for the case told us about séances there that Peg hadn't been part of. There'd been so many groups and paranormal teams at the hotel, I don't think she kept count or even registered it. My sense was that she was much too casual about it to keep track.

Prior to our arrival, Peg specifically asked that we not bring up the deaths and injuries in her family. If the activity was real, though, that would likely be an important part of any emotional factor here, so I brought it up anyway.

Peg, to her credit, responded. She told us there was a particular party they'd held in the hotel. "It was an anniversary party for my in-laws," she explained. "We had a wonderful party. I looked and saw an image go through my kitchen. It was like a dark image. It was a frightening thing to me. I didn't know what it was."

Her husband, Myrle, told me that within the next week or so, four or five major things happened among their family and friends. Peg's father-in-law had a heart attack and had to go to the hospital. One of their guests had a brain aneurysm. Another relative fell down a staircase and died. A fourth person died within weeks of the party. It seems too much for concidence, but these were all older people, making it possible their suffering was just happenstance.

Peg, though, told me she was worried it had something to do with her and the hotel. "I just started thinking, if there's something here, did I bring it? Because I started seeing all these people that I love have all these horrible things going on in their lives."

Whatever else might be going on, I was convinced she was absolutely genuine about that fear and her beliefs. To try to set her mind at rest, I explained to her that it was extremely rare for someone to be physically hurt as the result of a haunting. There were usually some *very* bad phenomena associated with hauntings in those cases, not just a couple of knocking sounds or even a few apparitions. In my experience, here there wasn't any connection likely. But Peg seemed convinced it was linked to the fact that they'd all been at the party.

It was understandable. The thought that "I could have done this to them" can become so overpowering you don't stop to think, "Well, they were all in my building because I *know* them all." It's hard to separate yourself from the underlying grief.

I held a regroup with the team and shared my concerns about Peg's emotional state. I was also worried that all the psychics might be provoking things, fanning the flames. Katrina brought up the notion that they might also be putting ideas in Peg's head, as we'd seen in "Haunted School House." One thing was clear: While none of us were sure there were spirits present, Peg was.

I'd gotten in touch with some of the psychics who had previously been in the hotel, hoping to learn something more about the haunting, but here they only reinforced my bias. I'd asked one woman to come alone and conduct a séance for us on-camera, but she brought along a troop of followers, a group that seemed to hang on her every word.

There was a séance held. We had recorders and a thermal camera running. At one point, a woman claimed she was feeling extremely cold on her right side, but the thermal cam showed her right side was hotter. In the end, nothing much else came of it, so it didn't make the episode. It did add to my general feeling of doubt about the haunting.

Part of the problem with the paranormal field is that because it has yet to be legitimized, or organized with any set of standards, it's one of the few areas where any crazy or fraud can pronounce himself an expert. Without a standard, you have to rely on belief, which is what I feel Peg Knickerbocker was doing. While I do rely on my own faith, I don't believe that anyone who walks up to me speaks for Jesus Christ just because they say so.

Since I was worried that Peg's conviction might interfere with the objectivity of the investigation, for the first night I asked that she not participate in Dead Time.

Usually, we go into Dead Time with some sense of who we're trying to contact. Here that just wasn't the case. We didn't discover much in the way of historical research, but not because we didn't try. There were rumors the hotel was part of a train station where there was a fire, but we didn't find much more.

For Dead Time, Serg, Josh, and Heather handled tech. I thought about spending time near the staircase Peg had singled out, but the area was too noisy. Even though this was a big location, the place was very creaky and we needed quiet areas to pick up activity. Instead, I decided to move around, starting on the first floor with Heather, while Eilfie and Katrina were on the third floor, another active spot.

As usual, we tried to communicate, particularly with the black cloud that appeared to Peg.

In an unusual turn, Katrina and Eilfie heard a voice, very clearly. What made this particularly strange was the fact that Eilfie didn't generally experience things. Some people do; some don't. I often don't have experiences when others do. Here what they both heard had the cadence of a small sentence, but they couldn't make out any words.

Not much was happening on the first floor, so Heather and I moved up to the second. I thought I heard a tapping in response to a question, but it was indistinct. Meanwhile, back on the third floor, Katrina was hearing the voice again, so Heather and I headed up there and we all tried to communicate.

Yet again, Katrina heard something that sounded like a woman speaking, very nearby. I didn't know what to make of it. It was one thing to go into a house I thought might be haunted and get something, but another when I *didn't* think the house was haunted. Even crazier was that we were able to hear the voices on the audio recording.

The next day, Josh and Serg presented the most distinct of the recordings. A voice, mumbling or speaking gibberish, could clearly be heard. It sounded to Katrina like the same voice, but fainter.

"It was the same pitch, but what I heard last night was really, really loud," she said.

As I've mentioned, we'd experienced that before, hearing things loudly only to have the tape either not pick it up, or pick it up faintly. There are two theories I know about why that happens. The first is that the spirits are able to manipulate the recording equipment so they're not recorded. But why would they? I can't imagine so many spirits being so camera shy.

The second is that if the sound a spirit makes isn't generated by normal means, it can't necessarily be recorded by normal means. As I've experienced them, the knocks and bangs, especially in poltergeist cases, don't exactly sound like knocks and bangs. They seem more like a distant popping with an echo, not quite natural. So some theorize that our recorders just aren't designed to pick up whatever medium the sound is generated through. When a paranormal sound *is* recorded, it may be because at times the spirit does use physical means to manifest.

I don't find any of that very satisfying. It strains my credulity to think a spirit can control what you can and can't hear, and no research at all has been done on the subject.

Josh brought up radio interference as a possible explanation for what we'd recorded. The only problem was that we'd originally heard it audibly. I didn't think they were faking anything, but I did wonder if there was a TV or sound system nearby. We couldn't find anything.

That made it possible, in my mind, that the hotel did have *some* supernatural activity. Given the other explanations we soon came up with, I'm convinced Peg was misinterpreting its severity.

As we continued gathering data that afternoon, I called Peg's sister, Kathy. She described how, at the top of the third floor, where we'd heard the voices, she'd seen a lady in white. Kathy said she couldn't see her face because of a veil, but she also smelled a sweet perfume.

"She speaks," Kathy said. "But I don't understand what she's saying. It's like a foreign language." That seemed to jibe with what we'd recorded.

Katrina also spoke with Amber, Peg's daughter-in-law. She told us about an experience on the staircase. As she was walking down, she said, it sounded as if someone were running on the stairs right behind her. Amber kept looking back, but no one was there. She realized the house was old and creaky, but the sound kept getting louder and louder. She described a cold sensation down her back and felt pushed. By the time she reached the third step, she felt as if she'd fall.

Amber said she'd never had a paranormal experience before. I'm always a little surprised when someone says that. Everyone generally has *some* sort of ghost story to tell. Oh, my grandmother appeared to me, or something.

After that, the team spent some time looking for more natural explanations for the activity, and that night we regrouped to discuss them. Serg told us how the steps on the active staircase bent really low as he stepped on them, then snapped back loudly after he removed his foot. As he walked down, he was continually releasing pressure from the previous step. A second later, it would snap back, sounding like a footstep. As Serg sped up, so did the snapping, making it sound to him just like like someone was running behind him. Once someone is convinced something is running at them from behind, as Amber said she was, a cold shiver is a natural reaction.

I tried the steps myself. The snapping and cracking really did sound like someone following me.

Next we discussed the "choking" room. Josh explained that as they were monitoring our surveillance cameras, they saw Peg enter the room to make a phone call. She was afraid to sleep there, but with production occupying a lot of the house, it was one of the few places she could have some privacy. While she was there, she stirred up a lot of dust that floated around the camera lens.

"We saw clouds of dust," Josh said. With poor air circulation, the dust could easily cause a sense of suffocation.

The apparitions couldn't be debunked, since that was based on Kathy's personal experience, nor could our EVPs, but they were faint and inconclusive. We had, however, come up with some solid natural explanations for some of the major recurring phenomena.

That night, CJ Sellers arrived for a psychic walk-through. She picked up on a female presence. In one room she said she kept getting the name "Katie" or "Katherine." On the third floor, she sensed a female wearing a white gown, who had a servant feeling to her. Lastly, in the kitchen, she "heard" an entity warn we were not supposed to be back there, to keep out.

On the surface that seemed to confirm what Peg's sister had seen, but I remained unimpressed. Every state and nearly every town has a "lady in white" story. My jaw is not going to drop because a psychic mentions a legend that's been repeated over and over all across the country. Again, I respect the psychics we use on our show on a regular basis. Obviously I'm not going to invite someone back who I believe doesn't have the potential of providing legitimate information. That said, despite working with her on two other cases during season one where she gave impressive results, I honestly felt that CJ didn't give us a whole lot to go with this time.

After the walk-through, I introduced CJ to Peg. When I

told her about the woman in white and the name "Katie," Peg seemed to get terribly excited. She said she thought CJ had been in touch with Katie Hickey, a woman Peg believed worked there in the 1800s. If memory serves, Peg said she'd first heard the name from neighbors, but we were never able to confirm it.

When CJ described the angry entity near the kitchen, Peg gasped.

"Is it a spirit that shows itself before negative things happen in my life?" she asked.

CJ couldn't answer, but Peg seemed convinced, saying, "It's an angry spirit that *is* here."

As always, CJ attempted to empower Peg. "Whatever angry spirit feels that you're being intrusive, it really should be the other way around," she told her. "It's no different than a human being walking in here and pushing you and your family around. You wouldn't put up with that. You shouldn't put up with this."

Peg listened, but I remained concerned that she was still blaming the spirits for negative events at the hotel, and took CJ's reading as validation of that belief.

Then something happened that brought things to a head. On the afternoon of the last day, I was gathered with the team in tech HQ, reviewing the EVPs again, when the electricity suddenly went out. Peg was in the kitchen alone, in the area she'd seen the entity. Apparently, she was extremely excited by what happened.

"I told it what she told me to say," Peg said. "She said to tell it to leave. This was right where it was and I did that. And this whole building went black! Maybe it *left*."

When I suggested we look into the possibility of a power outage, Peg remained adamant that she'd gotten a direct response. She spoke with great emotion. "It could've just been a power surge, but maybe it was a way of confirming that I was telling it to get out."

"Maybe," I said. "I'm just concerned about making sure there's rational thinking and making sure that you're fine emotionally."

"If a priest was standing here and it did that, *he'd* take it as a sign. I'm sure," she said.

That took me aback. "You're right. He would," I told her. I admitted that if I were standing there at that moment, I'd suspect it was more than a power outage. I also insisted I'd still investigate whether or not it was something that could be explained.

But it seemed that Peg felt so good, so excited about what had happened, her mind was made up.

It was a very awkward moment for me. The result seemed positive, but to my mind she was making such a powerful logical leap.

Meanwhile, my team was already investigating. Serg was making calls to determine if the blackout was natural or possibly supernatural. Katrina and Josh had gone out to the local stores to see if their power went out as well.

I had the sense that as far as Peg was concerned, there was no point, but they did return with answers. Not only did several stores experience the same thing, they told us it was a common occurrence, and that power outages happened a few times a week. I was now certain it wasn't paranormal.

For me, though, the question became how to present that to Peg. A lively conversation ensued. Katrina wondered why Peg hadn't mentioned the frequency of the power outages. She must have experienced them, after all.

At the same time, Serg wondered if we should say anything. "If believing in something false makes you feel better, why should someone come by and tell you it's false . . . ?"

"Are you saying we should withhold this information from her so she feels better?" Eilfie asked.

"If we withheld that from her, though, we wouldn't be doing our job," Katrina responded.

I wasn't sure what to do. It was such an odd twist on things, something I hadn't encountered before. Yes, I'd devoted my life to believing clients when no one else would, trying to empower them, but here I felt we had a *lot* of evidence suggesting there was no major paranormal activity going on. I was also frustrated that the client didn't seem to accept what we were saying. By the time the power outage occurred, I'd had it up to here with Peg's insistence that it was spirits. "Look, Peg," I said, "you can't really say it *was* paranormal." I just couldn't understand why she wouldn't accept that.

The problem hit me on a deep level. It was a role reversal. After being disbelieved when I was a child, I'd spent my entire career trying to be sympathetic to people who'd encountered these things, and here I was on the other side of the argument. I was trying to explain something away to someone who absolutely believed, trying to argue against their experiences. I had to be alone for a while to think this through.

Peg had presented me with an argument I knew very well, because I'd made it myself so many times. You can say there's an explanation, but I can still believe the root cause is something else, and nobody can take that away from me. Even recently, in "The Name" and "The Devil in Syracuse," it'd been a series of coincidences that convinced me the case was demonic—a name appearing on television, radio, and in the newspaper. That was very extreme, very specific, but wasn't it somehow the same sort of thing, where I decided for myself what the truth was based on faith? Who was I to draw that line for Peg?

Many of us who are spiritual see signs in everything we do and here I was trying to take that from her. It was a good moment for her, a healing thing, something that was resolving a situation. So why was I trying to take it away?

I do think a line needs to be drawn. Say you're recording EVPs but someone proves you're picking up a radio signal. Now, someone could still argue that a spirit manipulated the radio signal so that only those parts relevant to the questions being asked were recorded. If you're getting answers to ten or twenty questions, along with names and addresses, then you've got something. But, if it's one or two ambiguous answers, that explanation becomes very unlikely.

It was the same thing here. Of course, a spirit could have tripped some switch teetering on the edge just to respond to Peg, but a random power outage seemed a better fit. It's Occam's razor: The easiest explanation is usually correct. I was comfortable with the reasoning, but I still had to come to grips with the fact that I was a lot more skeptical than I used to be. I was no longer the wide-eyed high school student who wanted to believe so badly that there was *something* there, that I would I overlook more obvious natural explanations. It was a realization, an awakening, something I had to wrestle with.

In the end, I realized it wasn't up to me what Peg believed. I could only give her the information I had. It was up to her to accept, reject, or interpret it. Insisting on one explanation was selfish, based on how pleased I was that we *could* explain things.

I went back to her and told her that while I believed it could have been a sign, we also had an alternate explanation.

Peg was resolute. "I don't care if it happened in the whole universe. It happened while I was speaking. That was *my* signal that it was out of here."

I recommended that in the future, she be careful about who she let in to explore the spirits. Peg said she was "100 percent happy with what happened."

That night we stayed on the third floor. There was no activity, but in the morning, we heard Prince blasting through the entire hotel. On the surveillance monitors I saw Peg dancing and singing like crazy. Before we left, her husband, Myrle, pulled me aside for a moment that wasn't caught on-camera and thanked me. He pointed at Peg, who was obviously very happy and more energetic and said he hadn't see her like that in a while.

So I think she found some real comfort. Later she said that while there was still activity at the hotel, the negative entity had vanished entirely. Peg hosts a Web site devoted to the history and the hauntings at: www.knickerbockerlinesville.com.

I learned some things about myself as well. Working on the show had changed me. Questions that used to be important weren't so important anymore. Interacting with people across the country was making me rethink things. There were a lot of different viewpoints to explore. I was questioning my role more. Should I always be an interventionist? Some people don't need to definitively understand everything. They just want help. It seemed that Peg didn't really care about what was going on exactly, as long as it wasn't harmful.

On the flipside, I'd become more confident, better able to express what I wanted to do for the show, how best to do it, and to stand firm for what I believe in.

"The Knickerbocker" started an ongoing discussion about debunking. There were concerns that if a case turned out *not* to be paranormal, that viewers might hate it. I tried to argue that other shows featured debunking all the time. I think it shows the other side of the investigation process. If every episode provided paranormal evidence, especially on a documentary show, I feel that that would make people more skeptical. I'm proud to say that every so often, we take on a case that we legitimately feel isn't paranormal and it's turned out to be an excellent episode. For instance, in season two's "Smoke and Shadows," we concluded that some photos of a black shadow had been faked.

Looking back, this was one of my favorites because it forced me to face my own skepticism. It didn't provide the payoff everyone wanted, but it was, in a lot of ways, a better payoff. Because of "The Knickerbocker," I grew.

22

In the End, to Honor the Dead

There are seven . . .

After "The Knickerbocker" we went straight in to filming the last episode of the season, "The Asylum." It was mid-November 2007, just under a month before the series would air on A&E. Following the premiere of "The Name" at UNIV-CON, our interest in trying to collect more evidence in new ways, led to the appearance in this episode, of the controversial Frank's Box.

As for the case itself, PRS almost chose not to get involved, due to some objections from my team. Some time earlier, the producers had been contacted by Melvin Williams, superintendent of the Willard Drug Treatment Center in the Finger Lake region of upstate New York. It was a ninety-day program for prisoners with drug issues, but in the past it had been one of the largest insane asylums in the country. It was a sprawling complex, well over a century old, with a rich history.

There'd always been reports of paranormal activity, but recently a section in the oldest building had been reopened as a staff dorm. Two employees, former military people, said they'd sees an apparition—a screaming woman dressed in red. After that, these tough prison guards refused to return. And they weren't the only ones having experiences. With all the employee complaints, Mr. Williams was interested in seeing what we could learn.

The producers and I were very excited. It was a fantastic location—an archetypal haunting scene—with tons of atmosphere and a lot of activity. They felt it would be great for our final episode. Surprisingly, though, the team, mostly Eilfie and Josh, were against it. It took me a while to understand why.

Part of the reason was that Eilfie feels very protective about places like Willard. It's a somber space, where thousands suffered over the years, and many died. There's a sacredness to that sort of location. Because ghost hunting is hugely popular, there are those who disregard that and turn places like it into gaudy amusement parks, making a mockery of the people who'd lived there and the pain they'd endured. What's worse is that they have no desire to move the spirits on, because then they would stop making money. The mindset is offensive to PRS. It's why we don't go to ghost "hot spots" where they only want publicity so they can continue to make money from paranormal tourism.

Granted, on our own show, popularizing haunted locations sometimes worked to our clients' advantage. In "Beer, Wine & Spirits" the reputation brought business to the bar and helped it survive. In "Pet Cemetery" our client wound up renting the home to ghost seekers. In both of those cases, however, the clients wanted the spirits to move on. This case was the same. This was still a functioning government location. They had no interest in opening it up to ghost hunters or selling Willard Asylum Ghost T-shirts. They called us in because they wanted whatever was in there removed so their employees could remain without fear.

The other issue my team had was that we didn't know who we were there to help. The guards who'd seen the apparition wouldn't give us their names or appear on the show. Going in, we didn't even have a witness. What were we going to do there? How were we going to make a difference?

The team felt so strongly about it that I went back to production and said we didn't want the case. For my team, it was a moment when we had to sit back and evaluate who we were and what it was we wanted to do. It did seem like an opportunity, but could we investigate this asylum and be okay with it? The right reasons weren't immediately apparent.

After thinking it over, I came to two conclusions. First, the clients could be the spirits themselves. The asylum patients had extremely difficult lives. If their ghosts were suffering, we could try to bring them resolution. Second, just because others exploited similar places didn't mean *we* had to. If others did something we consider wrong, did that mean we shouldn't try to do the same thing correctly? It took a day or two to convince Eilfie, Josh, and the others, but since then, "Asylum" has become one of their favorite episodes.

Willard is in a very isolated area, so isolated we had to stay about forty-five minutes away. During the drive, we passed literally nothing for miles. Finally we reached a really tiny town. I don't even remember seeing a restaurant. Willard, which takes up hundreds of acres, really *is* the town. The locals depend on it for their employment. The only area bank is at the facility.

There was a Soldiers Memorial Library where we shot the briefing. We'd already discussed the case at length, but here was a chance to review some of the history, which I mentioned earlier. Then we headed to the facility, passing barbed wire, walls, and scores of buildings of different ages.

There we met with Mr. Williams for the tour. Activity had been reported in several buildings, but since it was a prison, there were many areas we weren't permitted to enter: sections where the inmates stayed, sections where private records were kept and so on. Other unused buildings were very run-down and unsafe. We were allowed to enter one of those rickety structures, but only with a guide.

Our investigation focused on the oldest building in the compound, built in 1860. It was a huge stone giant, three stories tall, with a basement and an attic. When Willard was an asylum, it housed patients. As I've said, I don't often feel things when I enter a site, but it was hard *not* to feel things there. There's a sense of sadness, isolation, fear. As I walked through the basement the first time, I felt it very heavily. The underground hallways formed a long maze, sometimes cinder block, sometimes old stone arches with wooden supports, and a series of drywall rooms. Even when it was daylight, down there it was pitch dark.

There was no activity reported in the attic, but I went up there anyway. It was pretty clean, except for all this bird crap.

A huge, thin ladder took us to the roof for a nice wide view of the massive property.

The rec room in this building, a common area, was where the two guards said they saw the screaming woman. They packed up and left the next day, about two months prior to our investigation.

Though those former guards didn't want to speak to us, others did come forward. Michael LePage, a former employee who was now a schoolteacher, told me about a similar experience he'd had. When he first started working there, he was in one of the classrooms and heard a noise. He walked toward the sound and saw a slender woman, who started screaming. We never got a detailed description of her, but others had seen her. And when they did, they would run.

One of the current guards, Lisa Bordeaux, also agreed to an interview. She said she'd been sitting in the rec room watching the news when she felt as if someone were standing over her shoulder. She heard the lock on a doorknob click and the door swing open. When she turned, no one was there. That had happened just a week before our arrival.

The best overview of Willard came to us from Chris Carroll, a former asylum nurse, who'd worked with the patients there for thirty-seven years.

"They were a sad, sad group of folks," she said. "Mental illness is very difficult. It's difficult for the person who has it. It's difficult for the person watching it." I asked how she dealt with it. She said she just grew with the place. "You become a part of it and it becomes a part of you."

Among the painful events at Willard, there'd been suicides.

Eugene, Chris's husband, also a former employee, confirmed he'd once had to search for a female patient, known to be depressed, who went missing. He found her dead, hanging by her neck in one of the other buildings.

All these moving stories were the tip of an iceberg. The visit to the Psychiatric Center's cemetery had the most profound effect on me. It was an enormous, wide field by a lake, where over five *thousand* people had been buried over the years. Only two areas showed some sort of recognition, a small Jewish memorial and two dozen or so marked graves for soldiers, who'd died in battle. The vast number of graves, belonging to the patients, were all unmarked. I understand that there used to be little iron markers listing the patient number, but even these had been pulled out and thrown away, to make mowing the field easier.

"These were unwanted people," Mr. Williams explained. "They were sent someplace where their families didn't have to see or deal with them anymore."

I was overwhelmed. Haunting or no, I felt a need to try to do something for all these unrecognized dead. We all did. I had the idea of putting together a memorial service. The producers agreed to try, but with such short notice we knew it would be difficult to arrange.

That night, Chip arrived for a psychic walk-through. He'd seen the barbed wire surrounding the grounds on his way in, so he had some idea of what was going on, but he quickly zeroed in and asked, "Did this place used to be a mental facility?"

Like me, he felt an omnipresent sadness, but also an anger, which seemed to peak for him in the rec room. "I'm getting yelled at. Stop!" he said.

I asked what they were saying. "Let me out," Chip responded.

Down in the tunnels, he picked up on a female spirit. "She's a nurse. It's almost as though she's a guardian in this building, or someone who's come back to try to help some of the people here physically leave. This is their prison."

This nurse didn't seem to be the same as the screaming woman our witnesses saw, but the overall sense that the spirits felt trapped made sense. Much in the same way the ghost from "Requiem" may have felt he still had Alzheimer's, patients who'd spent their entire lives not only suffering mental illness, but also incarcerated, might easily assume that even in death, their situation was the same.

"They're ready to go," Chip said. "You going to help them?"

Of course I was. The question remained: How?

The next day, Chris Moon arrived. We'd previously contacted him and asked him to demonstrate Frank's Box at the site. This was a new piece of equipment at the time, and everyone in the paranormal community was excited about it. It's not as though the paranormal field is so big that every new invention gets covered on CNN. Aside from our new focus on evidence gathering, I felt a responsibility to introduce and examine these things. Given the huge number of potential spirits present, it seemed a perfect opportunity to test a device that supposedly allowed them to speak.

You couldn't go into the store and buy one, either. The box was only seen if you built one yourself, or when being demonstrated by Chris. It was invented by Frank Sumption, a paranormal enthusiast with an electronics background. He'd never intended for it to be used for commercial or media purposes.

He basically gave it away, despite seeing others, such as Chris, making money from promoting it.

Apparently Frank knew Chris as a fellow enthusiast, and gave him one to try. Chris told me he'd left it on the shelf for a while. Then one day, bored, he remembered it, turned it on, and was blown away.

Chris sometimes called it a "telephone to the dead" saying, "It runs on a random voltage generator. Basically it pulls white noise, pink noise, and radio fragments all through the same unit. It takes the raw signal and runs it through an echo box that's in the unit and that's where the voices will actually come back out, essentially. It randomly picks a radio frequency, and when the words come out it's supposed to be a response from a spirit."

After flipping it on that night, Chris explained it would take a minute to warm up. Soon, static and bits of voices came through the speaker.

"How many sprits do we have here with us?" Chris asked.

Surprisingly, the box responded, clearly, "There are seven here."

That was an impressive display, but not proof the box worked. I asked, "What are the spirits' names?"

This time, the response wasn't completely clear, but to many of us it sounded like, "Lucy."

"Is there anything else here?" I asked.

To the rest of us, the next answer was indecipherable, but Chris nodded and said, "Demon. There's a demon. A strong demon."

"Is the demon what's holding them here?" I asked.

Again, the answer was garbled to my ear, but Chris said, "Yes, yes. Lucy's speaking for all of them."

According to Chris, Lucy was begging us all to come down to the basement. In demonic cases, the entity often tries to separate the group or bring you to a place where they were stronger. I was concerned it might be a trap, but of course, we went down to the tunnels.

The place was pretty drafty and I often felt a breeze as we moved along. "There's something bad, bad down here," Chris said. He claimed to see a moving shadow. "It shot across the wall, came back, and went straight through."

Chip suddenly announced, "I know where it's at." And he was off and running.

I caught up with him at a door that had been boarded up.

"I would love to see what's on the other side of that," he said.

We'd heard rumors, off the record, that some patients had been abused. I was never sure if the door Chip had singled out led to a room or a way out, but he felt that the area behind it might have been the site of some of that abuse. With the space so large and secluded, it made sense.

Meanwhile, we weren't getting much more from Frank's Box. Chris tried to contact Lucy again in a bathrom. He moved near a window to try to pull in some radio signal, which apparently the spirits needed to speak, but claimed the demon was blocking it. Amid the static, I did hear a low guttural sound, which Chris felt was the demon.

Chip began spraying holy water. Chris, translating for the box, said, "It says to stop that fucking spraying."

It made sense that a demon would enjoy the company of the damned spirits stuck there. Their pain would be its food, so it certainly wouldn't want us to interfere.

With no other signals coming through, Chip said, "We need to get out of here." Chris agreed and turned off the box, ending the session.

By then it was a little after 1:00 A.M. I regrouped with the team to discuss our opinions of the box. At times its response had been so uncanny; it was very impressive.

"Why isn't it saying different, random things?" Serg asked. "Why does it give you a number when you ask for a number?"

Josh was the most skeptical, but even he felt there were a few clips that were undeniably clear and responsive. At the same time, there were many others that were not, answers Chris heard that none of the rest of us could make out.

While we were all fascinated with Frank's Box, it's important to mention that some of Chris's beliefs about the box were not shared by the inventor, Frank.

Basically, Chris has said he believes there were only twenty or thirty people in the world who've been chosen to operate the box. They are the only ones who can accurately interpret what's being said. If you get a little gurgle from the box, Chris claimed to understand what that gurgle meant. He likened it to hearing a language spoken in a bad accent.

Chris, of course, believes he is one of the chosen. He said that Chip was another, and that while I was a candidate, I wasn't ready yet. Throughout the test, Chip did confirm the sort of information Chris got from the box.

But there was more. Chris also claimed that while we try to communicate with the other side, technicians on the other side work to communicate with us. He was teamed with a specific spirit technician, or operator, whose name, I think, was Larry. Larry was the one supposedly communicating through the box.

Admittedly, that's a lot to swallow. On the other hand, I heard the box say some things that were hard to deny. Yes, if you get a bunch of random frequencies coming through, you can misinterpret them as responses, but when you specifically ask how many spirits are there, and a voice says "seven" that's very compelling. Do you discount that or say it's just coincidence?

In an incident that doesn't appear in the episode, for instance, I asked, "What do I have on me?"

"Crucifix," it answered. I didn't have a crucifix per se, but I did have a cross.

It's impossible to test whether or not Chris is one of the "chosen" and he's undergone a lot of criticism on that front. At UNIV-CON the following year, Dr. Michael Shermer, a skeptic, brought up those arguments with him. In any case, having worked with Frank's Box several times now, in the end I don't feel it's a reliable piece of technology.

To get back to the investigation, we now had a name to verify, "Lucy." Doing any historical research proved to be the most difficult thing about the case. Even though the asylum was closed and most of the people involved were dead, the state wouldn't release any patient information due to confidentiality. At the same time, many records were misplaced. Others were stored in a town a few hours away. We had a hard time finding anything.

There were some patient records that were just lying around, so we reviewed them, hoping to find a Lucy who'd worked as a nurse. After hours of poring through them with the whole team, nothing came up. We did find a tape recording of a doctor discussing a patient. We also visited the morgue, where patients were autopsied.

On our third day, I asked Mr. Williams about Lucy. By this time we'd already heard her name from Frank's Box. So I was curious to know if he'd ever heard anything similiar. To my surprise, he said that several employees and inmates have talked about her.

"What do they say?" I asked.

"That she's a ghost," Mr. Williams responded rather quickly.

I asked if he could provide any other details, but all he said he knew was that she sometimes appeared in a red dress. Mr. Williams didn't know anything further, so I went back to Chris Carroll. While she was sure there must have been someone named Lucy there at some point, she couldn't recall anyone specific.

At that point, an interesting development led to an entire secondary investigation. Once people in town knew we were there, we received a number of local calls involving hauntings. It was a tiny town, but we had half a dozen or so people claiming activity. They felt that whatever was happening in the asylum was happening across the town, too.

Mr. Williams explained that once the asylum was shut down, a lot of patients who didn't have anyplace else to go began wandering the area. The homeless population exploded, and some died in the town.

We didn't have the manpower to investigate all these claims, but I did look at a house right across the road. A woman there was hearing knocking, banging, and, sometimes, screaming. It was a very sad case. Her two-year-old son had a birth defect and had passed away. The anniversary of the child's death was coming up, and she wanted to know if his spirit was there, too. The family also had an interesting photo they felt showed a face in the window.

The owner told me they'd not gone to the attic since they bought the place. There was a little hole in the ceiling, through which they'd put things to store, but they had never gone up themselves. Naturally I decided to go up and take a look.

At the far end, I found a number of personal items belonging to an old woman who died at the house. We later found a photo of her in an old school journal. She was born and raised in the town and we believe she worked for the asylum. We can't be sure. Again, the lack of records dead-ended our research. This was already a very full investigation, so we weren't able to include any of this in the episode.

As for the main case, we couldn't track down Lucy or the screaming woman, but given the possibility of demonic activity, I called in Lorraine. As I walked her through the tunnels, she, like Chip, felt a number of voices crying out for help. She sensed something demonlike, and felt the human spirits couldn't escape because of it.

This wasn't a possession, so an exorcism or deliverance wouldn't be appropriate. Our challenge, then, would be to free the spirits there from whatever held them back.

As you might imagine, Dead Time was difficult given the sheer size of the place. Katrina, Eilfie, and Josh were in the basement, tech HQ was set up in a former classroom with Serg, while Chip, Lorraine, and I were stationed in a patient room. I told everyone beforehand to explicitly challenge the dark spirits, to try to push them away, so the living spirits would have a chance to move on.

Chip's psychic reading had a powerful effect on me in this case, and now he tried to get Lucy to come to him, but had no luck. He sensed her approach, but she refused to commit. Meanwhile, in the basement, as they asked for a sign a thud came from upstairs. Katrina and Josh heard some talking, a higher-pitched voice, like a woman.

We tried to pick the best locations for our camera, but nothing showed up on video. We did get some unusual sounds, footsteps, and a howling of some sort, but couldn't determine if it was wind. It was definitely windy. We had a thunderstorm at one point.

We also heard some strong, clear footsteps from the first floor. Those came out clearly on the tape. We knew no one was there, but the floor was locked because prisoner records were being held there, so we couldn't track it down.

I heard really loud, bizarre sounds coming from a locked room. I was able to have someone from the staff unlock the door. Once they did, I kicked it in.

All at once, all these birds came flying out. It was a really intense, creepy scene.

During his walk-through, Chip had sensed a very negative, nasty presence, a male he felt had hurt a lot of people during his time there. It was possible this was one of the abusers. One of the goals for this Dead Time was to try to contact him.

Chip believes he did, but it was very intense. He grabbed his throat and seemed to be in pain. "He's choking her," he said.

"Who?" I asked.

"You know."

"What's the name of the person near Chip now?" I asked.

"Fuck you!" came the response. The energy became too intense. He called for Lorraine. I asked if he wanted out. "Yes."

Chip concluded that Lucy died trying to protect the people there.

Whether this other spirit was an abuser or the demon, it seemed to me that this was the time to rally the trapped spirits. I told them that if they wanted help, they had to ask for it. "You need to be determined. You need to be strong. You can get out of this place." Basically I said the same sorts of things I say to human clients when I'm trying to empower them. Here I wanted to empower the spirits.

Chip suggested we all focus on making a circle of energy, then draw the spirits into that circle, and send them up. Eilfie, with the group in the basement, asked the spirits to move upstairs to us.

As part of the effort, we chanted the St. Michael prayer:

Saint Michael the archangel,
Defend us in battle,
Be our protection against the wickedness and
*   snares of the devil.*
May God rebuke him, we humbly pray,
And do Thou, oh prince of the heavenly host,
By the divine power of God,
Cast into Hell Satan and all evil spirits
Who roam throughout the world seeking the ruin of souls.
*   Amen.*

I told any spirits that if they wanted to leave, they could. "There's a door here now. You're all free to go."

I have no way of measuring, but I genuinely felt we'd managed to open a path for them. Afterward, there were fewer reports of activity. With so many spirits, so many forgotten people, you can't be sure, but I felt we did something at least for some of them. When it comes to the spirit world, it's hard to measure what's actually effective. Maybe just the thought and act of bringing people together to honor their memory and to acknowledge their suffering was enough? Maybe it's truly is that simple, though it's something we living rarely do. Maybe that's all it takes to give them closure.

As for the memorial, we had contacted the local newspapers and tried very hard to get the word out, but essentially it was announced the final day, the day we did it. Despite the short notice, we managed to bring a good number of people from the town for this final ceremony. There were many who'd worked there, or knew someone who'd died there. Four faiths were represented: Catholic, Muslim, Presbyterian, and Jewish. I hope we helped the people there move on with dignity. By acknowledging them I hope in some small way we corrected some of the mistakes of the past. I found it very moving, the best ending we could've had, not only for the episode, but also for the season.

Others have done good work on behalf of Willard's unknown patients. When patients arrived, their belongings were checked in and put in an attic. When they were renovating the place for the prison, some staff members and a museum curator wanted to preserve some of the artifacts. They went up to the attic and found scores of suitcases from a span of a hundred years. They were all literally forgotten, until the staff found them. They helped put together a traveling museum exhibit, and there's an online version at www.suitcaseexhibit.org/indexhas-flash.html.

As for the first season of *Paranormal State*, there was a small "that's a wrap" ceremony I actually missed. Eilfie and I had gone back down to the basement, to place blessed medallions in the four corners. Sometimes the job is more important than the fanfare.

One other thing happened, which I mentioned earlier, providing a darker coda for the season. Through Chris, Frank's Box gave me a warning from the demons. It said, "Watch out, I'm going to come after your family." I thought the worst of the attacks were over, but apparently the box said, "No, we've got a lot more planned for you." The way Chris delivered it, the demon said it would get my soul when I least expected it, that there were other cases I'd be called to, that they wanted me to go to, and that they'd be waiting.

Nothing's happened to my family since, but that night I was truly scared. I made jokes, but I was freaked out. I wanted to call Chip to talk to him more about it. Eventually I just told myself there was nothing I could do.

Obviously you can respect the information, but other than being frightened, there's not much you can do. I did call my family the next day and said, "Hey, just be careful."

Originally, we planned to spend the night, but we decided against it. We didn't feel safe in the building. It wasn't just the prisoners. Everyone in town knew we were there. We could have our equipment locked up, but if we wanted to be locked up as well, we wouldn't have been able to get out. So I was like, "I don't know about this." Instead, everyone went back home.

There's a nice song over the closing credits, "In the Shadows," by Sofi Bonde. It was written just for that episode, to give us a good send-off. At the time, the show's future was uncertain, but this had been a two-and-a-half-year project, a two-and-a-half-year journey. Even if it wasn't the series finale, obviously things were going to change. To cover the possibilities, the final episode text is phrased as if it might be the end of the series:

> PRS *now receives more cases than ever . . . They remain committed to their mission statement: To Trust, Honor, and Always Seek the Truth.*

A Short History of Willard Asylum

The area that was to become Willard Asylum first opened as an agricultural college in 1860. It closed a few years later when most of its staff went off to fight in the Civil War. In 1869, Dr. Sylvester D. Willard, after studying the poor treatment of the insane, wanted to convert it to an asylum. As he was addressing the state legislature, he had a heart attack and died, but the new institution was named after him.

Willard wasn't the kind of asylum you hear about in horror movies. They weren't doing experiments or treating people badly. In fact, it was a first step in treating the mentally disabled more humanely. On October 13, 1869, the first patient, Mary Rote, arrived—naked and in a cage. Prior to that, she'd been chained for ten years without a bed or clothing. At Willard, she was allowed to clothe and feed herself. While it wasn't the same standard of care we expect today, it was an improvement.

It didn't always work out that way though. As the asylum grew, by the late 1880s, people were running sightseeing tours. Tourists would take boats to the grounds where they'd eat picnic lunches while making fun of the patients. The situation became such a problem that Willard was surrounded with barbed wire, gates were installed, and additional security was hired. It wasn't to protect people from the patients, but to protect the patients from the gawkers.

By the 1890s, Willard housed 2,000 patients at a time, covered two hundred acres, and had seventy buildings. At one point it was the largest asylum in the country. At its height in the 1960s it held 3,500 patients. Shortly after, the invention of antipsychotic medication combined with a lack of funding brought Willard into a slow decline, until finally there were only 135 patients left. Because it was keeping the town alive, though, it remained open until 1995, when it became a state prison and drug treatment facility.

FRANK'S BOX EXPLAINED
BY JOSH LIGHT

The concept is relatively simple. If it sounds like a broken radio, that's because it more or less is. The box generates a random voltage and the base acts as an antenna allowing it to tune in to A.M. frequencies. The signal is filtered for the audio, which is amplified and fed through a speaker, which, in turn, is received by a microphone connected to either another speaker or a line out for your listening pleasure.

As for how it "works," my first thought is that the device, by changing stations quickly, acts as a biased noise generator. The theory is that entities can use the noise to form words and phrases. My second thought is that spirits may influence the random voltage generator to use existing voices on radio broadcasts.

Both theories have huge holes. In the first case, like EVPs, the "words" are very subjective. Unless a large group spontaneously picks out the same words, the data is meaningless. On the other hand, some claim successful results from this very method.

The second theory is even worse. For a spirit to be able to use a radio broadcast, it must first access all the possibilities and, second, hear them at least a few seconds into the *future* in order to determine what *will* be said. Third, it must be able to influence the voltage to select the station that's about to have the phrase it wants to communicate.

There's a third theory: It doesn't work. Frank's Box then becomes a tool a psychic can focus their conscious mind upon to allow their other talents to come through. That makes it much like rubbing a stone or crystal, or watching *Plan 9 from Outer Space*.

That final theory relies less on science and more on psychic phenomena, which is just as questionable as the existence of entities in the first place. You can't hire the Jersey Devil to track down Bigfoot. Since the box conforms to what the inventor wanted it to do, in that sense, it does indeed "work." But by now you see the degree of my skepticism. How was it different from employing a spirit board?

Though little that we heard was instantly recognizable, there were a few instances when something relatively distinct came through. The trouble was that Chris constantly interpreted the messages, making it nearly impossible to remove the element of suggestion.

Not everyone was present during each session, though, so we

had some objectivity. We had at least three PRS members listening on headphones to the recorded audio, and then writing down what they heard (if anything). Each reviewer marked the appropriate time, folded the paper, and placed it in a secure location for later tallying.

The results cannot be shared due to the availability of some of these clips on the PRS forums. Once more it's all about suggestibility. Despite my skepticism and reservations, it's truly nice to see someone injecting new life into the paranormal field.

23

The Beginning

All of a sudden, I'd be the one being asked the questions.

The majority of this book deals with the cases and the film crew, but a third factor in my journey as an investigator was coming into play in a big way. Despite a few interviews here and there, up through "Requiem" we were all unknown. Beginning with "Asylum," though, the first rumblings of A&E's impressive press tour could be heard. For instance, a local TV station covered our investigation, but I wasn't allowed to speak with them because my first "official" interview had been promised to a major news show. Press tours were about to start; trailers were running in theaters; billboards went up. With the cases to focus on, I hadn't been thinking much about the show coming out.

Even as we finished "Asylum," it all seemed very far away. The end of season 1.5 was very calm, understated. No big party, just a thank you. Our producer said something like, "The show comes out in three and a half weeks. Let's hope this was a great end."

Then we packed up and started the six-hour drive to college. As the sun was about to set, suddenly it became scary. All at once I felt I was on my own, a feeling that was echoed physically, because production was no longer around.

After we got back to State College, we found a bar and drank a bit in silence. We'd finished shooting the day before Heather's birthday. We shared some memories and laughed a bit, but I was beginning to feel a little nervous.

The show had given me a distraction. While I was focused on filming, the onslaught of the press sounded cool. Now I didn't know if I could handle it. It was one thing to be documented, another to go out and do the PR game. I didn't know if I could handle going out in front of ten million people to talk about the show. After years of interviewing clients, all of a sudden I'd be the one being asked the questions.

The real strangeness hit me in the days that followed, when I arrived to do a live interview at Fox News, for their late-night show, *Red Eye*. Exhausted from being awake nearly twenty-four hours, I was waiting, getting ready to do my five-minute promotion, talk about the seriousness of the work, and maybe share a spooky ghost story.

When the interview started, I realized that wasn't what they wanted me for, especially when the host asked if "a creepy uncle" was responsible for my childhood haunting. It took me all the way back to when I first started thinking about doing a show, and I realized how the media thought of the paranormal as a novelty. I wanted to do something better. I thought we had, but would anyone listen?

December 10, 2007, was the day of the premiere for *Paranormal State*. A&E had had me in NYC for five days after doing a steady round of press interviews all over the country. That night the rest of the team was with me in New York for a party hosted by A&E. We hadn't been on an investigation in a while. Instead of skulking around in the shadows searching for the unknown, we were putting on suits and dresses for a bash full of executives.

My nerves were pumping. Throughout the day I was getting text messages and phone calls, all wishing me good luck for the launch. My parents called to tell me how proud they were.

As Serg and the others finished getting dressed, I took a moment to stand alone by the windows and stare out at the nighttime view of the city. Manhattan is beautiful. I tried to calm my nerves, but every time I thought I had it under control, all these questions flooded out: What if it's a bomb? What if everyone hates it? What if the clients get upset at watching the episode?

I was more nervous about the show coming out than I'd ever been about the paranormal. Now our work would be something the entire world could see. The realization that I was about to lose a piece of my privacy, possibly forever, began to sink in.

A hand clapped on my shoulder. I looked up at a reflection of Serg and me standing in the window.

"You ready to do this, man?" he asked.

It was almost like being at the pier down south, before the tornado hit.

"Not really, but I don't have a choice, do I?"

"Not really," he said.

We had Eilfie, Katrina, and Heather come up to the room. I broke open the minibar and we all took out a variety of liquors and beer (thanks, A&E!).

"A toast!" I declared, holding up my Corona. "Guys, we've come a long way. I don't know where the hell we'll be going after tomorrow, but I'm pretty sure it'll be a fun ride!"

We all cheered and drank. And, with that, we headed to the door.

We arrived at the party with less than an hour to go before 10:00 P.M. Chip Coffey, Jamie Hernandez, and Lorraine Warren were all there to help celebrate. They congratulated me, told us how excited they were.

"Think of all the millions of people who'll be watching," someone said.

In response, my stomach made a strange gurgling sound, not unlike some of the things I'd heard from Frank's Box, only easier for me to understand.

Before I knew it, the words that would become so familiar to many finally came on the TV screen for the first time: "These are the real stories of Penn State's Paranormal Research Society . . ."

Well, here we go, I said to myself. My worries about the inevitable future disappeared. Whatever was coming, I'd find out tomorrow. Why waste the night fearing the future?

Epilogue:
Mothman's Last Word

You want a sign?

In a way the story of the first season, or, technically, season one and "1.5," completes a circle. After being thrown into the hectic pace of television production, things became exhausting. There were times I couldn't even speak to the clients until I met them for the first time, times when I felt too drained to give my all. Thrilling as it was, and as much as I feel I stuck to my ideals, trying to get at the truth and help people, the day-to-day experience was very far from where I'd started as a paranormal investigator.

With the last six episodes, a lot of it came back, though. The new pacing of the shooting schedule helped. It felt good, more laid back, more like the sorts of investigations I did before the series began. I think it showed in the final product, too.

As I mentioned, *Paranormal State*'s first year isn't aired in the order in which it was shot. The six episodes from "Pet Cemetery" to "Asylum" were jumbled throughout the season, but if you watch them as we shot them, I think you'll see a huge difference as the series progressed. I'm very proud of many of our first thirteen, from "Sixth Sense" to "Mothman," but the last six were sharper, better, leaner, and they get to the point faster. We had time to develop them and make them great. Is it perfect? No. In some ways, I'd love it if we were doing ninety-minute movies every three months instead of a weekly series, so there'd be time for everyone to get the cases and the episodes just right.

But nothing's perfect.

It's in the nature of the process that nothing in this book will convince people one way or another about the existence of ghosts. These are the things I experienced and what I felt and thought about them. What I hope to have done is to have given fans of the show some added depth about who I am, what PRS is, and what we're about, and, for newcomers, to present a behind-the-scenes story about what it's really like to be a paranormal investigator.

In trying to serve that purpose, this book is filled with stories: ghost stories, personal stories, stories about what it's like to work on a show. I tried to cover my successes and failures, what was kept, what was left out, the evidence that was most exciting, the mysteries we never got to the heart of, the clients we managed to help, and the rare one or two who felt in some ways dissatisfied.

That's the what and the how and the where and the when, but the big question always left over is the why. Why get involved in paranormal investigations, and maybe more important, why stick with it for so long? In part I remain motivated by that first strange encounter I had when I was nine, but it's since become something more, something that can't easily be put into words.

I have one more story, a story that I think gets close to it. It was left out of the episode since it was so personal. I've told it at a few conferences. Like a lot of what we've experienced, it's open to interpretation.

As you may recall, while shooting "Mothman" we were inside one of those weird concrete igloos that supposedly once housed experimental explosives, trying to contact an ultraterrestrial being. I asked Chip Coffey if whatever he was in touch with could give me some kind of sign that it was really there, that it existed.

"You want a sign?" Chip asked.

John Frick, the Mothman expert who was guiding us, quickly said, "Well, I want a sign."

"No," Chip said. "They'll only give Ryan a sign, and only if he wants one."

He turned to me. "They will give you a sign, but you have to decide: yes or no."

I was already pretty creeped out by the way Chip had been acting. I rarely believe in psychics, but here I had the sense he was in touch with something. To me, it felt like a legitimate offer for a Mothman prophecy. I had to think about it. Did it mean I'd get a weird phone call from a higher intelligence, the way John Keel described in his book?

I paused, gulped, and said, "Okay, I'll take the sign."

"Okay," Chip said. "They'll give you a sign."

After that, I was like, fuck, what did I get myself into?

Serg, Josh, and I shared a hotel room, so after the shoot we headed back there. I was so on edge; I couldn't get to sleep. After tossing and turning for hours, I felt a presence in the room.

Slowly, I turned over. By the doorway, I saw a silhouetted black shape . . .

I almost screamed until I realized it was my overcoat hanging on the closet door!

After that, I was like, "Okay, I've really got to get to sleep here. It's all in my head, I'm not going to get a visit."

Just in case, though, just in case, I put one of my audio recorders on the night table and set it to RECORD. The next day I woke up—no sign of Mothman, no sign of any ultraterrestrials. Nothing.

It was the last day, so we had to pack up and leave the hotel before heading to the final shoot for the case. After that, we'd be going back to State College. I was just about done packing when I noticed something. My tape recorder wasn't on the night table where I left it.

I thought it was gone, but I opened the drawer, and there it was. Somehow, it'd been moved. I asked Josh and Serg if they had moved it, but neither had any idea I had put a recorder out to begin with.

That was back in 2007. It's nearly the end of 2010 and I haven't listened to that recording yet. People think this is crazy. There could be some solid evidence on that recorder, a message from an ultraterrestrial. Why *not* listen to it? They think it's like Mulder having a box with a piece of a UFO inside, but never opening it up to take a look. They ask if I'm afraid.

It's not about fear, and I like to think I'm not crazy. The question for me is whether I really want that mystery unraveled right now. If there were a message from the ultraterrestrials, or whatever, what would they say? Maybe I won't hear anything, or just a weird bird sound. Who knows?

Yes, the possibility that all I have to do is hit PLAY to maybe hear something from another realm excites me, but at the same time I don't want to press that button. It's like a present, a gift I don't want to open yet, a door I'm not quite ready to go through. Part of me believes I'd never be able to shut it. It'd be another moment like seeing that creature at the foot of my bed, or those demonic cases before *Paranormal State* began, something else that would change my life forever.

I'm not naïve. I know that I haven't fully gone through all the doors the unknown has to offer. I could keep going darker and deeper into the tunnel, but at what cost? When I do cases, I do cases, but if there's a door that's going to open for me, it'll open for me on its own. I don't plan on pulling the handle.

At the same time I don't think that if I play the recording an ultraterrestrial will say, "Hi Ryan, well, here's our bio and a Web site where you can learn more about us." The excitement is that maybe they did communicate with me and all I had to do was ask. I still have a long life to live. I don't want the mystery to be over this quickly just because I was impatient. It almost feels like cheating.

So, I want to let it sit there and see how the rest of the decades of my life pan out. It's a recording. It's not going anywhere. Unless I delete it accidentally. That would suck. But I've got it in a safe spot, carefully marked.

Maybe when I'm seventy I'll listen to it.

Won't it be scary if I listen to it and it says, "We'll see you tomorrow." And that's when I *die*?

There's a quote from Oscar Wilde that sums it up: "The suspense is unbearable. I hope it lasts."

SUGGESTED READING FROM RYAN BUELL

Belanger, Michelle. *The Ghost Hunter's Survival Guide*, 1st ed. Woodbury, NY: Llewellyn Publications, 2009.

Blum, Deborah. *Ghost Hunters*. New York, NY: Penguin, 2007.

Martin, Malachi. *Hostage to the Devil*. New York, NY: HarperOne, 1992.

Mercado, Elaine. *Grave's End: A True Ghost Story*. Woodbury, NY: Llewellyn Publications, 2001.

Owen, A. R. G. *Can We Explain the Poltergeist?* New York: Garrett Publications, 1964.

Playfair, Guy Lyon. *This House Is Haunted*. Lanham, MD: Madison Books, 1984.

Roach, Mary. *Spook*. New York, NY: W. W. Norton & Company, 2006.

Sagan, Carl. *The Demon-Haunted World*. New York, NY: Ballantine Books, 1997.

Warren, Ed and Lorraine. *The Demonologist*. Bloomington, IN: iUniverse, 2002.

Appendix 1
What to Do If You Think You Are Experiencing Paranormal Activity

Don't panic!

In 99.99 percent of all cases, whether the phenomenon is truly paranormal or not, the worst thing a person experiences is fear. Simply being frightened doesn't mean you're in any danger.

Do not use spirit boards or other means to communicate with spirits.

As illustrated in several cases discussed in this book, such efforts can actually attract spirits, and, in rare cases, lead to more dangerous activity. The spirit world is not a toy to be played with.

Seek natural explanations.

Creaking floorboards may be the result of heat coming on. Voices could be someone talking outside. As illustrated throughout this book, there are many natural explanations for what at first seems strange. Even in many true hauntings investigated by PRS, at least some of the activity is explainable.

Beware of pareidolia.

As described in this book, the human mind loves to find patterns, even when they're not there, as in a shadow that looks like a figure, or a wind that sounds like speech. Don't talk yourself into believing the supernatural is present when there may be other explanations, especially when you're lying in bed. Human beings can easily slip in and out of dream states without even being aware of it.

Keep a journal of your experiences.

What is it? Where is it? When did it start? What time of day does it generally occur? How often does it happen? Is there any history of activity? Are others experiencing it as well?

Don't be afraid to discuss things with someone you trust.

One of the major goals of PRS is to do away with the taboo of discussing these experiences. If something is genuinely happening, have faith that you will be believed.

On the flip side, don't necessarily trust hired psychics.

There are many charlatans, some self-deluded, willing to prey on the emotionally vulnerable.

If you've followed the above steps and believe something is genuinely going on, contact the Paranormal Research Society. See our FAQ on the following page for more details and contact information.

Appendix 2
The Paranormal Research Society Services FAQ

This FAQ is frequently updated online at
www.paranormalresearchsociety.org/services_haunted.php.
Important Notice: Since December 10, 2007, PRS has received thousands of case requests and inquiries. At this time, we do not have the manpower to respond to all these requests, especially in a timely manner. Please note that the likelihood of getting a response within a month is very low. We are keeping a lookout for urgent cases, however. It pains us that we cannot respond to all the requests at this time, but we will do our best.

Some Frequently Asked Questions

What kinds of cases do you accept?
We accept all claims of paranormal phenomena. This includes, but is not limited to: spiritual and demonic hauntings, psychic ability, poltergeist phenomena, occultlike phenomena, angelic encounters, miracles, UFO sightings, alien abductions, monster and cryptozoology phenomena, etc.

How do you determine what cases you accept?
In accordance with our handbook and the Ius Scriptum policies, cases with the most severe or threatening activity take precedence. That is to say that claims of supernatural phenomena

that involve clients who genuinely feel they are being threatened will get priority. Additionally, cases that can provide opportunities for research of scientific or moral benefit will also be considered a priority.

What is the process of getting an investigation?

We here at PRS are very sympathetic to all claims of supernatural activity, and we try to give our clients the benefit of the doubt. Anyone who watches our A&E television program, *Paranormal State*, can see this. That said, clients must be prepared to agree to *confidential* psychological evaluation from trained counselors before we can fully consider a case. If you already have professional specialists involved, then we may ask for permission to speak with them to rule out certain psychological and physiological factors for your protection. We are not here to judge, but we need to pursue certain avenues for ethical and scientific purposes. When we conduct interviews, we may ask very personal questions, such as asking about any history of drug or alcohol use, occult use, etc. (responding yes to any of these does not necessarily mean we won't accept your case). Again, everything remains confidential, but we ask clients to be very open and honest with us so we can do our job to help you figure out what's going on. It's important for both you and PRS to consider natural, logical explanations first. We may also ask clients to submit to a criminal background check for the protection of the society and its members.*

Keep in mind that each case is different and unique, so the guidelines on how we accept and pursue a case vary.

---

* All of the above is done in accordance with state and federal laws.

Clients who are being considered for an investigation will generally undergo a series of telephone interviews before the next step, which is a physical meet and greet. Information gathering and medical checks come next before the actual investigation. Some investigations might require an overnight stay. Overnight stays are done in order to observe the household environment while at the same time trying to witness paranormal activity. We try to embed ourselves with the clients and household so we can try to experience what the clients experience firsthand.

As you can see, the whole investigation process is very in-depth. We are selective with our cases because they are very time consuming.

How much does it cost to get an investigation from PRS?

Nothing. We do not charge clients for anything.

What will PRS do for me and the phenomena I am experiencing?

There's a lot we will try to do. One, we can bring in scientific, medical, and paranormal specialists. We can also conduct historical research. *Most important, we're here to listen without judging you.* We believe in the possibility of the supernatural and we're here to help, whether it's paranormal or not. We're not here to debunk your claims or to simply collect evidence. Our goal is to try to help you understand what is happening. Sometimes we can find a logical, rational explanation. Sometimes we cannot. We will also work within the client's religious, spiritual, and cultural beliefs. Despite the fact that PRS has a national TV show, we are quite capable and trained at keeping investigations discreet and confidential.

Do I have to consent to being on TV in order to get your help?

No, you do not. We still accept a certain amount of cases a year that are not taped or filmed in any capacity for the media.

Does distance affect your decisions about which cases you pursue?

Unfortunately, yes. We are not yet at the point where we can fly a team of investigators all over the country for every case. We are able to consider a few cases that are distant, but most of the cases we investigate are in the northeastern area.

CONTACTING PRS

Paranormal Research Society
P.O. Box 403
State College, PA 16801
e-mail: cases@the-prs.org
Web site: www.paranormalresearchsociety.org
Official Web site: www.ryanbuell.net

Acknowledgments

This book wouldn't have been possible if not for the patience and commitment of Stefan Petrucha, who worked with me and helped me slay the deadline demons.

Additionally, the film crew, producers (Gary and Betsy), the executives at A&E (special shout-out to Elaine Frontain-Bryant), and the awesome people at HarperCollins all deserve a special acknowledgement for supporting the work that went in to this book.

Thank you to Michelle Belanger for taking the time to not only write a foreword, but to also read the book and share your thoughts.

Special thanks to my editor, Jennifer Schulkind, for being patient and supportive during this entire process, and to my lawyer, Richard Thompson, and manager, Curt Smith, for being amazing!

All the clients, guest investigators, and experts featured in this book deserve a special thank you. For the clients—thank you for allowing us to go in there and tell your story. Whether you realize it or not, you helped influence someone out there.

Lastly, this book had to tell some hard truths and honest perspectives. I'd like to thank my family for being supportive about my decision to open up about some particularly dark moments. And if you weren't supportive, well, I hope that someday you'll forgive me. I did it in the hope that one day, someone else who went through something similar will find encouragement in these pages.